HIRE with your HEAD

HIRE with your HEAD

third edition

Using Performance-based Hiring(sm) to Build Great Teams

Lou Adler

John Wiley & Sons, Inc.

Published by John Wiley & Sons, Inc., Hoboken, New Jersey.
Published simultaneously in Canada.

Wiley Bicentennial Logo: Richard J. Pacifico

For general information on our other products and services or for technical support, please contact our Customer Care Department within the United States at (800) 762-2974, outside the United States at (317) 572-3993 or fax (317) 572-4002.

Wiley also publishes its books in a variety of electronic formats. Some content that appears in print may not be available in electronic books. For more information about Wiley products, visit our web site at www.wiley.com.

Library of Congress Cataloging-in-Publication Data:

Adler, Lou.
  Hire with your head : using performance-based hiring to build great teams / Lou Adler.—3rd ed.
      p. cm.
  ISBN 978-0-470-12835-0 (cloth)
  1. Employee selection.   2. Employees—Recruiting.   3. Employment interviewing.   I. Title.
  HF5549.5.S38A35 2007
  658.3'11—dc22

                                                              2007012416

Printed in the United States of America.

10 9 8 7 6

Foreword

Since the early 1990s, I've been advising business leaders in organizations ranging from JC Penney to JP Morgan Chase on how to leverage talent to meet their business objectives. One piece of advice that is a slam dunk is this: Buy a copy of Lou Adler's *Hire with Your Head* for yourself, read it, and then buy copies for every hiring manager, every recruiter, and every human resources professional in your organization. Why? Because this book offers a systematic approach to Performance-based Hiring and that is the most important thing you'll ever do to build your team.

As much as things change in the business world from week to week and year to year, there is one fact that isn't going to change: Talent is the number one asset in every organization. That has always been true, but the value of talent is even more important in the changing economy than ever before.

Organizations in every industry are trying to increase productivity and quality and they cannot rely on technology alone to achieve those objectives. As employers cut waste, introduce new technologies, and streamline operations, they put even more pressure on individuals to "add value" on a daily basis. Every operation nowadays must be lean, flexible, and high performance. Every supervisor is under pressure to get more *and* better work out of fewer people. That means those few people had better be really, really good.

High performance under pressure is what the *real new economy* is really all about. Technology implementation will continue, organizations will become even leaner, the pace of change will get even faster, competition will be even more intense, businesses will become even more customer focused, expected response times will get shorter, and productivity expectations will grow. The whole game is moving to a higher level.

That's why there is a growing premium on people—at all ends of the skill spectrum—who can work smarter, faster, and better. You want your people to be innovative (within guidelines), passionate (within reason), and armed with sufficient discretion to make mistakes (as long as they are not too big). In lean, restructured companies, the best employees are handling more responsibility, using greater technical skill, and applying more precious human judgment than ever before. Every individual, like every business, has his or her own value proposition to offer employers in the free market for talent, which really means simply: "Here's what I can do." That value proposition is strictly business. One really good person is worth a whole pile of mediocre people. Really good people "can do" real things (very well and very fast) that add real value to your bottom-line. They know it just as well as managers know it.

We're talking about that senior executive talent who can turn around a division in 18 months. The programmer who can write two lines of code for every one that an ordinary programmer writes. The call-center operator who can dazzle every customer, gather market research on the front lines, and routinely suggest improvements in the whole system. The salesperson in the field who can sell anything to anybody and who also monitors warehouse inventory and the production schedule from his palm computer. The warehouse manager who knows everybody by name and also knows the new database inside and out. The nonphysician health professional who delivers care previously reserved only for doctors. And the soldier operating a laptop computer mounted on a tank in the midst of battle who turns around, as soon as the battle is won, and plays the role of peacekeeper.

Regardless of fluctuations in the labor market, demand for those great people is going to outpace supply for the foreseeable future. And hereafter, in the real new economy, there's going to be a perpetual struggle in the marketplace to leverage the value of labor. How do *you* go about sourcing, attracting, and selecting the best people?

Business leaders, managers, and hiring professionals who fail to take a long-term strategic approach to hiring in today's rapidly changing business world will face a perpetual staffing crisis. You may be understaffed one day and overstaffed the next; the problem is, you won't be intelligently staffed with the right people in the right places at the right times.

If you want to be intelligently staffed, you have to hire with your head. Seize control of your talent supply chain, just as you have with other critical resources. That means you need the kind of systematic approach Lou Adler offers in this book.

Throughout most of the industrial era and until recently, the dominant staffing model for most employers was based on long-term, full-time, on-site employment relationships. But in today's quickly changing marketplace, where employers can never predict what is just around the corner, the old-fashioned, stable, til-retirement-do-us-part employer-employee relationship just doesn't fit. The key to continued success for companies today is the ability to adapt rapidly to new circumstances—staffing may have to expand rapidly in one skill area, or contract rapidly in another—or do both at the same time. Staffing strategy must be geared to face this reality.

People in today's workforce want to know what you want from them today, tomorrow, next week, and next month and exactly what you have to offer them in return. Create a compelling recruiting message by answering the fundamental question people want answered: "What's the deal?" To be effective in today's labor market, you need to be communicating that message through an aggressive and year-round effort to a wide range of well-chosen candidate sources. Why? If you attract an applicant pool that is sufficiently large, you can be very, very selective when it comes to the ultimate hiring. You must be prepared to implement a rigorous selection process that is all about collecting proof that potential hires have the skills they need to get up to speed and start contributing right away.

What you'll find in this book is a step-by-step process with detailed instructions for taking a logical, systematic approach to getting the right new-hire in the right place at the right time every time. We all owe Lou Adler our thanks for the third edition of this gem.

BRUCE TULGAN
Author of *Winning the Talent Wars* and
founder of RainmakerThinking, Inc.®

Preface

I became a line manager for a Fortune 100 company in my mid-20s. Within days, and with no interview training, I was sent on a corporate recruiting trip to a few of the top MBA schools in the country. The vice president of human resources (HR) called me before leaving and gave me three minutes of advice on how to interview. What he said still sticks in my mind today. It was wrong, but it was the only training I had, and it seemed reasonable at the time.

He said to consider only candidates who possessed the 4A attributes of success—assertive, affable, attractive, and articulate. With this benchmark and a decent resume, I could determine competency in 15 minutes. Or I thought I could. As I look back, this process was about 60 percent to 65 percent effective in predicting subsequent success. This was true for the 30 to 40 people I hired to work for me personally and for the 50 to 100 I recommended to work for others. I hired some duds, but I hired enough great people that I got promoted very quickly. Within six years, I was a business unit manager for a division of a Fortune 500 company. One thing I did learn was that hiring great talent is the key to a manager's career progression. I also found out that being a headhunter and helping other managers hire great people was a far more lucrative career.

THE BEST ARE DIFFERENT THAN THE REST

Despite the weak predictive value of the 4A interview approach, I still used it with great success as a headhunter in my early days. Because I started out as a contingency recruiter (i.e., I only got paid when a candidate was hired), it wasn't too hard to find people who met the superficial 4A criteria and who could last the short 90-day guarantee. At the time, most of our competitors offered only 60 days, so this was a competitive advantage. Everything changed when I became a retained recruiter and offered a one-year guarantee. Under this provision, the person had to actually be competent, not just appear so. A decent resume and the 4A criteria were no longer sufficient for judging talent. Finding the correct criteria for assessing talent was how Performance-based Hiring came into being. It took about five years to figure out the basics. Now, 20 years later, I'm still perfecting it. This book is pretty close.

As I studied the recruiting and hiring process, I found out some other interesting things. First, the most suitable or the best person rarely got the job; instead, the person with the best interviewing and presentations skills did. This is the old 4A conundrum: The most attractive, affable, articulate, and assertive person who was reasonably qualified generally got the offer. Worse, when people were hired this way, money typically became the primary decision criteria. Although these people were competent, they typically were unmotivated to do the actual work required since this wasn't the basis of the selection criteria.

There were some other interesting things I discovered along the way about the differences between top people and everyone else:

➤ There is no correlation between interviewing and presentation skills and on-the-job performance. Judging people on how well they interview is a terrible way to assess ability.

➤ Top performers don't use the same criteria or methods when looking for other jobs. Now that it's so easy to find new jobs, more and more passive candidates now look online. However, these people are looking for bigger jobs or better jobs and more career opportunities. When they do look, they spend less time at it. Unfortunately, most advertising and screening methods are targeting the wrong pool of candidates—those who have ample time to look for similar jobs.

➤ The best people use more decision variables when deciding whether to accept an offer. They also drop out quickly along the way if things seem incongruous or unprofessional. When getting an offer, they also take longer to decide, and they consult with more advisors. Unfortunately, most hiring processes are geared around the needs of the average candidate, not the best. For the average candidate, a new job is a tactical move based on short-term criteria. For the best, it's a strategic move. This fundamental difference is rarely considered in a company's hiring processes.

➤ The best candidates don't typically have the exact mix of skills, experience, and education described in the job description. They make up for this with traits that can't easily be filtered—potential, self-motivation, leadership, tenacity, and vision. So if a company advertises and filters totally on skills, the best are wrongly excluded from consideration.

➤ Boring job descriptions exacerbate the problem. Unless a company is an employer-of-choice, top people aren't going to apply for run-of-the-mill jobs that seem the same as everyone else's.

➤ Many top people get nervous when being interviewed. This reveals itself as poor eye contact, short or shallow answers, lack of poise, and less self-confidence. This excludes many good candidates for superficial reasons.

Companies that don't design these differences into their hiring systems wind up seeing fewer top people and, by default, hire the wrong type of candidate. The best people really are different from the rest, not only in how they perform on the job, but also in how they look for new jobs and the criteria they use to accept one offer over another. Few companies take these fundamental differences into account.

The candidate-facing side is only half the problem though. Here are some other things I discovered about hiring managers and those on the hiring team that need fixing:

➤ Most hiring managers and other members of the selection team aren't very good at interviewing, yet they all think they are. Each one also uses his or her own pet criteria to judge competency. Much of it is downright illogical, a lot of it is prejudicial, and most of it is a waste of time.

➤ Most members of the interviewing team don't understand the real job, but they all have an important say, even if they're unprepared or conduct superficial interviews. In these cases, a no vote is the safer decision, and no votes have more weight than yes votes. This is why some of the best candidates are bypassed. It's also why many of the best people pull themselves out of the process, not wanting to work at companies that conduct superficial interviews.

➤ The assessment process is in worse shape than the interviewing process. Too many interviewers make quick decisions about the candidates they're interviewing, then they collect facts to support this initial biased assessment. Matters are made worse when all of the interviewers get together and use an up or down voting system with little debate or analysis to decide whether a person is hired or not. The lack of a formal evidence-based assessment process, comparable to how other major business decisions are made, is inexcusable.

➤ When anyone on the interviewing team finds a candidate they think is hot, they go into immediate sales mode. They also stop listening and stop evaluating competency in a transparent attempt to excite the hot prospect on the merits of the job. This not only cheapens the job and drives many top people away, but also requires premium pricing. More times than not, the hot candidate is just an overpaid flash in the pan.

➤ Very few people know how to deal with the current legal environment. Stupid things are said and done, causing companies to pay outrageous defense and liability fees that could have been simply avoided. Other companies overreact to the fear of these costs and establish policies and procedures that preclude them from hiring the best.

➤ Few managers know how to negotiate salaries and make offers. Hiring the best requires a consultative process addressing a number of short- and long-term career management and personal issues. The best candidates must balance these against competing alternatives. Few companies put their salespeople in the field without some type of extensive formal training. In most companies, comparable hiring and recruiting training seems to be unnecessary or too costly.

If a company wants to consistently hire superior people, it needs to implement a system that everyone uses that is designed to find and hire superior people. By default, most companies use a system that is designed to fill jobs. It's hard enough to hire one great person. It's even harder to hire 5 or 10 great people. But somehow when we get to thinking about hiring tens or hundreds, we lose sight of what it takes to hire just one great person. In this book, we show you how to hire one great person hundreds of times. For this to work, all of the problems noted earlier need to be overcome.

While I've observed all of these problems over the years, I've also observed a number of managers, HR people, and recruiters who seem to get it right most of time. They've mastered the rules of the game. Most have learned through trial and error. I've watched them in action, then tried their ideas out. I then further refined these ideas and tried them out again. I've also tracked candidates for years to determine the best predictors of subsequent success. Eventually, a few fundamental principles became clear, which formed the foundation for a systematic process for hiring top people. This became the Performance-based Hiring methodology described in this book.

Then came the Internet, job boards, new referral programs, candidate tracking systems, new types of assessment testing, and passive candidate name-generating systems. With all of these great tools now available, everything was supposed to change. Hiring the best would be as easy as posting an ad or making a phone call. These tools overpromised and underdelivered.

In many ways, these tools made it more difficult to hire top people, not easier. For one thing, the hidden job market is no longer hidden. The new tools make it easier for a passive candidate to find another job within days. This adds more competition into the mix. For recruiters, passive candidates are now easier to find, but harder to attract with everyone emailing and calling the same people. These tools have broken down the barriers to leaving a company, increasing workforce mobility while decreasing company loyalty. There is no longer a stigma to looking for other jobs and accepting counter-offers.

In this third edition of *Hire with Your Head*, I describe how to use these tools to your advantage, but this represents a small change in tactics, not a change in philosophy. The primary goal of this book is to show every manager and every recruiter how to hire one great person. The secondary goal is to show how to do it over again, and again, and again.

Here are seven ways to get it done:

1. *Stop using traditional boring job descriptions for advertising.* Top people don't look for jobs based on their skills and experience. They look for jobs based on the challenges and opportunities involved.

2. *Make the job description the real job.* Most job descriptions list skills, required experiences, academics, competencies, and personality traits, with a little about duties and responsibilities. This is more a people description than a job description. Instead, define what people need to do with their skills and experiences. These are called performance profiles. You'll use them to screen, assess, and recruit every one of your candidates.

3. *When the supply of top talent is less than the demand, you need to design your advertising and sourcing programs and systems based on how the best look for new jobs.* Somehow, most companies have not considered this fundamental principle of marketing and economics when creating their hiring and recruiting processes.

4. *During the interview, forget the clever questions.* Instead, dig deeply into a person's major accomplishments to observe trends of growth and patterns of behaviors. Then compare these to the performance objectives stated in the performance profile. This is the core of the performance-based interviewing process described in this book.

5. *Hire people who are both competent and motivated to do the work.* It's easy to measure competency, but don't stop there even if the person is affable, outgoing, and interested in your job.

To assess true motivation, you'll need to look for multiple examples of where the person has excelled and the underlying environment and circumstances.

6. *During the interview, put your emotions in the parking lot.* Implement an evidence-based assessment process, which means use the interview to collect information, not to make a decision. The decision is made later in a formal meeting where all interviewers share this unbiased information to reach consensus. Watch your accuracy soar with this simple system.

7. *As the competition for talent intensifies, strong recruiting skills are essential for hiring top people on a consistent basis.* This requires strong consultative selling skills in combination with great jobs, an interviewing process based on deep job-matching, and the hiring manager's total involvement. Too many companies still rely on a transactional approach to recruiting based on money, charming or pushing a candidate into acceptance.

Collectively, these ideas and principles are embedded in the Performance-based Hiring process described in this book. However, this book is not about principles; it's about tactics. It describes how to hire one great person again and again. Don't lose sight of this concept as you build systems to hire dozens or hundreds of great people. Each great person is unique. Treat him or her this way. Implemented properly, Performance-based Hiring can become your systematic process for hiring top talent.

LOU ADLER

Laguna Beach, California
January 2007
louadler@adlerconcepts.com

Contents

HIRE with your HEAD

Chapter 1

Performance-based Hiring: A Systematic Process for Hiring Top Talent

> Hire smart, or manage tough.
>
> —Red Scott

■ A RUDE AWAKENING—WHAT IT REALLY TAKES TO GET AHEAD

I still remember the following situation like it was yesterday. I got the call sometime in the morning on a mid-October day in 1972 at my first management job, financial planning manager at Rockwell International's Automotive Group in Troy, Michigan. At the time, I was working on my first presentation, due the next day, to the Group's president and vice president of finance. It was going to be a very long day and night. I didn't mind, since my new wife hadn't made the move to Michigan yet. My boss, Chuck Jacob, and the reason for my being in Michigan, was on the phone with a desperate plea. Chuck was a 29-year-old Harvard MBA whiz kid, just out of Ford Motor Company, trying to prove to everyone that he deserved his position as controller for this multibillion-dollar automotive supplier. He was also my idol. I listened. He was over at the University of Michigan interviewing MBA students for planning analyst positions to fill out our department. We needed these people urgently. The good news—too many had signed up for the interview, and Chuck needed me there to interview the overflow. We were going head-to-head with Ford, Procter & Gamble, IBM, and every other top Fortune 500 company, who wanted the best candidates from this prestigious MBA program. He told me there were stars in this group that we needed on our team. The bad news—I didn't have a minute to spare. I protested, vehemently, pleading 14-hour days, a long night, and a critical presentation the next day. There was a momentary delay. Chuck's response still blasts in my ears today: *"There is nothing more important to your success than hiring great people! Nothing. We'll somehow get the work done. Get your _____ over here now."* He then hung up.

I was there within the hour. Together we interviewed about 20 people, took eight of them to dinner that night in Ann Arbor, and hired three of the top MBA students within two weeks. I've lost track of Russ, Joe, and Vivek, but I want to thank them and Chuck (who passed away at a too-early age) for an invaluable lesson: *There is nothing more important—to your personal and company success—than hiring great people. Nothing.* Chuck and I got back to the office at 10:00 P.M. that night and worked together until 3:00 A.M. to finish the report. The handwritten version was presented the next day to Bob Worsnop and Bill Panny. We apologized for the format and lack of preparation, but told them we were doing something more important. They agreed.

■ BENCHMARKING THE BEST

I learned 50 percent of what I needed to know about hiring that day. Since then, I've been trying to understand the rest. I'm not quite there yet, but close. For the past 30-plus years, I've been fortunate to be able to work with other people, like Chuck, who always seem to hire great people, year in and year out. Few have had any formal training. They learned through trial and error. Equally important, I've lived and worked with managers who've made every possible hiring mistake in the book. This is their book, too. It's the collective stories of the good and the bad, sharing what to do and what not to do. There are some great techniques in this book, but none are more important than your belief that hiring great people is the single most important thing you can do to ensure your own success.

Many years later, I heard Red Scott's adage, "*Hire smart, or manage tough.*" As far as I was concerned, this summarized everything. I've never met anybody who could manage tough enough. No matter how hard you try, you can never atone for a weak hiring decision. A weak candidate rarely becomes a great employee, no matter how much you wish or how hard you work. Instead, hire smart. Use the same time and energy to do it right the first time. Brian Tracy of Nightingale-Conant fame said on one of his audio programs that effective hiring represents 95 percent of a manager's success. This seems a little high, but from what I've seen, 70 percent to 80 percent seems about right to me. This is still enough to keep hiring top talent in the number one position.

Every manager says hiring great people is their most important task; however, few walk the talk. Although important, it never seems urgent enough until it's too late. When it really comes down to the actual hiring process, our words don't match our actions. Here's how you can quickly test yourself to see how well you score as a hiring manager. Rank the performance of every member of your own team. Are most of them top-notch and exceeding expectations on all aspects of their work without being pushed? If they are, consider yourself a strong manager. Unless you're hiring people like this 80 percent to 90 percent of the time, you need to throw out everything you've learned about hiring, and start with a fresh new slate. If you're already in the elite 80 percent to 90 percent, don't relax. We're undergoing some major workforce shifts that will make it even more difficult to continue to hire great people every time.

Ongoing demographic changes, global expansion, the Internet, and the great dot-com boom and bust changed the hiring rules forever. This resulted in a cultural shift of major proportions. Changing jobs every few years no longer carries the stigma it did pre-2000. Company loyalty is no longer a hallmark of character. It is no wonder, considering that reductions in pension plans, the shifting of the cost of health care to the employee, and the outsourcing of whole departments have forced each employee to look out for him- or herself. Companies no longer set the hiring rules, the best people do. While this has always been true, evidence abounds that this shift is accelerating. Just consider the increase in turnover. Retention is now the new buzzword and focus, as companies attempt to stem the tide of their best people leaving for greener pastures. Unfortunately, most companies are still using outdated hiring processes to find top people in a modern world. Posting boring jobs on a major board is out of date.

This book is about hiring top people. Finding them, interviewing them, and recruiting them to work for you. Many of the techniques presented in this book have been developed by observing people who consistently hire top people. This is a process called *benchmarking* and much of the material in the book has been developed this way. Some of the concepts were developed through trial and error as part of my search practice and then tested and validated in the field. Benchmarking and modeling the best practices are the cornerstone of the Performance-based Hiring process described in this book.

Modeling your hiring practice after the managers and recruiters who consistently find and hire good people is similar to modeling after the good performers for any type of job. This is pretty simple. Just find out what the most successful people do that makes them successful, and find other people who can do the same things. It turns out you don't need to be a trained psychologist to hire good people. Psychologists look for the underlying traits of high performers. Why bother? Just look for high performers. They'll possess the necessary underlying traits.

As a result of these benchmarking studies, an interesting pattern has been observed: The best hiring decision is not intuitive or based on gut feelings. Instead, it involves a three-step process:

1. *Remain objective throughout the interviewing process, fighting the impact of first impressions, biases, intuition, prejudices, and preconceived notions of success.* This way, all information collected during the interview is both relevant and unbiased.

2. *Collect information across multiple job factors, rather than deciding quickly if the candidate is suitable for the job based on a narrow range of traits, like technical competency, intelligence, or affability.* Collecting the right information before deciding yes or no is the key here.

3. *Use an evidence-based approach to determine whether the candidate is motivated and competent to meet all job needs.* This involves some

type of formal decision-making process based on evaluating the evidence rather than using an up/down voting system.

From my observations, it appears that weaker interviewers and those managers who make many mistakes violate one or more of these rules. A large percentage of these mistakes are made by smart people who make quick simplistic judgments largely based on first impressions and personality. Not unexpectedly, their hiring results are random. The overly intuitive interviewer short-circuits the process, superficially assessing only a narrow group of important traits. Every now and then, a star is hired, but more often it's a person who is strong in only a few areas and not broad enough to handle all aspects of the position. If you've ever hired someone who is partially competent, you've fallen into this common trap. The technical interviewers are at the other extreme. These people go overboard on validating technical competency, ignoring other critical core skills like working with others, planning, budgeting, and meeting deadlines. While the result is a solid team, many of them lack the motivation to do the real work required. The key to hiring both competent and highly motivated people is to collect enough of the right facts. Trouble occurs when this balance is broken.

■ HIRING IS TOO IMPORTANT TO LEAVE TO CHANCE

If you want to hire superior people, use a system designed to hire superior people, not one designed to fill jobs. Even with all of the new available technology, most companies do not take full advantage of it. The emphasis seems to be on reducing costs and filling jobs as rapidly as possible, not hiring stronger people or minimizing hiring mistakes. Hiring the best must drive every aspect of a company's hiring process, especially if you want to redesign the hiring process you now have.

If you want to hire superior people, use a system designed to hire superior people, not one designed to fill jobs.

Throughout, I cite some great books on management and hiring, specifically:

➤ *Execution: The Discipline of Getting Things Done* by Larry Bossidy and Ram Charan, with Charles Burck.

➤ *Good to Great: Why Some Companies Make the Leap . . . and Others Don't* by Jim Collins.

➤ *First, Break All the Rules: What the World's Greatest Managers Do Differently* by Marcus Buckingham and Curt Coffman.

➤ *Winning* by Jack Welch and Suzy Welch.

➤ *Jack: Straight from the Gut* by Jack Welch, with John A. Byrne.

Each of these books should be read by everyone who is a manager or wants to be one. They set the stage. The one common theme is that hiring top people must be the primary task of all managers, and companies must establish the tools and the resources to do it right. While these books emphasize the importance of hiring top talent, none describe how to actually do it. That's what this book is about.

Hiring the best requires a system designed around the needs of hiring the best people. This is what Performance-based Hiring offers—a simple and scalable business process that can be used by small companies with just a few people or large corporations that employ tens of thousands. Even better, it works whether you're hiring large numbers of entry-level people or one CEO.

Wells Fargo is now rolling out Performance-based Hiring in their retail stores to hire tellers and bankers. American International Group (AIG) is now using Performance-based Hiring to hire managers, insurance sales reps, and customer service reps for their call centers. Broadcom, Cognos, and Quest are using the process to find and hire software development engineers throughout the world. HealthEast Care System in Minneapolis uses it to hire nurses and nurses aides. The YMCA is using Performance-based Hiring to hire area CEOs and branch managers to manage their facilities, as well as thousands of camp counselors every summer. And the list goes on at companies large and small, in the United States and abroad. These companies recognize that hiring top talent is not the same as getting requisitions filled, and they have found that Performance-based Hiring is the solution.

At its core, hiring the best is about understanding how the best people look for new jobs and how they decide to accept one job over the other. It's about why they decide to take, or not take, a counteroffer. It's about why they take one job over another even if the pay is less. Hiring the best is not about setting up an applicant tracking system or posting a traditional job description on some job board. Hiring the best is not about managing data more efficiently, but about managing the *right* data more efficiently.

Not understanding what motivates recruiters, managers, and the best candidates, and how they make decisions is the reason hiring is more challenging now than it was pre-Internet. Top candidates now have more choices than ever before, and it's easy for these people to find new jobs. The openness of the job market has made it far easier for a top person who is a little frustrated with his or her job to find something better. Unless you take into account this major increase in workforce mobility in your hiring and retention process, you are doomed to forever play catch-up.

The following 11 reasons are some easily correctable problems that prevent companies from attracting enough top people. As you read through the list, consider how many are representative of your company's hiring processes:

1. *Hard-to-find job openings*: Do you push jobs to candidates or do they still have to hunt to find your openings? With so many choices, the best candidates won't waste their time looking for needles in haystacks. Few companies use standard search-engine techniques to allow top people to quickly find their open positions. We had one client whose ad for 20 call center reps was on page 37 of a 40-page Monster.com listing. More candidates now Google to find possible opportunities, bypassing career boards altogether. What would happen if a potential candidate put a few keywords and skills into Google, the name of your city, and a standard title? It's important that your openings are prominently featured on the first page of your corporate website.

2. *Poorly designed career web sites*: When candidates click on your company's web site, ensure that they can find all available jobs without using generic, time-consuming, pull-down menu choices. Most career sites make it too difficult for good people with little time to explore career opportunities

and check out open jobs. There are many interactive web features available today to attract people and keep them involved. Unfortunately, few HR/recruiting departments have kept pace with technology in this important area.

3. *Boring ads*: Most posted job descriptions are nothing more than lists of skills, qualifications, and required experiences. These commodity-like jobs certainly aren't written to compel a top person to apply or check them out. In many cases the prospect can't even check them out or explore them further unless he or she formally registers with the site. If it was a marketing site, those interested could send emails or call for more information. Something similar could be offered to the career section. For the call center position noted previously, the ad itself was boring, demeaning, and exclusionary. We rewrote it, made it fun and compelling, got it to the top five on the Monster.com listing, and had 280 people apply in one day.

4. A *cumbersome application process*: Applying for most jobs is so cumbersome and time consuming it precludes the best people from even applying because they don't have time to waste. This makes no sense. The application process used by most companies is designed around the needs of people the company doesn't want to hire. Monster.com revealed a study that indicated that if the application form is automatically filled in using techniques to extract information from the candidate's resume, there is a 75 percent chance the person will actually apply. If the form is blank, there is only a 20 percent chance the person will apply. Incorporate these ideas into every step of the process.

5. *Lack of basic consumer marketing expertise*: Most companies don't track the end-to-end yield of those initially viewing an ad to those actually applying. This is a common technique used by all marketing groups that use Internet advertising to maximize their advertising effectiveness. Somehow, HR/recruiting think all that's needed is to post a boring ad and the best people will knock down their doors.

6. *Lackadaisical managers*: Every manager believes the answer to hiring stronger people is having their recruiters source

more passive candidates. These same managers forget that these passive candidates want better jobs, better careers, and more money. More important, they want more time to explore these opportunities with the hiring manager before committing. Then these same managers get aggravated when the passive candidates aren't all that enthused about the boring jobs being offered, and they then have to spend more time convincing and recruiting them.

7. *Lack of clear understanding of the real job needs*: Recruiters and hiring managers are not looking for the same candidates. Most recruiters are screening candidates based on skills, while most managers are looking for something different. This covers the gamut from technical competency, drive, intelligence, potential, affability, or the always troublesome, "I'll know it when I see it." The best candidates then leave the interview sessions disappointed that no one they spoke with really understood what the job was.

8. *Lack of objectivity*: Emotions, biases, prejudices, and first impressions dominate the hiring decision. Too many interviewers make quick judgments about candidates in the first few minutes of the interview, then use the balance of the time looking for facts to confirm their initial biased reaction.

9. *The wrong perspective*: The best candidates, passive or active, are looking for careers, not jobs. Yet most companies offer identical jobs and wonder why they can't find enough good people. Under this basis, selecting one identical job over another is all about the money. And someone can always pay more. *Suggestion*: Don't differentiate on money, differentiate on opportunity.

10. *Weak interviewing and assessment process*: Everybody interviews differently, and few managers and recruiters are trained to do it right. There is also little understanding of real job needs. Then everyone on the hiring team votes yes or no. Since a unanimous yes decision is required, the no vote carries more weight. If an interviewer is untrained or unprepared, it's safer to vote no. Why not require more justification for a no vote than a yes vote? This alone will improve interviewing accuracy.

11. *Thinking recruiting is selling*: Most hiring managers don't know how to recruit and close. Recruiting the best is not about selling or charming. It's about providing big challenges and career opportunities and a little money thrown in.

You don't need to look too hard at your hiring process to observe a few of these obvious problems. Surprisingly, they are not that hard to solve. The key is to examine all aspects of your hiring process from the perspective of a top person who has little time to spare and multiple opportunities. First, you need to consider whether the jobs you post online or on your career website are compelling and interesting. You also need to determine whether top people can easily find these opportunities when your listing is competing with every other job for visibility. Next, consider whether your application process is a deterrent. Making these simple changes will instantly increase your pool of top candidates. Inadvertently, most companies have set up their hiring process to prevent bad people from getting in. Maybe it would be a better idea to focus on how to attract the best.

Hiring is comprised of a few core steps—defining the job, sourcing, interviewing, assessing, and recruiting. Redesign each of these steps from the perspective of a top candidate, and then integrate them into a systematic business process. While each step is relatively easy to solve, fixing all of them and making sure they stay fixed for all candidates is the secret to making the hiring of top talent a systematic business process.

At the core of this whole process is the job itself. Most of the previously noted problems are a result of short-circuiting the requisition generating process and deciding to use the job description as the selection standard. If the job itself isn't compelling and interesting, you have very little to offer. In some ways, it's like using the sticker on a car window as the primary advertising piece. This is dumb. Not only must real job needs be understood, it's also essential that everyone on the hiring team, especially the recruiter and the hiring manager, clearly understand these real job needs. This way, everyone who has to make a decision about a candidate's suitability for a job is on the same page. I refer to these real job needs as a *performance profile*.

A performance profile is not the job description or the list of skills or qualifications. A performance profile is what the person taking the job needs to do to be considered successful. Some companies call these *success profiles, performance-based job descriptions,* or *performance plans.* Whatever you call it though, it needs to describe the real job, not the person taking the job. Ask yourself why a top person would want the job.

Once you know the real job needs, hiring top talent is both possible and much easier. You'll use this information to post ads, select candidates to interview, assess competency and motivation, and negotiate the offer based on opportunity rather than compensation. When people on the hiring team don't know what's really required for job success, they assess the wrong things and attract the wrong people. Worse, they can't interest the right ones. By default, they substitute their biases, perceptions, and stereotypes in assessing candidate competency, not the person's ability and interest to do the work. This is why different people can meet the same candidate for the same job and each come up with a different assessment. At the end of the process, if candidates view all jobs as the same, the only differentiator is the money, not the opportunity to grow.

For the past 15 years, my company has trained over 30,000 people to use Performance-based Hiring as their sourcing, interviewing, and recruiting process. During these workshops, we take a quick survey of the hiring challenges facing managers and recruiters. I find it disappointing that despite all of the promises of the Internet and technology, not much has changed since we started taking these surveys. The gap even seems to be increasing as companies fall further behind in attracting the best, while their turnover increases. Following is a summary of the results over the past 15 years:

Performance-based Hiring Survey of Hiring Challenges, Practices, and Attitudes

> ➤ Almost everybody agrees that their online job postings are not very compelling. They certainly wouldn't induce someone sitting on the fence to apply.

> ➤ Most people say they never see enough good candidates and the situation is worsening.

➤ There is a belief that the quality and quantity of candidates from the major job boards has significantly declined since 2004.

➤ Turnover is increasing, and it's taken an upward spike since 2004.

➤ More candidates are rejecting offers or accepting counter-offers. This has increased dramatically since 2004.

➤ Most managers said they've made bad hiring decisions, especially hiring people who are competent, but not motivated to do the actual work required.

➤ Ninety-five percent of hiring managers indicated that hiring is number one or number two in their order of importance, but they only spend 10 percent to 15 percent of their time on the process. Of course, they complain about it. Few managers are measured on how well they perform on the hiring side and their ability to develop talent.

➤ Ninety-five percent of hiring managers don't like their company's hiring process.

➤ While over 50 percent of the companies indicated they had a formal hiring and recruiting process in place, most said their hiring managers disregarded most of the rules, especially on how to interview.

➤ Almost everybody felt that the interview process wasn't very accurate. Few were surprised to learn that a study conducted by John Hunter of Michigan State University and Frank Schmidt of the University of Iowa indicated that the typical employment interview is only 57 percent effective in predicting subsequent success, or 7 percent better than flipping a coin.*

➤ Most managers thought they were personally very good interviewers, yet they rarely agreed with their associates when assessing candidates. Not surprisingly, they all used a dif-

---

* John Hunter and Frank Schmidt, "The Validity and Utility of Selection Methods in Personnel Psychology," *Psychological Bulletin*, 1998, vol. 124.

ferent interviewing method and selection criteria, and each felt his or her approach was superior.

➤ For most jobs, it takes from three weeks to three months after a candidate starts to determine true competency, although most managers think they can make an assessment pretty quickly.

Despite all of the books, articles, and wealth of evidence supporting the importance of hiring the best, little has changed. Everyone is still looking for the magic fix. The Internet wasn't the answer. Neither were the job boards or applicant tracking systems. While hiring the best on a consistent companywide basis is not easy, it's no harder than setting up a worldwide distribution or accounting system, designing a new product, launching a new web site, or starting a business. It's only a process that needs to be implemented, just like any other process. Most important, it requires a commitment from the executive management of the company that hiring is important, and the resources and time will be devoted to making it happen.

■ THROW AWAY EVERYTHING YOU KNOW ABOUT HIRING

When thinking about hiring, let's start from scratch. For one thing, the typical interview, the one most managers use, is a flawed means to hire anyone. Emotions, biases, chemistry, and stereotypes play too big a role. The competency of the interviewer is questionable. True knowledge of the job is weak. Some candidates give misleading information because they're not asked appropriate questions. Others are nervous. Standards fall as desperation grows. Some of these problems can be eliminated just by knowing their causes.

One of the biggest problems is that too much emphasis is placed on the interaction between the candidate and the interviewer, and too little on the candidate's ability and motivation to do the job. This is the primary cause of hiring mistakes (see Figure 1.1). Over the past 30 years, I've been personally involved in over 4,500 different interviewing situations. Without question, most of the hiring decision is overly influenced by the interpersonal relationship

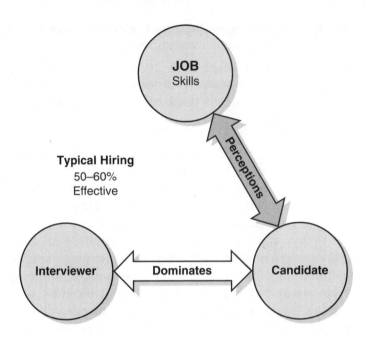

Figure 1.1 Hiring accuracy is random when relationships dominate the decision.

developed early in the interview between the applicant and the hiring manager. Sometimes this can be in just a few minutes. This has to do with chemistry, first impressions, emotions, biases, stereotypes, the halo effect (i.e., globalizing a few strengths), and the tendency to hire in your own image.

In most cases, real job needs are poorly understood, and even if they are well understood, they're filtered through these interpersonal relationships and biases. This is how randomness enters the hiring process. If you like a candidate, you tend to go into chat mode, ask easier questions, and look for information to confirm your initial impression. If you don't like someone, you put up a defense shield, ask tougher questions, and try to end the interview quickly. You go out of your way to find information to prove your initial belief that the candidate is incompetent.

In both cases, the hiring assessment is inaccurate because the wrong things are being assessed. The candidate's ability to *get* the job is what's really being measured, not the candidate's ability to *do*

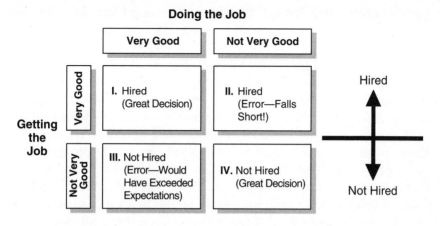

Figure 1.2 The impact of doing the job versus getting the job.

the job. Presentation is overvalued in comparison to the candidate's ability to handle the job successfully. Getting the job includes things like personality, first impression, handshake, affability, social confidence, assertiveness, appearance, extroversion, and verbal communications. Doing the job includes factors such as drive, team skills, achieving objectives, technical competence, management and organizational skills, intellect, and leadership, to name a few. There is a natural tendency to overemphasize the "getting the job" skills when assessing a candidate, rather than the person's ability to "do the job." The impact of this is shown in Figure 1.2.

➤ When Getting the Job Is More Important Than Doing the Job

When the hiring decision is based more on a candidate's ability to get the job, rather than do the job, two bad things happen. One, we frequently hire people who fall short of expectations (Situation II in Figure 1.2). These are the people who are good interviewers but weak performers. We also don't hire people who are strong candidates but weaker interviewers (Situation III). Two good things can happen, but they're inadvertent. We hire people who are good at both the getting and the doing (Situation I), and we don't hire those weak at both (Situation IV). You don't even need to read this book or take a single training course to get these two parts right. It's all luck. As my former partner once said, "Even a blind squirrel finds a nut every now and then." It's how you handle the other 50 percent that will improve your hiring effectiveness.

Everything changes when the hiring decision is based primarily on the candidate's ability to do the work. You still hire those good at both (Situation I), and don't hire those bad at both (Situation IV). More important, you eliminate the other two major hiring errors. You stop hiring those who always fall short of expectations (Situation II), and you start hiring those who are really great but might be a little weak on the interviewing side (Situation III). You need to hire people who are very good at doing the job, not those just very good at getting the job.

➤ Substitute the Job as the Dominant Selection Criteria

Moving the decision-making process from "getting" to "doing" is the key to increasing hiring accuracy. Part of this is remaining objective, overcoming the natural tendency to judge people based on first impressions, personality, and a few select traits. Overcoming this problem will eliminate 50 percent of all common hiring errors. Understanding real job needs will eliminate most of the rest of them. Figure 1.3 illustrates the shift in decision making based on the candidate's ability and motivation to successfully do the work required, not the person's relationship with the interviewer.

➤ Increase Objectivity during the Interview

Since we're mentally wired to make instantaneous judgments about people based on first impressions, it's not easy to make the performance requirements of the job the dominant selection criteria. This emotional reaction is part of the fight versus flight response. If you like someone, you relax. If you don't, you get uptight. Within 10 to 15 minutes, this normal emotional reaction is neutralized. Unfortunately, by this time, many of us have already

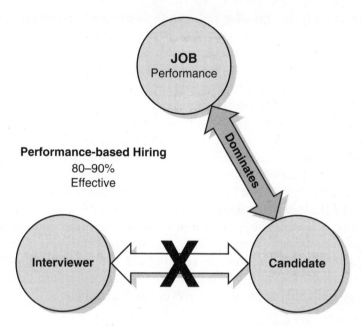

Figure 1.3 Hiring accuracy increases when performance is the selection criteria.

made the yes or no hiring decision, and we then spend the rest of the interview collecting enough facts to support our initial flawed impressions, good or bad.

Bring this emotional reaction to the conscious level to minimize its effect. If you buy in too soon, you tend to ignore negative data, globalize strengths, begin selling, and stop listening. You may dismiss a lack of skills as something easily learned and start selling, trying to convince the candidate why this is such a great job. You won't ask tough questions covering real job needs. You assume that the candidate can do them all because he possesses a few, apparently important, characteristics. You go out of your way to find easier questions to ask, and you even unknowingly give your favorite candidate the answers. This approach not only gives the person who makes a strong presentation the upper hand, but you waste time considering candidates who are more fluff than substance. From our experience, 30 percent to 50 percent of the candidates you meet who make strong first impressions are just average performers.

Conversely, if you don't like the candidate, you immediately feel uptight or disappointed. You grit your teeth and begin thinking of how you can end the interview as soon as possible. Sometimes boredom sets in. If you listen at all, you ignore all positive data as being a fluke or unrepresentative. Weaknesses will be magnified. Different approaches are instantly judged as worthless or ill-conceived. If the candidate is actually pretty strong, but you don't like the person, you undersell the job as something beneath her, hoping she'll exclude herself. We have also discovered that 30 percent to 50 percent of the candidates you meet who make a bad first impression turn out to be much stronger once you get to know them and their accomplishments.

There is a solution to this dilemma. As you start following the performance-based interviewing techniques presented in this book, you'll be able to quickly see through the candidates who initially seem strong, and you'll find a few stars you would have normally overlooked, when you give them half a chance.

A Short Course on Interviewing

A few years ago, the CEO of a fast-growing marketing company cornered me before I was to speak at his trade group breakfast seminar. He had an interview with a vice presidential candidate the next day and wanted a few quick tips on hiring. In response, I gave him the most important secret of hiring success. I told him not to make a hiring decision in the first 30 minutes of the interview. More hiring mistakes are made in the first half-hour of an interview than at any other time. I told him that if he could delay his decision, favorable or unfavorable, he would eliminate 50 percent of his hiring mistakes.

The shortest course in interviewing: Wait 30 minutes before making any decision about a candidate's ability to do the work.

To increase your objectivity during the interview, use the following six ideas:

1. *Measure first impressions at the end of the interview.* As part of our structured performance-based interview methodology described in Chapter 4, we include a step comparing first impressions before and after the interview. At the end of the interview, you can then determine whether the candidate's first impression helps or hurts in the person's performance of the job. By then, you'll discover it probably doesn't matter.

2. *Disallow the yes/no decision unless the candidate is a complete dud.* Make it a rule that you must suspend any decision for at least 30 minutes. During these 30 minutes, conduct a work-history review and get some details about the candidate's major accomplishments (e.g., breadth, scope, scale, size, complexity, impact). A "no" is okay if the person is a complete mismatch, but if you have any doubts, put the person into a "further evaluation required" pool.

3. *Delay the decision by redefining the purpose of the interview.* Use the interview just to collect information, not to make a decision. This forces you to suspend your judgment. Go out of your way to ask the same questions to all candidates. Then collectively debrief with the complete hiring team. If the interviewer recognizes that he or she doesn't need to provide a yes or no opinion, the focus will be on obtaining stronger evidence.

4. *Give partial voting rights.* Since most managers have a tendency to rush to judgment based on very narrow selection criteria, only let them vote on these factors. Don't give anyone full voting rights. Instead, set up a process where the collective judgment of the whole hiring team prevails. This way, everyone must share information before deciding.

5. *Demand evidence before you accept gut feelings.* Facts, examples, and details must be provided to justify a ranking, good or bad. "I don't think the person would fit," is inappropriate. However, a comment like "the environment, pace, available resources, and the lack of a formal decision-making process at the person's last two companies is a clear indication that the person would not survive here," is certainly sufficient. After you've shared all available information, then it's okay for gut feelings to override the evidence. The subtitle of the

first edition to this book was A *Rational Way to Make a Gut Decision*. While you can never learn everything you would like to about a candidate, you should try to find out as much as possible before you resort to your gut.

6. *Make a "no" harder to justify than a "yes."* A "no" is safe and easy. It encourages laziness, and it rewards interviewers who are weak or those who were unprepared. To eliminate this potential problem, demand more detailed information and evidence from those invoking the "no." A "no" is okay as long as it's based on factual information. Too often, it's based on weak interviewing.

It's hard to overcome our initial reaction to a candidate. On top of this, add biases, preconceived ideas, prejudices, and the halo effect to the list of why managers make dumb hiring mistakes. Following the previous steps to increase objectivity eliminates many of these. Using the performance-based interviewing process described in the book on a consistent basis eliminates most of the rest of them.

➤ Get Candidates to Give Good Answers

There is one other big issue that needs to be addressed to improve interviewing accuracy. It took me about 10 years before I figured out that the best candidates aren't the best interviewers. After about 1,000 interviews, it became pretty clear there was no correlation between interviewing skills and job competency. The best candidates aren't generally the best interviewers, and the best interviewers aren't generally the best candidates. This is pretty amazing, and scary, because most interviewing methods measure interviewing skills, not job competency.

This is a huge problem. Part of the problem is minimized by controlling our biases and the impact of first impressions, but this is only a partial solution. Interviewers need to proactively take responsibility for obtaining complete information about job competency from each candidate. Interviewers need to train candidates to give complete information. If you leave it up to candidates to provide this information on their own, you're measuring interviewing and presentation skills, not job competency. If you Google "behavioral interviewing questions," you get 1.1 million hits. Most of these are geared to candidates who want to learn to ace the behavioral interview. The performance-based interviewing methodology presented in this book allows you to get past the well-prepared, articulate, and confident candidates who are getting offers based on presentation, not substance.

Interviewers need to proactively take responsibility for obtaining complete information about job competency from each candidate.

■ USING A SYSTEMATIC PROCESS FOR HIRING TOP TALENT

Every company wants to hire top talent, but few succeed. Those that do succeed rarely keep it up on a consistent basis. Sometimes success is due to a hot company that establishes a great, but short-lived, employer brand. The best then flock there. If a bit of negative news hits, they then fly away to the next hot prospect. A company needs to be able to hire top people during the ups and the downs. This takes a systematic approach to hiring based on solid principles and strong processes. Every other business process has improved profoundly over the past 20 years. Consider distribution, inventory management, call center management, order processing, product design, accounting, and manufacturing if you need some examples. However, hiring seems to be stuck in a time warp.

The primary reason for inconsistency on the hiring front is the lack of a simple and scalable hiring process that line managers will willingly use. In this book, the case is made that Performance-based Hiring can become the underlying business process for hiring top talent. This is attributed primarily to the fact that it represents a commonsense approach that meets the needs of all stakeholders—recruiters, executives, line managers, everyone on the interviewing team, and most important of all, top candidates who don't look for or accept new jobs in the same way average candidates do.

When a company is not an employer of choice, if it's not a well-known company, or when candidate supply is less than demand, it takes enormous resources to consistently hire top people. This situation is more difficult when technology doesn't integrate well with new and existing tools, when every manager does it his or her own way, when recruiter competency varies from strong to weak, and when best practices are ignored due to lack of time or leadership. This pretty much describes most companies in the world.

However, the tools available today make hiring more businesslike if they are effectively tied together. Consider this: The marketing knowledge to quickly find and source top people is available today, but it is very underused. The technology to process information efficiently and improve recruiter productivity is available today, but it is poorly implemented. The recruiting skills to recruit and close top people are available today, but most recruiters, especially those in corporations, are unwilling to learn new techniques. The interviewing and assessment tools to accurately assess candidate competency are available today, but managers don't want to use them. Learning what tools are available today and making them easier to use is what this book and Performance-based Hiring is all about.

Performance-based Hiring is based on two core concepts. First, everything involved in hiring must be designed around the needs of how top people look for jobs and accept offers. Second, each of the individual steps must be integrated in a systematic fashion that is easy to use. Putting these pieces together means that you must follow four steps:

1. *Write compelling job descriptions that describe real job needs, not ads that emphasize skills and qualifications.* A top person should be able to look at your job description and say, "Wow! That's a job I want to consider." It should be so clearly written that your top candidate could show it to his circle of personal advisors and easily convince them this is a true career move, with the compensation of secondary importance.

2. *Design every aspect of sourcing to attract top people (whether active or passive), which includes where you place the exciting job descriptions, how you design the career web site, how you get referrals, and when you make phone calls.*

3. *Organize the interview to assess competency and create opportunity at the same time.* You do this by asking tougher questions, not by overselling or overtalking. Interviewers must use the information obtained to collect evidence that the candidate is both competent and motivated to meet all real jobs. Top candidates must leave the interview knowing they have been assessed completely and properly. More important, they must leave knowing the job offers a true career opportunity.

4. *Make recruiting, negotiating offers, and closing a natural, integrated part of each step in the hiring process.* Do not save these for the end. It starts by creating a compelling opportunity. It continues through the interviewing process, testing and closing at each successive step. It ends when the candidate agrees to your offer based on opportunity, not compensation. Professional recruiting is how you overwhelm the competition and minimize counteroffers.

The four steps that comprise Performance-based Hiring are graphically shown in Figure 1.4.

Figure 1.4   The Performance-based Hiring Process.

In these pages, you learn that Performance-based Hiring is a practical and easy-to-learn methodology that provides any manager the ability to consistently hire top people.

■ PUTTING THE PIECES TOGETHER: A ROAD MAP TO THE ORGANIZATION OF THIS BOOK

A little about the organization of this book is in order. Performance-based Hiring involves the four separate stages, as previously described—defining the job, finding top candidates, interviewing and assessment, and recruiting and closing. While there is a definite time sequence to the process, many of these tasks are conducted in parallel. Most important, each step is linked in a logical fashion. This is how you convert the separate steps involved in hiring into a business system. While the focus is on hiring top talent, it's also critical to incorporate the specific needs of recruiters, hiring managers, and everyone on the hiring team. In most companies, one group's desires dominate the process design, negatively impacting the overall system's effectiveness. This lack of integration can cause severe problems.

This past year I worked with a consulting firm that didn't want to be too specific about the type of projects their new consultants would handle. They were doing a pretty good job of hiring enough top people, although in my mind they were paying too much and offering more sizzle than substance. I made the point that top people want to know the specifics of the job they're being offered, even though this might require the company to prepare a performance profile ahead of time. Top people use this job information to compare one job to another and even whether to accept a counteroffer or not. From the top candidate's perspective, these specifics are essential, even though there is some extra work required on the company's part to put them together. However, the extra work required is not nearly as much as looking for another candidate when an offer is turned down, or dealing with an underperforming employee who accepted a job for the wrong reasons, or having to fill the job again after the person leaves within the year for something apparently better. This then puts the company in the position of putting together a counteroffer in an attempt to lure the person back in. I contended that all of this can be avoided when a performance profile is prepared at the outset. My client conceptually agreed, although I suspected they wouldn't be as rigorous as they should be when opening new requisitions.

However, now the story gets more interesting. Coincidentally, I happened to share a taxi ride that afternoon with one of the company's new hires on the way to the airport. She was a very talented young woman from a top MBA program. Since it was a long ride, I had the chance to ask her about her job. After a bit of hesitation, but not much, she told me she really didn't like the job, or her current boss. She said she was underutilized, quite dissatisfied, and planned to leave within the year if things didn't improve. She had been with the company about six months, and felt she was misled about the types of projects she would be involved in. She told me that if she could do it over she would have taken an offer with a less prestigious firm, handling bigger projects, as some of her classmates had. She also told me she was not alone in her feelings about the company. I caught up with her a few months later via email and she responded that the company had finally given her an exciting project. However, she indicated she would explore opportunities outside her firm if additional exciting projects weren't forthcoming.

I didn't reveal this confidential information to my client, but this type of stuff goes on every day. Not understanding real job needs and conducting an interview based on matching competencies and interests against real job needs is at the core of this problem. This is the root cause of the rise in turnover companies are experiencing. You can't be myopic when designing hiring systems. Everyone's perspective is important, but the most important of all is the one of the top person you're trying to hire. This doesn't mean you have to give away the farm or roll out the red carpet. Throughout these pages, you discover that these techniques are old-school and counterproductive. Making the job hard to earn but worthy of earning is how you hire top people.

➤ Chapter-by-Chapter Summary

Performance-based Hiring is a hiring system, not an interviewing method, recruiting technique, or sourcing process. It's all these woven together. To make it work, you need to understand all of the separate parts first. However, as long as you've prepared a performance profile, you can start trying out everything within hours. A performance profile is the foundation of the whole process. There is a step-by-step guide included in Chapter 2 on how to do this. With a performance profile, you're now in a position to find more top talent. Some of the latest sourcing techniques are given in Chapter 3. Chapters 4, 5, and 6 collectively represent the interview and assessment piece. As you'll discover, how each interviewer collects information and shares it with the team is the key to increasing assessment accuracy. Do *not* use the interview to make a yes/no decision, use it only to collect information. Eliminating individual voting privileges is a great way to increase assessment accuracy and prevent dumb hiring mistakes. While recruiting and closing has its own chapter, these techniques are woven throughout the process. In Chapter 7, they're brought together, showing how to negotiate offers based on opportunities, not compensation. More important, the recruiting process we recommend is also how you increase retention and improve on-the-job performance. Chapter 8 ties everything together describing a simple rollout plan that can be used by a single manager or a whole company. The key here is to pilot the process, get the right metrics, calculate the return on investment (ROI) of hiring top people, and then begin the implementation process.

For quick reference, be sure to refer to the following chapter-by-chapter summary:

Chapter 1—Performance-based Hiring: A Systematic Process for Hiring Top Talent. Hiring top talent needs to be an integrated business process that meets the needs of all participants including top candidates, line managers, recruiters, and everyone on the hiring team.

Chapter 2—Performance Profiles: Defining Success, Not Skills. If you want to hire top people, define first what they need to do in terms of accomplishments, not what they need to have in terms of skills. Then ask, "Why would a top person want this job?"

Chapter 3—Talent-Centric Sourcing: Finding the Best Active and Passive Candidates. There is no longer a hidden pool of top candidates. Now everybody can find them. You need to use the latest technology, aggressive consumer marketing advertising techniques, and advanced recruiting techniques if you want top candidates to consider your open opportunities.

Chapter 4—The Two-Question Performance-Based Interview. It only takes two questions to determine the 10 best predictors of on-the-job success. Repeating them over and over again to develop trend lines of performance is how you assess consistency, growth, and potential.

Chapter 5—The Evidence-Based Assessment. Interviewing accuracy can soar when information is shared and consensus is reached. The 10-Factor Candidate Assessment template is used to assess a candidate's competency and motivation in comparison to real job needs.

Chapter 6—Everything Else after the First Interview: Completing the Assessment. There's much more to assessing competency than just interviewing. To get it right, you need to conduct reference checks, assessment tests, background checks, drug tests, and then throw in a take-home problem to boost your odds of getting it right.

Chapter 7—Recruiting, Negotiating, and Closing Offers. You'll need to offer at least a 30 percent increase if you want to hire the best. However, to do it right, most of this needs to be in job stretch and job growth, not compensation. Recruiting, negotiating, and closing focus more on career counseling and creating opportunities than selling.

Chapter 8—Implementing Performance-based Hiring. By the time you finish this book, you'll be able to hire a great person every time as long as you follow the steps as described. It takes a little more time and effort to make sure everyone else in your company follows them, too.

Performance-based Hiring is as much about good management as it is good hiring. As far as I can tell, the two are inseparable. You become a better manager in the process of hiring better people— which, in turn, makes you a better manager. And if you want to keep the top people you just hired, you need to be a great manager. Creating a performance profile is the first step in hiring great people and becoming a great manager.

To *hire with your head*, you need to combine emotional control with good fact-finding skills and intuitive decision making. This whole-brain thinking provides the critical balance to match job needs, the interviewer's personality, and the candidate's abilities and interests. Combine this with state-of-the art sourcing. Without enough good candidates, everything else is futile. Once you start meeting strong candidates, good recruiting skills become essential. Recruiting starts at the beginning, not the end. It must be part of an integrated interviewing and assessment process to work effectively. This is the strength of Performance-based Hiring. It brings all of the critical hiring processes together. While each step is easy to use separately, its effectiveness lies in their integration. Overlook any aspect and the whole process collapses. Do all steps for consistently great hiring results.

HOT TIPS TO MAKE HIRING NUMBER ONE

✔ *"There is nothing more important to a manager's personal success than hiring great people. Nothing."*—Chuck Jacob

✔ Management is easy as long as you clearly know the performance needs of the job and hire great people to do it.

✔ Hiring is too important to leave to chance. Hiring is the only major process in a company that's random. Any other process that's this unreliable would have been redesigned long ago.

✔ The key to better hiring decisions is to "Break the emotional link between the candidate and interviewer and substitute the job as the dominant selection criteria."

✔ When you start the interview, wait 30 minutes before deciding yes or no. An even better approach is to measure first impressions at the end of the interview when you're not affected by them.

✔ Measure a candidate's ability to do the job, not get the job. Determine whether you like or dislike the candidate after you've determined his or her competence. Substance is more important than style, but it's sometimes hard to tell the difference.

✔ Great hiring requires more than just good interviewing skills. Performance-based Hiring brings everything together into an integrated, systematic core business process.

✔ *"Hire smart, or manage tough."*—Red Scott

Chapter 2

Performance Profiles: Define Success, Not Skills

Many people regard execution as detail work that's beneath the dignity of a business leader. That's wrong. It's a leader's most important job.*

—Larry Bossidy

■ IF YOU WANT TO HIRE SUPERIOR PEOPLE, FIRST DEFINE SUPERIOR PERFORMANCE

This chapter is about understanding execution. To understand real job needs, it's important to remember the following four key points:

1. *Everyone wants to hire superior people.* Yet the criteria most people use to define work, write ads, filter resumes, and interview candidates is based on a misleading job description that describes qualifications and requirements. In the majority of cases, these job descriptions don't define the job at all, they define the person who will ultimately take the job.

---

* Larry Bossidy and Ram Charan, with Charles Burck, *Execution: The Discipline of Getting Things Done* (New York: Crown Business, 2002).

Traditional job descriptions that list skills, experience, academics, and competencies are misleading, and are the primary reason companies can't find enough top people.

2. *If you want to hire superior people, first define superior performance.* Performance is about results, not about skills and qualifications. This is the execution part of the job. If someone can do the work, he or she obviously has the skills. Here's a historical example demonstrating the importance of results over specifications. When Teddy Roosevelt was Assistant Secretary of the U.S. Navy, he purchased a used Brazilian merchant ship, the N*ictheroy* for $500,000, under the proviso that it must arrive under its own power within a very short time frame to a specific port. The contract didn't have any of the normal technical specifications. Roosevelt knew that if the ship couldn't travel the distance required by the date specified it was worthless.*

3. *Once you've defined superior performance, all you need to do is find and hire people who are competent and motivated to do the work.* While these people will have many of the skills listed in the traditional job description, the mix will most likely be different, but comparable, to what was initially described.

4. *Don't compromise on performance; compromise on the qualifications.* This will expand the pool of top performers without giving up anything.

The job description is the performance profile and it's the foundation of Performance-based Hiring. A performance profile describes the six to eight performance objectives a person taking the job needs to do to be successful. It differs from a job description in that it doesn't describe skills or traits, but rather what the person needs to accomplish with his or her skills and traits. Instead of saying the person must "Have five years of accounting experience and a CPA," it's clearer to say, "Complete the implementation of the Sarbanes-Oxley reporting requirements by Q2."

By describing job success rather than skills, performance profiles can be better used to source and filter candidates, conduct

---

* Edmund Morris, *The Rise of Theodore Roosevelt* (New York: Ballantine Book, 1980).

comprehensive interviews, recruit the candidate, and negotiate and close offers. The performance profile can also be used as the foundation for the new employee's onboarding program. This increases the likelihood for success by clarifying expectations just as the person starts the new job. Taking this one step further, the performance profile can then become the cornerstone of a company's ongoing performance-management process by comparing real job requirements to what the person actually achieved.

The Internet has had a profound impact on increasing workforce mobility. Good people, even when they're slightly frustrated, can find seemingly better jobs relatively quickly. A properly prepared and regularly updated performance profile can be a useful countermeasure for this trend. This is a process called *continuous rehiring.* As you discover in this chapter, a performance profile is used to attract top performers by clearly demonstrating job stretch and job growth. Once the person is on the job, a manager can use this same tool to offer a continuous opportunity for personal development by adding new and bigger performance objectives as the initial objectives are achieved.

Table 2.1 lists the differences between traditional job descriptions and performance profiles. Compare the following two job descriptions for a product manager. The list on the left describes the more traditional skills and experiences. The list on the right defines the required results, or deliverables. Given only one choice, would

Table 2.1   Traditional Job Descriptions versus Performance Profiles

Experience and Skills	Desired Results, Deliverables
BS degree, MBA a plus	*Upgrade* the product marketing and new product launch process.
5 years of experience in consumer products	*Develop* new online and direct distribution channels.
Strong market research	*Prepare* a comprehensive competitive analysis report in the first month.
Heavy Web analytics experience	*Lead* massive buildup in online and multimedia advertising programs.
Good team skills a must	*Coordinate* all product launch activities with procurement and distribution.

you rather hire the person with all of the skills and experiences or the one who can deliver the desired results?

Over the past 10 years, I've asked this question to over 10,000 people. Ninety-eight percent want to hire someone who can deliver the results. If you agree, all you have to do is throw away traditional job descriptions for hiring purposes and define the results instead.

➤ Use the Same Criteria for External Hiring as You Do for Internal Moves

When performance is the basis for making hiring decisions, accuracy increases dramatically. Most companies by default already use this type of performance-based assessment approach for internal moves with great success. For a known internal person, the predictability of subsequent performance is very high, about 80 percent to 90 percent, even for a promotion. For the external hire, predictability is only around 55 percent to 65 percent. The reasons for this disparity are obvious. The internal move is more accurate because we know the person's past performance, attitude, work habits, intelligence, leadership and team skills, ability to learn, management style, potential, and commitment. All of these are educated guesses for the unknown outsider. A person we don't know is assessed differently, usually on experience, skills, academics, and personality as measured in the interview. All of which are poor predictors of success. This comparison is shown in Table 2.2.

The decision-making process between outside hiring and internal moves is fundamentally different. Personality and qualifications dominate the selection for outside hiring. Past performance, potential, and teamwork are the basis for the internal move. A performance profile bridges this gap.

Table 2.2 Criteria for External Hiring and Internal Moves

Outside Hiring Factors	Internal Move or Promotion
Degrees, certifications	Ability to deliver results
Excessive experience	Balance of strengths and weaknesses
Strong base of skills	Potential and capacity to learn new skills
First impressions	Team skills, attitude, character, and values
Interviewing personality	True personality, commitment, and motivation

It's What You Do with What You Have, Not What You Have That Counts

Underlying the concept of using skills-based job descriptions is the unstated hope that enough experience, skills, academics, and personality will be sufficient to meet the performance requirements of the job. On this basis, the more skills and qualifications the candidate has, the better. This is flawed logic and excludes many top performers from consideration. A candidate can *have* all of the skills required and not be able to *do* the job. There are many people who can do the job without having exactly the skills listed, especially if they're highly motivated. (These are the people who have been successfully promoted or laterally transferred.) Externally, these same high-potential people are automatically excluded from consideration because they don't have the skills. Worse, high-potential people who have the exact skill set required rarely want to do the same work, so they won't even apply. Limiting your sourcing to people who have all of the skills and qualifications is really a hunt for average performers.

Limiting your sourcing to people who have all of the skills and qualifications is really a hunt for average performers.

It doesn't need to be this way when you consider that it's what a person does with his or her skills, experiences, and abilities that determine success, not the quantity. By changing the focus to *doing* rather than *having*, the underlying concept of hiring can be altered with a focus on targeting top performers while dramatically increasing assessment accuracy.

Preparing Performance Profiles: Clarifying Expectations Is the Key to Hiring Success

Over the past 30 years, I've prepared over 1,000 performance profiles for jobs ranging from a person in a call center handling Yellow Page renewals to a COO for a Fortune 500 company. Every job, from entry-level to CEO, has six to eight performance objectives that define job success. These objectives spell out what the person in the job must do to be considered successful, not what the individual must have in terms of years of experience, industry, academics, or skills.

A CEO's performance objectives might include turning around a struggling division, leading the development of a new strategy to take on Google, and rebuilding the management team from top to bottom. For a camp counselor, the list might include preparing the next's day activities each night, being on top of each activity, ensuring that even the quiet campers are involved, and showing 100 percent total involvement in the camp's activities while in session. As a sample, here's a more complete example of a performance objective for a project manager:

> During the first 30 days, prepare a detailed review of the status of the project including an appraisal of all critical action items and potential bottlenecks. Develop and present a plan to the executive committee evaluating alternatives ensuring that this critical project is completed on time.

Creating SMARTe performance objectives as defined in the following list helps everyone involved in the selection decision better understand the real needs:

Specific: Include the details of what needs to be done so that others understand it.

Measurable: It's best if the objective is easy to measure by including amounts or percent changes.

Action-oriented: Action verbs build, improve, change, and help understanding.

Results: A definition that complements the measurable piece by clearly indicating what needs to happen.

Time-bound: Include a date or state how long it will take to start and complete.

environment: Describe the company culture, pace, pressure, available resources, and politics.

Other than defining the project and expanding on the environment, the project manager performance objective example is pretty SMARTe as it is.

In *First, Break All the Rules*, Buckingham and Coffman make a convincing case for the use of performance profiles rather than job descriptions for all aspects of management.* Based on extensive interviews with thousands of people, they describe the best managers as those who first clearly define performance expectations for every job. These positions are then filled with people who have both the ability and the motivation to do the work required. General Electric (GE) measures talent by those who can execute and deliver predetermined results. In *Good to Great*, Jim Collins examines how great companies emerged from the average.† His conclusion is that each had a leader who built teams of great people who could define and deliver the results. Hiring great people is about defining the desired results, and then finding people with the ability and desire to deliver these results. It's not about listing skills and qualifications.

While the specific performance objectives are different for every job, they fall within similar categories, including effectively dealing with people, achieving objectives, organizing teams, solving problems, using technology, and making changes. Creating these performance objectives starts by asking what the person taking the job needs to do to be successful, not what the person needs to have.

Trudy Knoepke-Campbell, the director of workforce planning at HealthEast Care System, has been using performance profiles for the past few years and has had exceptional results. We helped her put together performance profiles for nursing assistants and advanced practice nurses for a large hospital group in the St. Paul, Minnesota, area. She's done another 30 on her own and now calls them Success Profiles. And it is no wonder. Line managers have seen better candidates, made fewer hiring mistakes, experienced improved on-the-job performance, and experienced significant reductions in turnover. One clinical director was impressed the first time she started hiring RNs using performance profiles and the deep job-matching interviewing process. Not only was she better

---

* Marcus Buckingham and Curt Coffman, *First, Break All the Rules: What the World's Greatest Managers Do Differently* (New York: Simon & Schuster, 1999).
† Jim Collins, *Good to Great: Why Some Companies Make the Leap . . . and Others Don't* (New York: HarperCollins, 2001).

able to assess job fit, she also realized why she had made a hiring mistake a few months earlier using her traditional techniques.

Knoepke-Campbell calculates the cost savings due just to improvements in turnover at over $2 million per year—which she completely attributes to using performance profiles as the standard of measure. She also found that the line managers in all departments, including nursing, medical, and administration, accepted the use of performance profiles more willingly than her staff recruiters. She attributes this to the idea that recruiters are a very independent group and resisted the idea that there was a better way to select candidates than what they were currently doing. This is not an uncommon occurrence as corporations adopt Performance-based Hiring and the use of performance profiles. This is the beginning of a cultural shift converting hiring and recruiting into a formal business process rather than a bunch of loose independent activities.

➤ Performance Profiles Improve the Sourcing and Selection Process

When hiring managers, other interviewers, recruiters, and candidates all understand what a new employee needs to *do* to be successful, instead of what the person must *have*, the overall accuracy and effectiveness of the hiring process improves dramatically. Specifically, it shows:

➤ Interviewing accuracy is increased because the selection criteria are based on objective criteria. This is the first step required to create an evidenced-based selection process as described in Chapter 4. One of the major problems with assessing competency is that most interviewers don't use the same criteria to define it. A performance profile eliminates this problem.

➤ Candidate quality can be more easily assessed when all candidates are compared to a standard benchmark.

➤ Recruiters are better able to screen candidates based on measurable and objective criteria. A bad, and often deserved, rap for recruiters is their lack of understanding of real job needs. A performance profile helps everyone better understand the real job.

➤ Fewer candidates need to be seen because unqualified candidates are eliminated earlier in the process. Screening on performance rather than on qualifications also lessens the chance of eliminating a top person without the exact skill set.

➤ One of the major criterion top people use when selecting one position over another is the job fit. Using a performance profile as the basis for advertising increases the number of top people seen and, even better, more top people are hired since money is typically less important in accepting a job when the opportunities and challenges are clearly described.

➤ Managers become better managers when they clarify expectations.

➤ The number-one hiring mistake—hiring candidates who are competent but not motivated to do all aspects of the work—is reduced, by specifically measuring motivation across all key job needs.

➤ Using objective criteria is fairer and legally sound. This approach also broadens the pool for more diverse and high potential candidates.

➤ The performance profile can be used for onboarding, employee development, and performance measurement in a process referred to as *continuous rehiring*.

➤ Prepare a Performance Profile: Step-by-Step Guide

First, determine the top six to eight performance objectives in general terms, then get more specific. The hiring team needs to put the final performance objectives in priority order. When completed, a performance profile describes the results needed to be successful, the key process steps needed to achieve these results, and an understanding of the environment (e.g., pace, resources, professionalism, decision making, culture). The following list contains nine steps for creating a performance profile:

1. *Define the major objectives.* Determine what a person taking this job needs to do over the next 6 to 12 months to be considered successful. Most jobs have two to three major objectives (e.g., implement a new process, see 25 customers per day, conduct an analysis, reduce costs).

2. *Develop subobjectives.* For each major objective, determine the two or three things a successful person would need to do to achieve the major objective. For a new product design, one subobjective might be to develop the product requirement specifications during the first 90 days. Another might be to get the budget approved. While not all objectives end up in the final performance profile, this is a good approach to better understand how the major objectives will be implemented. This is the execution part of the job: don't ignore it, but don't go overboard. Some managers want to be very precise (micromanagers), while others don't want to know the details (hands-off managers).

3. *Ask questions to make sure you have all of the key objectives.* "Is there anything else that needs to be changed, fixed, upgraded, or improved over the next few months? What are the biggest challenges in the job? Are there any problems that need to be addressed right away?" These types of questions allow managers to better understand the major objectives for the job.

4. *Convert having to doing.* Review each critical skill and requirement on the job description and convert these into measurable performance objectives. Change "Five years of product marketing experience" to "Develop a product marketing plan for the new high-speed controller." The key is to determine how each skill or requirement will be used on the job to deliver results. This is a good way to move from subjective to objective selection criteria. Often the best performers can achieve the same results with less overall experience. This type of *having* to *doing* conversion ensures that you don't inadvertently exclude high-potential candidates.

5. *Convert technical skills into results.* Define the most significant technical challenges involved in the job. Then convert each major technical skill into a specific performance objective, or clearly describe how these are used during the job. Ask,

"How will the person use his BS and five years of C++ on the job?" It's easier to measure technical competency by understanding what the person actually needs to do with the skill. Technical managers tend to overvalue technical brilliance when assessing competency, rather than how a person's technical ability is actually applied on the job. This is one reason why many technical candidates feel they have been misled after taking the job.

6. *Understand team skills.* Though often overlooked, it's important to define team skills. After asking who the person will work with and about the types of projects, convert the most important team projects into performance objectives (e.g., "Work with manufacturing and quality to develop a complete testing protocol"). Draw a work chart describing all of the people the person will work with, including their titles and roles. As you find out in Chapter 4, you ask candidates to describe their most significant team projects, so this offers a great comparison.

7. *Understand management and organization objectives.* Every job requires some level of planning and organization. This could be as simple as completing the daily work schedule or prioritizing and completing multiple design efforts. Frequently, these organizational competencies are overlooked when hiring staff people. For managers, this is even more important. Not only do they have to build the team, but they also need to manage the group's activities to ensure that all milestones are met on time and on budget. When preparing performance objectives, consider the most important project as a representative sample (e.g., during the first 90 days, rebuild and reorganize the accounting department to improve the accuracy and timeliness of the monthly financial reporting package).

8. *Understand long-term planning and strategy issues.* A performance profile needs to address both short- and long-term job needs. The long term involves critical and forward thinking, strategic insight, and the creative aspects of the job. This could be a research and development project, the development of a multiyear product road map, the implementation of a new technology or process, or some new type of

advanced analysis. Don't ignore this type of work in staff jobs either. The best people evidence their ability to think strategically or creatively very early in their careers. Including these tasks in the performance profile is also a good way to demonstrate long-term opportunities. This is a key consideration people use when selecting one job over another. For example, for a design person, a critical-thinking task might be to conduct a trade-off analysis of two alternate design concepts. For a manufacturing person, a task like this might be to lead the effort to develop an international manufacturing and distribution strategy. For a mid-manager, a task might be to implement a succession planning program to increase the company's supply of sales managers to support a very aggressive sales plan. Next, determine whether these strategic, analytical, or creative objectives are more important than the tactical, technical, management, or team issues. This allows you to better match a candidate's interests and abilities with the full range of job needs.

9. *Benchmark the best.* For entry-level or process-type jobs, ask, "What do the best people in this job do differently than the average person? Think about your best person; what does he or she do differently?" By benchmarking the best person currently doing the job, you'll often discover some overlooked success factors. For example, at a call center for Verizon's Yellow Pages, we discovered that the reps who had the largest percentage of renewals were those who could keep existing customers on the line the longest when they first called. When asked to renew a $75 monthly ad, a "yes" response was more frequent than a "no" when asked later in the conversation. Previously, product knowledge, overcoming objections, and affability were considered the prerequisites to success. At HealthEast Care System, we found through benchmarking that the best nurse's aides proactively ensured patients were comfortable and met their personal needs without asking. Benchmark the worst people to find out what to avoid. This is how the YMCA discovered that the worst counselors were those who didn't spend any time planning for the next day's activities.

To complete the performance profile, select the six to eight most important objectives, make them as SMARTe as possible, and then put them in priority order. Use the final performance profile to write ads, source candidates, and conduct the interview. When managers understand the process involved in achieving success, they are better able to assess candidate competency and motivation. In addition, use this performance profile to help transition new employees into the job. Clarifying expectations has been shown to be an important element of continuing job satisfaction and on-the-job success.

➤ Case Study—A Performance Profile for a Product Marketing Manager

It's best if you can prepare and prioritize these performance objectives with everyone on the hiring team. Everyone then understands the real needs of the job to increase assessment accuracy. Getting everyone on the same page also has value beyond the interview, since they now have a vested stake in the candidate's subsequent success. The key here is to shift everyone's thinking from *having* to *doing*. The action verb is the critical part here. Actions verbs like *create, build, change, improve, establish, develop, design, analyze, identify, prepare, conduct,* and *lead,* are much better for describing the work that needs to get done, rather than passive verbs like *have to* and *be responsible for.* Using the previous step-by-step guide, here's some examples on how to uncover the performance objectives for a product marketing manager in a software company:

1. *Major objectives*: Include all the major requirements of the job like setting up a new department, developing new products, or increasing sales. For the software product manager position, it could be, "Develop and launch the new Internet buying program within 15 months with limited resources."

2. *Supporting or subobjectives*: Include some of the key steps needed to meet the major objectives. Often subobjectives are more important then the primary objective itself, since they describe the critical milestones and processes used to achieve the primary objective. Two supporting objectives

related to the product manager's primary task of launching the new product line include (1) "During the first quarter identify the size and buying patterns of the user community" and (2) "Despite the challenge with engineering and the limited research available, prepare the marketing requirements specification for review within 60 days." This second one also addresses the environment underlying the objective, which helps match the person to the job.

3. *Management and organization issues*: Consider all of the team and management requirements that are needed to be successful in the job. Often these are minimized or ignored. Consider the size, scope, and complexity of the management challenge. "Identify key resource requirements including team members and budget needs, and prepare a detailed plan of action within 45 days of starting" is a good example for the product manager.

4. *Changes and improvements*: Ask what you want changed, upgraded, or improved. Take everything into account, like systems, methods, processes, and people. Consider anything that could be done better and include it on the job specification. The product manager, for example, must "Improve the project tracking system to better identify critical constraints and bottlenecks."

5. *Problems*: Include any existing problems or those likely to be encountered. Minor ones don't matter, but major ones do, such as lack of time, resources, or special situations. The product manager needs to consider how to, "During the first quarter, develop alternate PR plans to penetrate the direct mail channel, since our current agency has missed some critical dates."

6. *Technical issues*: Focus more on the application, expected outcome, or use of these technical skills rather than on an absolute level. Instead of asking for five years of hardware design plus a BSEE, it's better to request that a new engineer "Lead the design effort on a new optical switching system." One for the product manager could be, "Complete the database interface requirements to ensure efficient online ordering by June." This is better than stating the product manager needs to have at least five years of experience writing marketing requirements for software products.

7. *Team and people issues*: Some of this might have been covered in the management category, but here include any special interpersonal needs or problems or cross-functional team issues. Dealing with another department or dealing with customers is an important component of many jobs that is often ignored. Here's one for a cost accountant, "Develop a new team approach with manufacturing to upgrade the cost and productivity reporting system." When the previous product manager had problems with an egocentric development manager, the objective became, "Develop a new communications approach to deal with a very dominant, yet talented, software manager." This was better than saying "have good interpersonal skills and a balanced ego." This is an ineffective classic found on many traditional job descriptions.

8. *Long-range, creative, or strategic issues*: Always consider the creative and strategic needs of the job. This could involve long-range planning or developing new approaches to conducting the work. For the product manager, a creative task was, "Quickly develop and implement a multimedia ad campaign using search-engine optimization techniques, social networking sites, radio, television, and billboard advertising." A strategic objective for this same job was "Develop an ongoing long-term marketing plan based on a comprehensive competitive analysis and doing whatever it takes to become the brand leader in this category."

Sometimes you won't have all the information necessary to fully complete each performance objective. In this case, start with an action verb, describe the task, and include the expected result. Here is an example for someone taking on an information technology (IT) project, "Assess the problem with the database architecture and within a few weeks put together a preliminary plan of action." Once the candidate starts, it's important to clarify these preliminary performance objectives and make them more detailed. While you should strive for complete SMARTe objectives, don't be too rigid. Describing jobs based on *doing* instead of *having* is a great first step.

Table 2.3   Performance Objectives for a Sales Representative

Category	Desired Result
Major objectives, projects, and key deliverables	Achieve quota within 60 days after training. Add six new accounts per quarter.
Subobjectives	Improve the close rate by 20% using the new solution selling system. Learn the complete product line within 30 days. Meet with the top 10 accounts the first month.
Management and organization issues	Maintain complete status of each open account, new accounts, and progress of open orders.
Changes and improvements needed	Upgrade the new contact report to reflect order size and timing.
Problems to solve	Ensure 100% customer satisfaction despite potential delivery delays.
Technical objectives	Learn to use salesforce.com and order-entry software to insure 100% accurate order processing.
Team, people issues	With shipping department, develop quick-response program for any order delays over five days.
Long-range, creative, or strategic issues	Develop new territory management techniques to improve identification of major new accounts.

Once you have all of the performance objectives listed, the hiring teams need to put them into priority order. The first six to eight should represent the bulk of the job.

These performance objectives are more than just a list of MBOs (management by objectives), which typically only cover the top-level performance objectives. A performance profile digs one or two levels deeper to understand the critical subtasks necessary to achieve success. Frequently, these subtasks are ranked higher in priority than the major objectives. The sample performance profile for a sales rep in Table 2.3 was prepared by benchmarking the best sales reps in the company. In this case, if the sales rep consistently and successfully handled each subtask or process step, the overriding quota objective would be easily met.

➤ Define the Job, Not the Person

Look on monster.com or any company's web site if you need proof that most job descriptions emphasize skills, duties, responsibilities, and experience. There are plenty of good examples of bad job descriptions. Qualifications-based job descriptions inadvertently exclude strong candidates with related, but not identical, experience. It also overvalues factors (i.e., skills, level of experience) that have been shown to be misleading predictors of success. You obviously want to motivate top performers to apply for these jobs, but a focus on skills and competencies introduces two unnecessary roadblocks. First, the best candidates don't look for work based on what skills they possess, they look for work based on what they'll be doing and learning. Second, the best want to do different things. So if the job is exactly the same as what they're currently doing, there's no incentive for them to check it out. A job description built around performance objectives eliminates these problems.

When you define the job, rather than the person, you fundamentally change the way you find candidates and assess their competency. It's better to understand the expected outcomes of a job, rather than the inputs. This is the fundamental difference between performance profiles and experience-based job descriptions. If the candidate can achieve the performance objectives, she obviously has enough experience and skills. She couldn't achieve it, or something similar, otherwise. Reversing the logic, just because someone possesses this arbitrary list of required skills and experiences doesn't mean the person can deliver the results. Lack of motivation is one reason. An inability to work in your culture is another. It could be the person is a weak planner, or doesn't work well with outside departments. We've all seen people with a different set of skills and experiences deliver the same results. With a performance profile, you'll be able to use the interview to obtain examples of comparable past performance to determine whether the person is both competent and motivated. This is the huge shift that's possible once you start using performance objectives to define job needs rather than a list of qualifications.

➤ Three Ways to Prepare Performance Objectives

There are some other ways to prepare performance objectives depending on the type of job and how much information you have available. The approaches, summarized in Table 2.4, are

Table 2.4 Approaches to Preparing Performance Objective

Method	Description	Examples
1. The big-picture approach *What will the person hired need to do to be successful?*	Get measurable objectives for each major factor in the job. Cover technical needs, management issues, team issues, projects, needed changes, and problems.	Launch three new products within the next 12 months. In the next 90 days, upgrade the planning system for manufacturing.
2. The micro-approach *Convert HAVING to DOING*	Relate actual skills to real job needs. Develop a measurable objective that demonstrates competency.	Develop an online project-tracking system. Have enough experience to design three new products per year.
3. The benchmarking approach *What do the best people in this job do differently from everyone else?*	Compare the best people already in the job and select traits that best predict success. Avoid the traits of under-performers.	Prepare complex spreadsheets covering pricing and cost issues for long periods. Use initiative in dealing with customer return problems and make quick decisions.

embedded in the techniques described in the previous step-by-step guide.

1. The Big-Picture Approach

Performance profiles for jobs with lots of projects or management positions are the easiest to prepare. Just start by asking what the candidate must do to be considered successful in the job, then work your way through the step-by-step guide. A time line can help clarify this process. Consider the job needs over a one- to two-year time horizon, starting with the first 30 days. Break the job into appropriate time segments and determine what the candidate must do or achieve at each point. Then determine what interim steps need to occur along the way. Determine what's the first problem, challenge, or issue the person will face. It could be something like, "break the bottleneck in order processing" or "determine the status of a major project."

Next, move out to the 90-day and then the six-month mark. Figure out what the person must achieve during this time frame. It could relate to staff assessment, rebuilding, or closing a few major deals. After a year, ask what other major things need to be accomplished. After you've developed a number of performance objectives, review them all and eliminate the less important ones. Then put the remaining objectives into priority order. The top six to eight are all you really need to define the performance requirements of the job. Make sure each performance objective covers a different aspect of the position (e.g., management, technical, decision making). This will help you conduct a more broad-based and balanced interview when you begin meeting candidates.

Figure 2.1 is an example of this big approach combined with a time line. The primary performance objective is to "Set up a new distribution facility over the next year." Two interim objectives are to "Coordinate with the design group to complete the physical layout of the site by a certain deadline," and "Negotiate a contract with the software vendor to meet critical system needs." Understanding these subobjectives is often the difference between success and failure on the job. By identifying them early, you'll eliminate major hiring and performance problems later on.

In addition to the time line, it's important to directly consider some of the *tactical* and *managerial* needs of the position. Tactical has

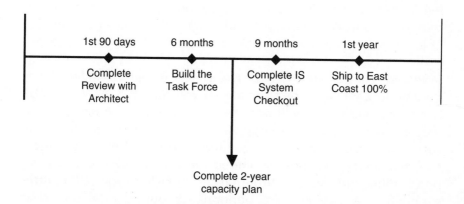

Figure 2.1   Distribution manager—Performance objectives for new facility.

to do with obtaining short-term results, either individually as a team member or as a manager. Here's an example of an individual tactical objective for a salesperson, "Improve the ratio of closes/calls by 15 percent by developing improved selling techniques." This gets at specific behaviors and traits much better than the classic, "have good sales and closing skills coupled with five years' experience selling office products."

For most management positions, the classic job description just lists the years of management experience required. It's better to describe what the manager needs to do to build, develop or manage the team. For instance, "During the first 60 days, establish an employee development program to support a 20 percent increase in order processing," is a clear tactical management task. During the interview, you'll ask the candidate to give real examples of comparable accomplishments. Generalities regarding these types of tactical tasks can cause problems later on when you assess managerial competency based on years of experience.

Many jobs require strategic or creative skills. You can get at these by describing the outcomes expected from these conceptual skills, long-range or creative skills. Some examples include "Architect a new system protocol," "Create a new technology to support high speed data switching," "Develop a long-range planning system," "Create a new marketing promotional program," and "Prepare a five-year global manufacturing plan." The verbs used in the performance objectives need to describe the creative or strategic nature of the work. When you prioritize all of the performance objectives, the importance of these conceptual skills will stand out.

Ignorance Isn't Bliss: Delegate Knowledge to the Candidate What do you do when you don't know what you want the person to do? Every now and then you'll want to hire someone with just a vague idea of what the person is supposed to do at the task level. In this case, make the creation of these requirements a primary performance objective. Suppose you need someone to take your existing product line into a new distribution channel where you've had little experience. An appropriate performance objective in this case would be, "During the first month, prepare a detailed action plan identifying all of the key requirements for a direct marketing channel for the XYZ product line." Let the candidate tell you the needs of the job, the appropriate resource requirements, and the time line. During the interview, have the candidate describe comparable accomplishments and discuss how she would implement the program if she were to get the job.

Here's an example based on this concept. One of my clients had a product that could potentially be used in the managed health care industry. They wanted to hire a vice president-level person to head the new program. The major performance objective for the position was to "Prepare a five-year business plan within six months." The second one was to "Build the team needed to launch the business." The CEO, while aware of some of the issues, needed a leader to take over this business segment and build the detailed action plan. During the first interview, the president and the candidate (who ultimately got the job) spent two hours together developing a detailed operational plan for this new business. This was after reviewing some of the candidate's accomplishments in setting up similar ventures. So even before starting the job, the candidate and the CEO worked together on this project. The CEO later told me that the candidate exhibited the same insight, organizational skills, and approach to problem solving on the job that he did in the two-hour session.

You can't be expected to know everything about every job under your watch. By delegating this "need to know" to the new person, it becomes the performance objective. Higher level jobs often have these kinds of needs. Setting up a new business, developing a new system, or creating a new product all fall within this category.

The big-picture approach starts by asking, "What does a person taking this job need to do to be successful?" Then just fill in the blanks to get from here to there. Preparing a performance profile this way will not only help you hire better people, but once they're hired, it will make you a better manager.

2. The Micro-Approach: Convert Having to Doing

This approach works for all jobs. Just go through each qualification listed on the job description and ask the hiring manager what the person needs to do with the skill to demonstrate competency. Rather than saying the candidate must have strong C++ software development skills, it's better to state that the candidate will be leading the development of a new series of business intelligence software products. For a technical design position, something like "Develop two new electro-mechanical devices to handle the measurement of fluid flow in high-speed oil lines" is better than "Have three years' experience in fluid flow controls and product design." This approach better relates actual skills to real job needs.

Behaviors, competencies, and personality traits can be redefined the same way. Rather than saying the person must "Work well with engineering," you'll gain more insight with "Develop a means to deal with a very technically oriented engineering manager in developing product launch plans." For "good team skills," it's better to describe the actual team situation by saying, "Lead the process improvement team for order entry to reduce cycle time by two days."

Using performance objectives instead of skills can change the very nature of the job. In Table 2.5, two skills-based requirements for a director of sales and marketing were converted into their performance equivalents. The differences were startling but not unexpected.

The skills-based criteria were not representative of the actual work that was required. This client had been looking for months to fill this position, yet no one could agree on what was required. It's not surprising. When you convert skills and experiences to outcomes, you clarify the real needs.

Most job descriptions fall short because they require an absolute level of skills, years of experience, academics, and required behaviors. This is a poor short-cut approach that ignores real job

Table 2.5 Comparing Skills Converted to Performance Objectives

Original Skill-Based Criteria	Actual Requirement	Comments
Strong one-on-one selling skills	Set up training program for new sales staff to penetrate national accounts.	The person needs to be a great sales manager and trainer, not an individual salesperson.
Very creative at the product level	Take the lead on coordinating the introduction of three new products per year.	The person doesn't have to be creative at all. He just has to coordinate the activities of creative people.

needs. Worse, specifying an arbitrary level of skills and experience inadvertently excludes the best candidates.

3. The Benchmarking Approach

Building a performance profile is relatively easy for a task- or project-oriented job. It's a bit more challenging for a process, transaction-oriented, administrative, or entry-level position. In these cases, the benchmarking approach works best. Determine what the best performers already in the job do differently from everyone else, then look for these same abilities in the people you hire. Also study the worst people, discover what they do that makes them poor performers, and then avoid these traits, skills, and behaviors in the people you consider.

Some examples will help you understand this approach. Many years ago we had a client in the jewelry manufacturing business that had a lot of turnover in its polishing department. It turned out that the best employees had a great eye for detail, could quickly determine which pieces were good and bad, and tended to stay in each previous job for more than two years. In the interview, we gave candidates some pieces of jewelry to evaluate in order to assess their eye for detail. Turnover was dramatically reduced when using these selection criteria. Using another example, an entry-level accountant must have the ability to learn new processes quickly and produce 100 percent accurate reports. The dominant selection criteria for a telemarketer involves the ability to handle rejection, make lots of calls, and be persuasive. The key in all of these situations was to find out what made others successful in the job and to look for these same traits in the candidates hired.

You can use this benchmarking technique for all kinds of positions, but it works best for jobs that follow a routine or a standard process. For REI, the outdoor products retail chain, we determined that the ability to engage customers quickly and constantly presenting the merits of various recreational products was essential to success. At Southwest Airlines, the ability to proactively engage with groups of customers was a critical performance trait. Marriott uses a similar approach to assess service personnel. At In-N-Out Burger, the best candidates for entry-level positions had perfect attendance records, had a high level of mechanical dexterity, and proactively and naturally engaged with people. At Red Bull, the best college students for jobs giving away samples were those who had a track record of reliability doing physically demanding work. In all of these situations, these core traits were developed by finding out what top performers did differently once on the job. In most of these cases, managers thought energy in the interview and affability were good predictors of on-the-job success. In most cases, this wasn't even a prerequisite.

■ SAMPLE PERFORMANCE PROFILES

Following are three performance profiles you can use as templates while you develop some of your own. You'll find more samples at the resource section on our web site, www.adlerconcepts.com.

➤ Organization Chart

As part of the performance profile, it is useful to include an organization or work team chart for the position. An organization chart describes the traditional superior and subordinate relationships. A work chart is more expansive by describing the internal and external team members typically interacting with the person in this job. This includes other departments, outside suppliers, and customers. During the interview, ask candidates to draw a work chart as they describe their accomplishments. This will help determine the comparability of previous team roles and management tasks. As part of the performance objectives, include any required organizational changes. This could include rebuilding or upgrading the team, training, supporting growth, addressing new responsibilities, or downsizing.

■ DIVERSITY, AMERICANS WITH DISABILITIES ACT, AND THE LAW

Rob Bekken, formerly a senior partner at Fisher & Phillips, one of the largest labor law firms in the country, estimates that the average cost of a wrongful discharge lawsuit is $600,000. This is a high cost for someone who should not have been hired in the first place. According to Bekken, most of these hiring mistakes would have been

PERFORMANCE PROFILE SAMPLE 1

First-Line Manager

Position Summary

A first-line manager is involved with some basic business process managing and supervising a small team. This usually consists of professional staff members and process and administrative specialists. The focus is usually on maintaining and improving the process.

Keys to Hiring

The best first-line managers are good developers of staff personnel; they possess a good balance of hands-on technical competency coupled with the ability to apply technical knowledge in resolving conflicts, evaluating trade-offs, and decision making. Organization skills are evident through the improving of department process and the implementation of new methods and systems. Preparing and managing projects by a budget is an essential aspect of good first-line managers.

Performance Objectives

By preparing performance objectives, the balance between team and individual competencies is better understood The following performance objectives represent the general scope of activity for a first-line manager:

1. *Primary objective*: The most important performance objective for this department is to [increase sales by, improve margins by, implement new systems, reduce costs by, improve efficiency by, design/develop _____ products, launch _____ products, conduct research addressing, improve performance in]. Within _____ days, assess the status of the objective and define the plan necessary to achieve the overall outcome.
2. *Secondary objective*: (With consideration to the primary objectives noted earlier, include here any important shorter term or interim objectives the person taking the position needs to achieve to meet the main objective.) An interim step necessary to achieve _____ [primary objective] is _____. During the

(continued)

first _____ days, identify the key resources needs to accomplish this, evaluate actual status against existing plans, and revise and implement as necessary to achieve the planned goals.

3. *Team building and staff development*: (A primary role of first-line managers is to build and manage or rebuild the team. It starts with a strong understanding of the needs and capability of the existing team.) During the first _____ days, meet all team members and evaluate capabilities in line with ongoing objectives and department needs. Establish developmental and reorganizational plans as necessary for each team member to rebuild and strengthen the whole group.

4. *Operational review*: (It's always good for any level manager to benchmark the operational effectiveness of the department's basic functions and responsibilities.) Conduct a comprehensive operational review of ongoing department activities including processes, systems, methods, and procedures. Especially consider _____. Complete this first review by _____.

5. *Technical competency*: (For most managers, the application of technical skills in a management situation is as important as the absolute level of technical knowledge. To get at this, prepare a performance objective that directly relates to what the person needs to do with a technical skill, not the skill itself.) One of our key technically oriented objectives is manage the [implementation, launch, design, development of] _____. Over the next _____ months, we must [complete, identify, plan, define resource needs] to ensure achieving planned results.

6. *Address major problems, changes, and improvements*: (Other sources of performance objectives involve eliminating problems or implementing changes. Consider the major objectives the person is expected to address if they have not already been covered.) Some critical problems to resolve and changes necessary to improve operational performance in this department are _____, _____, and _____. Quickly identify the changes required and create a series of recommended solutions. Implement a prioritized action plan to address these issues over the following _____ months.

7. *Strategic and planning issues*: (A top-notch first-line manager can think strategically, at least with respect to department needs, and plan and implement accordingly. It's imortant to tie this to a specific project in which the person will have direct involvement to validate

this ability.) During the first _____ days, prepare a strategic plan outlining all the needs of the department to meet the company's long-term objective of _____. From this, prepare a calendar-based monthly operating budget and implementation plan by _____ [date].

8. *Project management, organizational planning, and execution*: (The best first-line managers are very strong at managing cross-functional teams to achieve significant objectives. Include a project that incorporates these needs like a systems implementation, launch of a new product line, or leading the implementation for a new piece of equipment.) Develop [review, upgrade] the operating plan for the project by identifying staff needs, budgets, capital equipment, development expenses, technology requirements, and _____.

9. *Thinking skills, decision making, and conflict resolution*: (Good first-line managers have the ability to think tactically, technically, and organizationally within their team, solve related problems, and incorporate these in implementing solutions. Include an appropriate issue that demonstrates this type of decision making and/or problem solving.) One of the main issues facing the department is what to do about _____. By _____, identify the key issues needing resolution, and define the underlying problems. Specifically consider _____.

10. *Personality and interpersonal skills*: Identify any major personality demands of the position (e.g., tough boss, potential conflicts with other departments, cultural needs of company). Successful completion of the _____ project requires the cooperation with a very independent [or add some other interpersonal issue] _____ department [or person].

PERFORMANCE PROFILE SAMPLE 2

Customer Service Director

Position Summary

The director of customer service will be responsible for rebuilding the customer service department, organizing the group to handle the anticipated growth, and leading many of the efforts toward upgrading the customer service activity. The key to success in this position is to ensure a companywide focus on improving all aspects of customer service. This includes direct support, new systems, and better handling of complaints. The person selected will be responsible for customer service, order processing and tracking, returned goods, warranty sales, and technical support. The company's future growth depends on establishing new procedures in all aspects of customer service, especially online ordering and tracking. The position supervises 24 people through three supervisors.

Performance Objectives

1. Improve customer service from 93 percent to 99 percent and reduce customer complaints by 75 percent within 12 months.
2. Rebuild the customer service department to support a 25 percent per year growth rate. This includes upgrading supervisors, a reduction in turnover, and a complete process reengineering of the group.
3. Take a management lead on organizing a multifunction task force in developing companywide customer service improvements. This will support the 18-month IS conversion program now under way incorporating new technologies like EDI, bar-coding, and Internet catalog and ordering.
4. By June, conduct a complete process review of all aspects of the department identifying key staff issues, system problems, customer complaints, and bottlenecks. Coordinate with major customers addressing their needs and begin a corrective action plan immediately.
5. Develop a series of interim solutions to reduce back orders, improve returned material replacements, and improve communications with the field support team. Present action plan within 90 days.

PERFORMANCE PROFILE SAMPLE 3

Recruiting Manager

Position Summary

The recruiting manager is involved with recruiting and staffing for the entire company supervising a team of in-house recruiters. The focus is on hiring the best people into the company in an efficient manner.

Performance Objectives

1. *Improve the recruiting process and the quality of candidates hired.* The primary objective during the first year is to completely upgrade the existing hiring processes at the company. This requires the installation of new hiring practices, improved sourcing, better assessment tools, and an ability to quickly react to short- and long-term hiring needs.

2. *Conduct a hiring needs analysis.* During the first _____ weeks, meet with all hiring managers and determine the status of all open requisitions, and identify all hiring requirements for the next six months. Put this in priority order, and implement a staffing plan of action during the first month.

3. *Develop short-term staffing alternatives.* Given critical needs and time frames, develop alternative staffing approaches to eliminate existing open requisitions within _____ days. This plan needs to be completed within _____ weeks.

4. *Conduct a process review.* During the first _____ days, conduct a detailed review of all hiring practices and processes. Identify key constraints and problems and develop a plan to overhaul the process within _____ months.

5. *Train and rebuild the team.* During the first week, meet all staff members and assess capabilities against departmental objectives. Implement necessary training and during the first _____ days, rebuild the team as necessary to meet company hiring requirements.

6. *Reduce the time to hire.* Over the next _____ months, reduce the time to hire typical positions from an average of _____ days to _____ days.

(continued)

7. *Improve the assessment process:* Within _____ days, establish the staffing department as the benchmark for identifying and assessing competency. Provide tools and guidance to line managers throughout the company to upgrade the quality of all candidate assessments.
8. *Upgrade Internet recruiting efforts.* Within _____ days, ensure that the staffing department is on the leading-edge of Internet recruiting.

eliminated if performance profiles were used to establish the objective selection criteria, rather than traditional job descriptions. The firm has prepared a white paper describing the legal benefits and importance of implementing Performance-based Hiring. This is included in the Appendix to this book. In the white paper, Bekken concludes that "Hire with Your Head and Performance-based Hiring represents an important breakthrough from both a practical and legal standpoint. By utilizing this approach, employers are now equipped with the tools to hire the right employee and to legally defend their decision."

The preparation of performance profiles also offers a practical way to implement a diversity hiring program. While many companies have good intentions, success is limited without practical tools to eliminate normal biases and artificial barriers. For example, by imposing a seemingly fair baseline of qualifications (e.g., a BS degree from a top university and five years' industry experience), most companies inadvertently establish a nondiverse candidate pool. Few top universities are fully diverse, nor are most competitors. To overcome this lack of natural diversity, companies then must go to extraordinary means to find enough diverse candidates to meet their hiring objectives. A performance profile can reduce this problem by broadening the criteria without compromising candidate quality. As you discover in Chapter 3, ads can be written and placed to appeal to the best and most diverse candidates. But to be effective, they still need to emphasize the challenges and opportunities, not the qualifications.

While legally required, diversity has a more important practical side. Legally and morally it's important to give equal consideration to all potential candidates, both male and female, regardless of their racial, religious, ethnic backgrounds, or physical challenges. As the workforce becomes diverse, it becomes important to hire people who can work on a diverse team. As a part of this, it's also important to offer products and services to meet the demands of an increasingly diverse customer base. Performance profiles directly address these issues.

To address the legal/moral issue and avoid an arbitrary list of qualifications, make the candidate's ability to meet the performance objectives the dominant selection criterion. This is a fairer and more legally sound method to overcome the sourcing constraint subtly imposed when using qualifications to screen candidates. If a candidate can meet the performance needs of the job, meaning the person has achieved some level of comparable past performance, he or she deserves the new job, regardless of age, race, religion, gender, or physical challenges. Conversely, if a candidate hasn't done anything comparable, the person should not be offered the job regardless of age, race, religion, gender, or physical challenges.

With workforces and customers becoming more diverse, it's also important to directly consider these issues in the preparation of the performance objectives. This addresses the second important diversity issue. For marketing or sales positions, this might mean mentioning the need to create or sell products to an ethnic customer base in the performance objective. Rather than just saying, "Increase market share by five points," it's better to expand this to say, "Increase market share by five points, half coming from the Hispanic community."

Manufacturing positions often require management of multiethnic labor groups. In this case, the performance objective should include this important need, such as "Install a total quality management program addressing all the needs of a diverse labor team." This sets up the requirement for applicants to be proficient and aware of the cultural differences and needs of these important work groups. If you want to create a diverse workforce a performance objective might be, "Over the next two years establish a multiethnic workforce and training program that gives every employee an opportunity to grow." By incorporating these requirements into the performance objectives, companies can directly address diversity throughout the sourcing, hiring, interviewing, and evaluation process.

In the case of physical challenges, the United States has created the Americans with Disabilities Act (ADA) to prevent artificial criteria being used to eliminate otherwise qualified candidates. To comply with this act, companies are required to provide modifications to the workplace to ensure that people with physical challenges aren't arbitrarily excluded from employment. A performance profile can help minimize these problems. It also allows for a much fairer means to understanding the real physical requirements of the job. Identify all of the physical requirements of the job using the performance objectives as the guideline. Break these down into those that require some form of physical activity like standing, lifting, traveling, driving, or using equipment. If the physical tasks are not required, don't include them. For example, lifting anything other than a briefcase is not required for most office jobs. According to the ADA act, you don't have to compromise your performance standards as long as they're essential. However, you do have to provide a reasonable level of accommodation (ramps, access devices, larger screens) for those who can otherwise meet the performance objectives. If a physically challenged candidate can meet these performance objectives with some reasonable level of accommodation, he deserves the job. Conversely, if a person can't meet these requirements, or if you find someone who is better at the nonphysical aspects of the job, you don't need to hire the person.

Using performance profiles as the baseline to justify your hiring decisions will minimize your liability in this area since you have proven you've hired the best person without consideration to the physical challenges. Make sure this is documented and get specific legal advice if you have any questions. This area is constantly being evaluated in the courts, so it's important to have the latest advice.

■ IN BRIEF: THE SIX BUSINESS BENEFITS OF USING PERFORMANCE PROFILES

While this chapter focused on how to prepare performance profiles, you'll discover that they impact every aspect of the Performance-based Hiring process. Here's a quick six-point recap of the broader role and impact that performance profiles can have on helping companies hire more top talent:

1. *Helps advertise for and screen candidates.* When you write ads based on the having, rather than the doing, they appear boring and may exclude great candidates. When the challenges are emphasized the best people are drawn in, rather than turned off. Not only will you get more top candidates this way, but you'll also be able to screen their resumes on comparable accomplishments, rather than skills, experience, academics, and industry. One of our clients, a restaurant chain in Southern California, started looking outside of the restaurant industry for managers and serving staff, as a result of focusing on doing rather than having. Within six months, it was fully staffed with outstanding people, a first in seven years for the chain. Many of its new crop of stars came from a retail background, where service and support are essential to success. If sourcing is a problem, opening up the pool to indirect and functional competitors is a great way to find more top people.

2. *Helps recruit on opportunity, not compensation.* The best people are willing to make salary concessions if the job offers a strong career move. Performance profiles attract those that see the job this way. By describing the challenges and asking for examples of comparable accomplishments during the interview, candidates better understand the real job and the potential opportunities. When it comes time to close the deal, you'll discover your negotiating power is in the form of a great job, not how much money you can offer.

3. *Improves onboarding.* The performance profile can be used as a natural transition program for the new employee. Since you've discussed the performance objectives during the interview, the new employee has a clear sense of job expectations. During the orientation program, reprioritize and renegotiate the performance objectives. During this time, you can then make them as SMARTe as necessary. Lack of clear expectations is one of the biggest causes of employee

turnover and poor performance. This is what Ferdinand Fournies describes in his classic book on management, *Coaching for Improved Work Performance*, as the biggest problem with management.* A performance profile is a great way to eliminate a serious potential problem, and become a better manager in the process.

4. *Reduces employee turnover through continuous rehiring.* The Internet has profoundly increased workforce mobility by reducing barriers to leaving companies. The countermeasure for this is to provide reasons for an employee not to leave. The best way to do this is by offering a formal process of continuous growth and personal development. By using the performance objectives to constantly monitor a person's performance, managers can provide additional stretch opportunities as the situation warrants.

5. *Monitors performance management.* The prioritized list of performance objectives forms the basis of a complete performance management system. With these as a baseline, you'll be able to use them to monitor ongoing performance, implement targeted employee development programs, and conduct meaningful performance reviews.

6. *Saves time.* "It takes too much time" is the biggest complaint we hear when first describing the performance profiling process. It doesn't. It saves time. The list of performance objectives is essentially what you'd discuss with the new employee on her start date. Why wait? Discuss it three weeks sooner, during the interview process, and managers will hire fewer competent but unmotivated people. That is the real time waster. The time involved in managing an underperformer is far greater than the time it takes to prepare one of these performance profiles. The cost and time involved in eventually dismissing a person you should never have hired in the first place would justify any time added to the evaluation process. During a recent workshop, a facilities manager complained loudly about the time element. I asked him to name the five biggest problems he wanted his new plant engineer to address once he

---

* Ferdinand Fournies, *Coaching for Improved Work Performance* (New York: McGraw-Hill, 1978).

came on board. He put the list together in less than 10 minutes. Managers waste time every day by not clearly understanding what they want their team to do. Preparing performance profiles is the solution, not the problem.

HOT TIPS FOR HIRING WITH A PERFORMANCE PROFILE

✔ If you want to hire superior people, first define superior performance. Minimize the use of traditional job descriptions as part of the sourcing and selection process.

✔ A performance profile describes the required results, the process used to achieve the results, and the environment in which this happens.

✔ Define the job, not the person. Define success, not the skills. It's best to separate the job from the person. This allows for a more objective appraisal of true competency.

✔ Focus on the *doing*, not the *having*, to improve hiring accuracy. It's what a person does with his or her skills that determines success, not the skills alone.

✔ Experience and personality are poor predictors of subsequent performance. It's better to define and use the real performance needs of the job to screen and interview candidates.

✔ Every job has six to eight performance objectives that define on-the-job success. These range from dealing with people, meeting technical and business objectives, to organizing teams, solving problems, and making changes.

✔ To develop the list of performance objectives, ask the hiring manager what the person taking the job needs to do throughout the first year to be successful in the job.

✔ To expand the list of performance objectives, convert each qualification listed on the traditional job description into a measurable task.

✔ For entry-level or process-oriented positions, benchmark the best (and worst) people already doing the job. Use this to create performance objectives for any type of position.

✔ The performance profile establishes the framework for better hiring and better management by clarifying the expectations for the job. This improves on-the-job performance, requires less day-to-day management, and reduces turnover.

$$Chapter\ 3$$

Talent-Centric Sourcing: Finding the Best Active and Passive Candidates

> If you're trying to persuade people to do something, or buy something, it seems to me you should use their language, the language in which they think.
>
> —David Ogilvy

■ THE BEST PEOPLE ARE LOOKING—FINDING AND HIRING THEM IS THE CHALLENGE

The Internet has dramatically increased workforce mobility. Job satisfaction appears to be at an all-time low. Turnover is rising. People change jobs on a whim. Counteroffers are more prevalent and more are being accepted. No wonder. To find another job nowadays, all a top person needs to do is Google a few keywords, a job title, and a city. When combined with a huge reduction in barriers to leaving a company (i.e., portable pension plans, reductions in health-care insurance, and fewer fringe benefits), employees are capable and willing to leave for minor infractions or slightly better offers. Turnover is no longer considered a character flaw. In this environment, a well-positioned ad or a timely phone call is sometimes all it takes to find a top performer. To take advantage of this trend, companies need to move away from a classified ad mentality of listing boring, hard-to-find jobs and, instead, adopt a consumer-marketing approach to advertising.

In this chapter, we describe how to find top people whether they are active or passive. First, it's important to recognize that top performers don't look for new opportunities the same way that average candidates look. They're more selective, and even if they are looking, they will only consider positions that offer true opportunities. Even if they're not looking, most top people are still open-minded enough to explore something if it were better. The common ingredient among the best people, whether they're somewhat looking, potentially looking, or deciding whether to accept an offer is that their criteria to move forward or not involves a long-term goal and major career step. It is a strategic decision based on opportunity and growth, not just a tactical decision based on salary and location. Not understanding this difference is why so many companies lose so many good people. If you want to get more of these great people into the game, your job descriptions must describe career opportunities, not just skills and experiences. Then these compelling, career-oriented job descriptions need to be advertised and pushed to where the best people will see them.

Companies overlook the importance of the lowly, online job description. If the ad isn't interesting and compelling, most top performers will instantly eliminate it from consideration. Even referred and passive candidates will look at your online job description before getting too serious, so it's important that they are written to appeal to a top performer, not to an average candidate. As you soon discover, there are more top people going online every day just to check out the market. While the time spent looking is short, designing online advertising to address this group can be a good way to pick up some great people who are temporarily in the market. To attract this group though, your jobs must stand out, be compelling, and be at the top of every listing and you must move fast.

The mission statement for any sourcing program should be to find the strongest people possible in the shortest period of time at the lowest reasonable cost.

The mission statement for any sourcing program should be to find the strongest people possible in the shortest period of time at the lowest reasonable cost. Few companies get this part right. Far too many companies employ a simplistic, undifferentiated shotgun approach to sourcing that involves trying every channel possible, not offering anything different from anyone else, using boring qualifications-intensive ads, and hoping that something will work. This approach involves little planning and little thought. Then, these people complain that the job board they used is no good or that the manager is overly demanding. When every company uses the same advertising tools as every other company, posting jobs that are essentially the same, they should expect average results.

■ PRIMARY CHANNELS FOR A SEQUENCED SOURCING PROGRAM

In order to obtain a disproportionate number of top performers, use a variety of sourcing techniques. Develop a sourcing strategy that consists of multiple channels sequenced in some way based on quality, cost, and time. Then, optimize each channel to attract the best people possible, moving on to a higher cost channel only if needed. Here's a quick summary of the channels commonly involved in setting up this type of sequenced sourcing program for a corporate recruiting department:

➤ *Resume databases*: Whether private or public, the key is to develop a just-in-time source of candidates using drip marketing campaigns in combination with good customer-relationship management (CRM) techniques. Target 10 percent of jobs to be filled this way.

➤ *Internal transfers*: Companies need to take advantage of their existing employees through aggressive *continuous rehiring* programs. Twenty percent of open, nonentry-level jobs should be filled this way.

➤ *Internet-based advertising*: This is the core of every sourcing program and consists of compelling ads, targeted jobs boards, and web site optimization. Good people do go online to find better jobs, but they are more selective and they won't waste their time. Great advertising, an easy-to-use career site, and ads that can be found are the keys to finding some great people. Done properly, 25 percent to 30 percent of jobs can be filled this way with good, to very good, people.

➤ *Employee referrals*: Proactively asking your top employees for the names of the best people they've worked with in the past is a great first step in finding more top passive candidates. Few companies take advantage of top employees' networks. Companies should target 35 percent to 40 percent of their openings to be filled by a strong proactive employee referral program.

➤ *College recruiting*: This is how you build the farm team. Although many companies have done a good job here, they can't rest on their laurels. The key here is to develop strong relationships with the appropriate colleges and universities, targeting their best students. This needs to be an ongoing process, not just a one-time event on interviewing day.

➤ *Diversity recruiting*: The demand for diverse candidates in every field is outstripping the supply. This is not just an equal rights issue; it's a critical business decision. Your employee base needs to mimic your customer base. To obtain enough talented, diverse candidates, companies need to use and optimize every sourcing technique described in this chapter.

➤ *Campaigns and career events*: This is an old-time favorite that's coming back into vogue. Success here requires that top people be invited to a special hiring event where they'll have an opportunity to speak with hiring managers. Done properly, a company can fill a number of critical positions quickly with some top people.

➤ *Direct sourcing*: This includes passive candidate name identification, cold calling, and networking. Too many companies think this is the panacea. It's not. It takes skilled recruiters who have the time to do it right. Making matter worse, few companies have allocated the necessary resources to pull this off. It also requires hiring managers to get involved earlier and conduct more exploratory interviews. Regardless, do this for more difficult assignments, especially if the simpler approaches aren't working.

➤ *External recruiters*: Sometimes it's important to bring in a specialist. Paying a fee for an A player is always worth it. Paying a fee for a B player is not.

Corporate recruiting departments all want to find the silver bullet, or the next tech toy, to solve their sourcing problems. A one-stop solution does not exist. This is a management challenge that involves the effective use of technology, the implementation of a sequenced, multichannel sourcing strategy, and a strong team of recruiters and sourcing specialists who know how to deliver consistent results. However, few companies have implemented this type of comprehensive sourcing program. The balance of this chapter describes how to optimize the core channels mentioned earlier. It all starts, however, by making sure your job descriptions emphasize career opportunities, not qualifications.

If you want to hire better people, you'll need to offer better jobs. If you want to hire passive candidates, you'll also need to offer better careers.

■ OFFER CAREERS, NOT JOBS

Before you write another ad or speak to another candidate, it's important to recognize that top people don't use the same criteria when applying, considering, or accepting an offer. When considering whether to apply, top people want the ad to clearly explain the challenges and growth opportunities. During the interviewing process, they want to understand real job needs and gain a sense of the leadership skills of the hiring manager. When accepting a job offer, compensation is *not* the primary consideration. The opportunity and challenges inherent in the job are. In order of priority, the following are the top-five criteria that top people use when deciding to accept an offer:

1. *The job match*: The best people want to do work that challenges them and allows them to grow in areas they deem important.
2. *The hiring manager*: Top people want to work for leaders and mentors who can help them reach their goals. The quality of

the manager directly relates to the quality of the people hired. As you discovered in Chapter 2, preparing a performance profile and understanding real job needs can help average managers become stronger.

3. *The quality of the team*: The team is a very important consideration for a top person. Meeting strong potential coworkers can overcome other concerns and minimize the chance of accepting a counteroffer. The best people get concerned when they meet potential coworkers who are weak interviewers or who don't understand real job needs.

4. *The company*: A strong company with great employer branding certainly makes it easier to get someone initially interested, but these factors are less important when a top person makes the final decision to accept or not. Tying the actual job to some major company initiative is a great way to strengthen this link. This is called *job branding*. Even small or less known companies can do this.

5. *The compensation package*: As long as the compensation package is reasonable, most top people don't consider it the number-one criteria. Only when the comp package is very high or very low does it become the primary consideration.

Develop sourcing strategies and programs with these decision-making criteria in mind. The best people always have multiple opportunities. When evaluating new opportunities, the decision to accept is viewed as a long-term decision based largely on the criteria noted earlier. As a result, they take longer to decide and they want more information. They seek the advice of friends, family, and business associates. This is different for the average candidate who is interested more in the basic job content, the compensation package, and how long the commute is, not in the impact he or she can make. However, if you don't differentiate your jobs, if the hiring manager is weak, and the overall interviewing experience is unprofessional, you'll probably wind up competing on price. This is what always happens when a product or service is no different from its competitors. So if you want to find more top people, you need to differentiate your jobs and make sure that the top people you ultimately want to hire can find them.

Most advertising and sourcing programs are ineffective because they are targeting the wrong audience: those who *need* another job, not those who *want* a more challenging job or a long-term career. Top people will respond to compelling ads that are easy to find, especially if they focus more on opportunity rather than qualifications. Top people don't get excited when reading a list of requirements. Not once have I ever heard a top person say the reason he or she was accepting an offer was to get more experience doing the same type of work. Yet, that's what most job descriptions offer. Change this if you want to start hiring more top people.

➤ Sourcing Starts by Understanding Why Top People Look

Design your sourcing programs around the needs of top people, not average people. A great web site with boring jobs won't attract great people. A sophisticated applicant tracking system that causes top people to opt-out is counterproductive. A poorly administered employee referral program that targets everyone or overlooks high-potential candidates with a slightly different skill set is soon ignored.

It takes a great job to hire a great person. Whether you're hiring one person or one hundred, this fact must be advertised, discussed, understood, and paraded about by everyone involved in the hiring process, especially hiring managers. It needs to be built into every system, ad, process, letter, email, and form. Hiring the best is hard enough. Make sure you're not precluding them from even applying in the first place.

To hire the best people, you must find them and attract their attention with the right offer. Most sourcing efforts ignore these two concepts.

➤ The Sourcing Sweet Spot: Semi-Active and Semi-Passive Candidates

Forget the active versus passive candidate definition for a moment. Too many managers believe that active candidates are below average and all passive candidates are great. Realistically, there are some very good active candidates and some pretty bad passive candidates. By segmenting the market as shown in the following and developing more targeted sourcing programs, it's relatively easy to find the best of both:

Segmenting Candidates Based on Need for a Job

➤ *Very active*: These are people who need a job and are aggressively looking. They tend to be less discriminating and focus on short-term compensation and security issues when considering a new job. This pool represents about 15 percent to 20 percent of the total employment market. They are either unemployed, or severely underemployed. The best are underrepresented in this pool. Traditional, boring advertising is sufficient to attract and hire this type of person.

➤ *Semi-active*: These are people who are fully employed but who want a better job. They look infrequently, generally on bad days or just to test the market. However, while they use job boards, they are more selective. Compelling advertising and systems designed to bring these people to the top of the list is a key part of hiring them. This pool is big, about 25 percent of the employment market and it's growing. It doesn't take much anymore to get someone to consider leaving and start looking. This could be as simple as a boss who says something stupid, a project gone temporarily awry, or a simple inconvenience. This is the sourcing sweet spot, since the best people are overrepresented in this pool. To capture them, your ads need to be visible and you must move fast. For a corporation with limited resources, most of its efforts should be spent on sourcing people from this group.

➤ *Semi-passive*: These are people who want a better job and a better career. They are not actively looking, but they will accept a phone call to discuss future career opportunities. Who you call and what you say is a critical piece of hiring people in this group. The best approach is to prequalify all candidates before you call them; this way, you restrict your calls to only top people. This saves a great deal of time. The only way to prequalify someone is if he's been referred by someone else. Being great at getting referrals is the secret of sourcing semi-passive candidates. The best people are fairly represented in this pool, but it takes more effort and time to find them. This pool is big, too, about 25 percent of the employee market, and it's growing. Semi-passive candidates want to be found and pursued, so they'll post their names on LinkedIn.com and somehow get their profiles listed on ZoomInfo.com. Make sure you have something compelling to offer when you call or email people in this group, or else your efforts will be fruitless.

➤ *Very passive*: These people don't want another job. It takes too much effort and time to call and convince them to pursue your opportunity. The best people are fairly represented in this pool, but it's not worth the effort if you can find an equally strong person using a less-intense, lower-cost approach. These very passive people represent about 30 percent of the market, but it is declining in size. Everybody seems open to explore new opportunities.

In *Winning*, Jack Welch states:

*Hiring good people is hard. Hiring great people is brutally hard. And yet nothing matters more in winning than getting the right people on the field.**

Hiring the right people is much harder if you can't find any. It's a lot easier when you know how they look for new opportunities.

➤ Employer Branding versus Job Branding

Sourcing the best candidates is somewhat easier if you're an employer of choice. In good economic times, fast-growing, highly visible companies attract a larger share of top candidates. In slower economic times, solid, stable companies with a more secure future enjoy the spotlight. However, there is a counterbalancing effect that keeps the supply/demand of talent in relative balance. In slower economic times, the pool of semi-active and semi-passive candidates shrinks as these top people become reluctant to move from

* Jack Welch, *Winning* (New York: HarperCollins, 2005).

relatively safe jobs. In good times, more good people look since there are more opportunities to explore. To get a fair share of the top talent market, all companies need to aggressively target top people, regardless of the economic cycle.

From an employer-of-choice standpoint, Google is now the star. Microsoft is working hard to reestablish its earlier reputation. McKinsey is still the consulting firm of choice. And the big four (Deloitte Touche Tohmatsu, PricewaterhouseCoopers, KPMG, and Ernst & Young) are still the first choice if you want to be a CPA. *Fortune* magazine's "Best 100 Places to Work" helps companies attract more top people, so this certainly gives W. L. Gore, Wegmans, and Genentech a leg up. If you aren't an employer of choice, you can do two things: (1) try to become one, or (2) make each job you're offering a job of choice. In my opinion, you should spend more time on the latter.

■ USE A PERFORMANCE PROFILE AS THE FOUNDATION FOR BETTER SOURCING

If you're using a performance profile as the job standard and you're measuring a candidate's ability to do the job, rather than just get the job, the foundation for good sourcing is in place. This change alone will eliminate many of the sourcing problems most companies encounter. Good hiring is about hiring candidates who can achieve comparable results and are motivated to do it, so define great results and stop filtering out candidates for lack of skills. This eliminates many top performers who have 70 percent to 80 percent of the skills, but 150 percent of the desire and potential. By advertising on performance rather than skills, you'll increase the number of qualified candidates to select from. By selecting on performance rather than personality, you won't inadvertently exclude a great person. If you don't have these basics in place, better sourcing techniques won't result in better hires on a consistent basis.

Here's one example. A few years ago, I spent a day with a group of outstanding engineering managers at Intuitive Surgical in Mountain View, California. This is the company that is leading the development of less-invasive surgery with the da Vinci Surgical System. At the time, they were looking for a number of top senior design engineers. During the session on preparing performance profiles, I asked, "What does an engineer need to do in the fist six months for every person here to agree that the engineer hired is truly outstanding?" We converted the required skills into SMARTe performance objectives. We benchmarked some existing top engineers to better define competencies and to determine how problems were solved. In the end, we came up with about six deliverables around technology, quality, creativity, and team dynamics. I received a call the next day from their recruiter handling these assignments. He called to say thanks. He was very excited about one candidate who was initially excluded because he didn't quite meet the original skills-based profile. As a result of preparing a performance profile, the candidate was being brought back for another round of interviews. I later learned that an offer was extended and accepted. Six months later, this previously excluded candidate was performing at peak levels. This is not an unusual story. Unfortunately, too many companies never have a chance to experience it, because they eliminate good candidates based on an arbitrary level of skills, not on whether they can perform at high levels. From what I've seen over the years, sourcing problems are cut in half when you advertise and screen on performance rather than on skills and experience.

Sourcing problems are cut in half when you advertise and screen on performance rather than on skills and experience.

➤ How to Write Great Ads

A compelling ad is the next layer of an effective sourcing program; without an appealing, top-notch pitch, top people could look elsewhere. Whether posted on a job board, the company web site, or used as a verbal pitch to explain the opportunity, the ad serves as the first impression to prospective candidates, so you want it to intrigue a top person. Top people will explore career opportunities if the underlying message makes career sense. This has to do with the opportunity and growth—that is, what the person will do, what impact the person can make, and what the person can become. Don't post traditional skills-based job descriptions if you want to see more top people. This is akin to advertising the technical specifications for a consumer product and expecting people to buy it. Ads based on qualifications exclude top people from applying who might have a slightly different background. Those who do meet the qualifications won't apply unless they're desperate, because the job appears boring. The best candidates are not interested in doing the same job over again, even for more money. If the ad is compelling enough, then you'll attract more high-potential candidates and those great applicants sitting on the fence, waiting for the right opportunity to present itself. Compare the two ads for the same job in Figure 3.1 and Figure 3.2 to understand this concept.

The boring ad in Figure 3.1 was for a customer service person. I found it recently on one of the major job boards. It was posted by a recruiting process outsourcing (RPO) firm for one of their clients. (An RPO firm takes over the sourcing process for their clients. Their goal is to find better people more efficiently than the client can.) I found it by searching on the title and the city in the "Search for Jobs" section on the job board. To the company's credit, the ad was in the top five out of more than 1,000 that were available. Unfortunately, it was terrible in terms of the written copy.

Customer Service Representative

We are looking for a Customer Service Representative on behalf of our client, Acme Systems. This position is based in Dallas, TX.

Summary

Our customer service representatives will apply their strong communication skills to fulfill customer needs to ensure customer satisfaction.

Responsibilities

➤ Respond to a high volume of customer inquiries and requests
➤ Process orders and prepare various correspondences
➤ Two years' previous customer service experience, preferably in a call center environment
➤ Proven track record of stability and commitment to providing excellent customer service
➤ Strong computer skills, including proficiency with Windows
➤ Excellent communication skills, detail-oriented, and able to multitask
➤ Able to work in a team environment

Figure 3.1   Traditional boring ad.

Customer Service Rep, Juggler, and Master Organizer

Our client is growing fast in major part due to its focus on ensuring great customer service. As part of this expansion, the company wants to hire people who are looking for long-term careers in customer service, sales, or marketing. If you're interested in a career, not just a paycheck, then check this out:

1. You'll be put through a highly interactive three-week training course on using state-of-the-art CRM systems. (By the way, you'll probably make some lifelong friends as part of this.)

2. You'll need to juggle lots of tasks, track down orders, and solve tough-scheduling problems in order to keep our discriminating customers happy.

3. Attention to detail is critical. We take great pride in making sure every order is 100 percent correct. Hopefully, you help us get better here.

4. Our customers and your teammates are counting on you to be here, every day. If you've ever worked in this type of environment, you know how important teamwork and commitment are to personal success.

5. We'd like a year-or-so in a call center or customer service position. More important though is a commitment to yourself to be as good as you possibly can. We'll help you achieve this goal.

Figure 3.2   Compelling marketing-type ad.

The ad in Figure 3.2 shows the same ad rewritten to appeal to a top performer. We prepared something similar for a Verizon call center in Dallas, which resulted in a major increase in both candidate quantity and quality.

Which job would you apply to or recommend to a friend? Ads need to describe what's in it for the candidate, not what's in it for the company.

Figure 3.3 shows another example of a great ad. Over the past 10 years, we've used this type of ad format with great results, attracting technical and senior management personnel. This is a modified version of an ad we used to find CEO candidates for a not-for-profit charitable group in the Philadelphia area.

We posted the actual ad on TheLadders.com and used ZoomInfo.com's JobCast emailing program to broadcast it to anyone who had a not-for-profit background. The Ladders is an "employee pays" site for $100,000 positions and up. The fee is modest (less than $50 per month) and since the ad is free to employers, it's well worth checking out. We also placed a CFO from this site using a similar type of ad.

CEO (circa 2010) Fast-Forward One Year

We'd like to thank you for making Philadelphia a great place to live. Here's what happened under your leadership:

1. You raised $50 million to create a *City of Life* center as a safe place for inner-city kids to hang out after school.
2. You introduced a new program for single moms to enter the workforce with real jobs that offered real careers.
3. You got the top 50 companies in Philadelphia to make major commitments to being part of the city's revitalization program. The mentoring program you developed continues to receive national recognition.
4. Your programs helped stem the tide on drug use, reduced gang membership, and increased the graduate rate at all city high schools.

We can't wait until next year.

Now Back to Today

If you'd like this story to be yours . . .

Figure 3.3   Convert ads to stories.

ZoomInfo is a site that searches the Internet for names of people and categorizes them by title and company. Their JobCast emailing system allows you to automatically send the ad to anyone with an email address. Two of the final four candidates for the CEO position came from referrals from the JobCast email. The key was that the ad was so compelling that people wanted to send it on to others.

If you want to attract the best people, ads should be written from their unique perspective—they don't need a job, but they might check out a better opportunity. If you want to gain their interest, recognize they're smart, savvy, insightful, and discriminating, but not desperate. Choose the words for your ad copy with this concept in mind. Strong people who already have good jobs need a few compelling reasons to leave their current position. Your ads must clearly describe three to four reasons why a top person should bother to spend his valuable time checking out your job opportunity. Design and write your ad to stand out and attract top people who have multiple opportunities. If your posted job descriptions start out with the requisition number as the first thing a candidate sees when clicking on the title, you are losing good candidates for bad reasons. However, when your postings get constantly referred to other top people, you know your advertising is working.

In summary, great ads must meet three criteria:

1. *Have a compelling title that's quickly seen on the long listings of open opportunities.* "HR Wizard Required" is much more effective than "HR Director." This is a title we recently used with great results. Long titles are also effective since they stand out on the long listing of similar titles.

2. *Write copy that's focused on what the candidate will learn, do, and become.* "Use your HR magic to rebuild in only six months a department that's endured six years of neglect," is how we started our HR ad. You need to appeal to the candidate's underlying motivating needs.

3. *Describe the most critical skills in the context of how they're used.* For example, don't say "Five to 10 years of training and employment is essential." Something like this is a much better approach: "One of the biggest challenges you'll face is to use your training and employment expertise to set up a companywide effort to reduce turnover and improve customer service at our 350 locations."

An ad needs to overcome the inertia of not responding, or the pull of dozens of similar-sounding ads. To do this, the job and the ad must be different, interesting, and compelling. You want to attract as diverse a group of people as possible. The best-case scenario for boring ads that emphasize skills and qualifications, like most do, is attracting candidates who are competent but unmotivated. The best candidates are looking for something more than another job. Your ads must focus on the motivating needs of top performers. For most, it's a challenge or an opportunity. For some, it's better working conditions. For all, it's an opportunity to excel and to be recognized for doing outstanding work. Make sure your ads capture this concept.

Review a few of your most recent ads. Do they attract candidates needing another job or those open to explore new opportunities? I learned this fundamental rule about management from one of my candidates. He said, "If something isn't working right, don't keep on doing it. Keep on changing it until it works right." You might want to try this same technique with your ads, especially if they're not pulling as effectively as they should.

The Primary Rule about Posting Ads: Make Sure They Can Be Found

The whole approach to advertising on Internet job boards is changing. Niche boards catering to narrow job families are expanding, while generalist boards (i.e., Monster, CareerBuilder, and HotJobs) are losing traffic and rethinking their business models. Regardless of what the boards do, one thing will remain certain—if your ad is going to work, then it must be found by semi-active candidates. This requires three big changes. While the following steps are not common to corporate recruiting groups, most marketing departments would consider them the first steps in developing any advertising campaign:

Use Marketing Concepts to Give Your Ads More Visibility

1. *Reverse engineer your ads.* Less-active candidates don't spend much time hunting for jobs, so you have to make your ads easy to find. Reverse engineering is the process of optimizing your ad placement based on how these less-active candidates look. The goal here is to use the right key words and the best boards to make sure your ad is at the top of the listing.

2. *Use search-engine optimization techniques.* More and more candidates are bypassing the boards entirely and using search engines (e.g., Google, Yahoo, MSN, Ask) to find new jobs. Companies will need to redesign their career web sites so that their jobs can be found this way.

3. *Push your ad to the right audience.* There are many sites now (e.g., ZoomInfo, LinkedIn) and new Internet data-mining techniques that provide long lists of names of people with their titles, company names, and email addresses. Some of these candidates are semi-active, most are semi-passive, but if they receive a compelling email, they might be interested in checking out your offering. They also might refer

someone if the offer is interesting enough. These informal referral-like programs have great potential if the ad is well written and offers a clear career opportunity.

Create a Candidate Profile to Find Connections to Ideal Candidates
After you've put together a compelling ad, but before you start using any of these marketing concepts, draft a profile of your ideal candidate. Include all possible skills, keywords, connections, and links, as well as the types of people your candidate might know, potential places your candidate might have worked, vendors the candidate might have used, keywords your candidate would use to find a job, awards or honors your candidate might have received, and comparable past experience. Creating an ideal candidate profile is a great first step to finding an ideal candidate. Here's a checklist with a few examples and ideas:

- [ ] *Skills that the candidate needs*: Be broad enough to attract a wider audience.

- [ ] *Keywords the candidate would use to find your job listing*: Think out of the box here. Ask some of your recent hires for keywords they used to find your job.

- [ ] *Companies where the candidate would likely look to find a job*: These are probably your competitors. Buy these company names on a few key search sites and put them in your keyword list within the job posting.

- [ ] *Indirect or similar positions the candidate might have held in the past*: For example, for a workforce planning person in HR, we looked for someone in distribution and supply chain management.

- [ ] *Honors and awards the candidate has probably received*: When looking for salespeople, search resumes using "rookie-of-the-year" and "club." For an engineer, search resumes that have the terms "patent" and "white papers" in them.

- [ ] *Functional competitors*: These companies offer work and challenges comparable to your needs, but compete in a different market. For example, someone who has been a department manager at a retail store might make a great restaurant manager. We helped the Ruby's restaurant chain in Southern California fill many of their open positions this way.

☐ *Direct and indirect connections*: These people may have worked with your candidate directly in the past or they know someone who has. Previous supervisors, vendors, outside consultants, or someone on a cross-functional team are good places to get started. This is a great list to use to develop targeted referral messages.

☐ *Societies and alumni lists*: Determine what groups or schools the person belongs to or attended, and post your ads on niche sites that cater to these groups. The *Encyclopedia of Associations* is a great place to get the names of appropriate trade groups and professional societies. You can also get these names from the resumes you receive from your ads. Don't forget to call the association leaders for referrals. In my early search days, I used to get most of my leads for engineers from the Institute of Electrical and Electronic Engineers (IEEE) and the American Society of Mechanical Engineers (ASME) local chapter leaders.

☐ *Trade shows*: The candidate could either be a speaker or an attendant at the company booth. Regardless, search these names when sorting through a resume database. Once you find the conference title, look up the agenda for the list of presenters. These are great people to network with and recruit. Do this for every upcoming conference in your field to get a head start on your competition.

☐ *Blogs and web lists*: There are 23 million C++ blogs and 2 million Sarbanes-Oxley blogs. If I was actively recruiting, I would certainly use these areas to start getting names.

The opportunities to find the names of great people are almost endless. This by itself has changed how companies need to find and attract top performers. A great job is still a prerequisite. Speed, persistence, and professionalism are equally important. Great technology is not far behind. All of these activities need to be coordinated through the company's career web site, but few companies have taken this idea fully into account when designing sourcing programs.

➤ Career Web Site Design: The Central Control Point

Is your career web site underperforming? Does it act as a portal for top people to explore opportunities in an efficient and respectful manner? Or is it difficult to find jobs, hard to navigate, and overly complex? The primary objective of the career portion of a company's web site should be to provide quick access to jobs for interested top performers who have little time to spare. The second objective of the career web site should be to provide a means for companies to stay connected to these top candidates even when there are no current jobs available. Everything else comes next. Forget the shopping carts. Top people don't use shopping carts.

A career web site is the critical hub of a company's hiring efforts. Don't skimp here. A survey of over 500 candidates we took a few years ago showed that 65 percent to 70 percent of all candidates checked out a company's web site before applying for a job they found at one of the job boards. Half decided not to apply as a result, because the career section was weak. In our informal surveys, we also discovered that most passive candidates hearing about a job will generally check out the company's career site and read the specific job description before deciding to move forward. Seventy-five percent decided not to pursue the opportunity as a result, because the job descriptions were boring. People are being bombarded with new opportunities every day, so everything you do to capture their attention and keep it is critical. Your company career web site is the focal point of all of this activity. It is how you differentiate your jobs and your company. It is fast becoming your most important sourcing tool.

The following section details some basic rules to follow as you evaluate and redesign your company's career web site.

Marketing Advice to Improve Your Company's Career Web Site's Effectiveness

A company's career web site is one of the foundational pieces of effective sourcing. Few companies do a good job here and, as a result, miss some great candidates. New job-hunting trends combined with improved designs will allow candidates to go directly to a company's career site, bypassing job boards, and other intermediaries.

Done effectively, this can become a competitive advantage giving a company a jumpstart on attracting some top people.

It surprises me that some people dismiss the need for a good career site, suggesting that they just want to hire passive candidates. Even passive candidates will look on your site before considering a potential opportunity. More important, everyone is now looking, including more and more passive candidates. So if you want to take advantage of this increase in workforce mobility, you'll need to massively upgrade the quality of your career web site.

As you consider this, there are a few basic rules you need to follow to improve the effectiveness of your career site. As you read the following 10 guidelines, rank your company on a one-to-five scale for each of the factors noted. I ranked Deloitte & Touche, Microsoft, and IBM (during October 2006) on the first five factors to serve as a benchmark for this evaluation. These are highly regarded companies, and I wanted to gain a sense of how progressive they were. (Hint: they weren't.) The following 10 guidelines will improve your career site:

1. *Make the career web site easy to find from the company's home page.* Candidates should be able to go from the home page directly to the career section.

   I couldn't even find the IBM career site from the main company site (no points). Deloitte's link was easiest to find at the top (5 points), while Microsoft's was a little more difficult since it was at the bottom (3 points).

2. *Post jobs of interest that are easy to find on the career site.* In a customer service world, candidates shouldn't have to hunt and peck for jobs. One search box where a person can put a few keywords, a location, and a job title should be all that's required. Then *presto*, all of the jobs that match the candidate's interest should appear. That is Search 101, but somehow few applicant tracking systems have caught on.

   At IBM, it took four clicks to even begin looking for jobs and then the candidate would be confronted with a maze of pull-down menus (another goose egg). At Microsoft, it was easier to find the maze, but their approach was still disrespectful to a top person (1 point). Deloitte had no maze, yet their simple approach to find jobs still had some unnecessary pull-down menus and it was difficult to easily find jobs of interest (3 points).

3. *Use splash pages, also called talent hubs, to gain interest in a business unit or class of jobs.* Using splash pages can ease the conversion of your job descriptions from the traditional boring experience and skills-intensive approach to a compelling career opportunity. This is a good way to get candidates excited about a class of jobs by linking them to the company strategy and the broad career opportunities they provide. From the splash pages, candidates should then be quickly able to find a specific job.

   Microsoft did a good job with the splash page, highlighting the advantages of each type of job, but getting to the specific jobs wasn't easy. Once I was hooked on a class of jobs, they lost me when I was presented with the maze of all jobs, not just the ones I was interested in (3 points). Deloitte and IBM didn't have any splash pages that I could find (0 points).

4. *Compelling job write-ups to attract top performers who have multiple opportunities.* As described earlier, eliminate traditional job descriptions from your web site. These are not marketing tools.

   Microsoft's job descriptions were actually quite good, but they were impossible to find. Ironically, here's what I found after 15 minutes of looking for a software developer position at Microsoft: *"Have you ever thought about how much easier and efficient computers could be, if only you could easily find what you are looking for, or have the computer help you do what you want?"* Despite this, their advertising copy gets them 4 points. IBM's jobs were traditional and not the least bit compelling (0 points)—and I was willing to travel 100 percent of the time! Deloitte's jobs were a bit better, but not compelling enough for a top person with multiple opportunities to consider applying (2 points).

5. *Ensure a quick and easy application process.* Here's an interesting stat that I got from Monster.com: if your application form is auto-filled (i.e., most of the line items are parsed from the resume and placed into the application form automatically) when the candidate applies, there is a 75 percent

chance the candidate will complete the application. It's only 20 percent when the candidate has to complete the whole application from scratch. Good people won't waste time filling in the blanks. Technology is available to do this today, but not everyone uses it.

IBM's application process was pretty labor intensive, but not terrible (2 points). Deloitte's was more difficult than IBM's and seemed to be never ending (1 point). When I got to Microsoft, I was sent a message that I had to verify my email address, but when I logged back into the site, I had to start over trying to find the job I originally tried to apply to (0 points).

On these first five measures of career web site effectiveness, how many points would your site earn out of the 25 points possible? I would not use these major companies as benchmarks for designing your site. Deloitte had the most with a total of only 11 points. These fine companies are relying on their employer brands rather than considering how top people actually find jobs and have to navigate through their career web sites. For a better example of how a career web site should be created, go to the Toll Brothers site or Federated Department Stores. Toll Brothers, the luxury homes builder, has designed a very professional site that is easily worth a 22. Federated Department Stores treats its candidates as customers at every step. It's easy to find the site, it's attractive, and it's fun. If your career site is not at least in the 18 to 20 point range, then you're losing 50 percent or more of the best people who might want to just check out your openings.

6. *Call the best candidates within 24 hours.* If someone applies on your site, you'll need to make sure your backend search engine automatically brings this person to the top of the list. Someone in the recruiting department, or the hiring manager, needs to call this person within 24 hours. Semi-active candidates are a fickle lot. One day they're looking, the next day they're not. So when you catch them looking, you need to move quickly to get them into the game.

7. Add *customer-relationship management* (CRM) *capability.* Everyone who applies submits his email address and some basic career information. Make sure your site has the ability to send out mass, customized (i.e., some of the content changes based on the person's specific interests) emails to these people on a regular basis. If the messaging is done right, you'll be able to fill 10 percent of your open positions from people who just stopped by initially to see what you had available. Known as *drip marketing,* About.com defines this marketing technique as "a direct marketing strategy that involves sending out several promotional pieces over a period of time to a subset of sales leads." As part of the customization piece, it's important to include all potential job openings when they become available.

8. Be *careful how you use assessments and knockout questions.* If designed properly, these are useful for entry-level positions when candidate supply is greater than demand. Track how many people actually complete the test to make sure the best people don't opt-out for silly reasons. If you do use upfront questions, keep them short. Three or four questions are ideal. More than this and you'll notice a drop-off in the number of people who actually complete the questions. You also might want to use a performance-oriented approach to improve the effectiveness of the questions. For example, for a salesperson, the following might be a better question than, "Do you have at least two years of retail sales experience?"

> Performance-oriented sales question: *Would you be able to demonstrate that you've made quota at least 75 percent of the time for at least two years?*

You can make this type of question more meaningful by introducing the question with a little hype about the job. You could say that you're hiring experienced sales professionals to help launch a new product line. This will help induce more strong candidates to complete the questionnaire.

9. *Use web analytics to optimize your site's performance.* Use tools like Webtrends (webtrends.com) to track the effectiveness of each page in your career site. Knowing the opt-out ratios at each step in the process and where people spend the most time is invaluable information. This is what you'll use to ensure your career site is performing at an optimum level. Google Analytics is a free way to get started tracking this information right away.

10. *Take advantage of compliance requirements like the Office of Federal Contract Compliance Programs* (OFCCP). Since there are so many compliance issues to handle, companies just follow all the rules in bureaucratic fashion without consideration to the negative impact it has on top performers. While you must meet the legal requirements, this doesn't mean you can't be creative. The OFCCP has developed a definition of an Internet applicant that imposes some onerous reporting requirements on those companies that work as contractors for the Federal government. One of our clients used this to their advantage for a few jobs by sending emails to all candidates who applied. In the email, they described the job in compelling terms and requested that if the person was interested, he submit a short write-up of something he's accomplished that's comparable to the real job needs. Per the OFCCP, only those who respond meet their definition of an Internet applicant. Not only did this reduce the number of candidates that had to be tracked, it also induced the best to apply. These people were intrigued by the compelling nature of the job and the fact that the email was sent to them.

These 10 steps are no more than Internet Marketing 101 applied to career web site design. It's important to pass this course if you want to take advantage of the massive increase in workforce mobility. Everybody is now looking. Why not make it easy for them to find you?

Things are changing and there are other new techniques becoming available to drive more traffic to your job postings. Here are a few more ideas you should consider.

➤ Use Reverse Engineering and Search-Engine Optimization Techniques to Help Top People Find Your Postings More Easily

Fewer candidates are going to job boards to find jobs. Fewer still go directly to your career site to find a job. However, more people are using search engines to find a job. This entails nothing more than putting a few skill terms into Google, adding a title or two, including a city, and the word "jobs." Suppose a financial analyst was looking for a new position in the Chicago area and had 30 minutes to spare. Conducting a Google search using "MBA financial analysis Chicago jobs budgeting planning" the person would be presented with jobs posted on boards at Hewitt, PepsiCo, the University of Chicago, a number of generic jobs, a real good one on Craigslist, and three placed by third-party recruiters. There was also one from Indeed.com, an aggregator of job postings. Aggregators comb the major job boards and career sites and consolidate opportunities using a one-stop shopping approach. What was surprising is that not one job from a company's own career site showed up until the third page. This was from a local TV station, and the job had nothing to do with financial analysis.

The reason most company career sites don't show up on these listings is that they're hidden from the search engines. The way most job descriptions are formatted on career sites preclude them from ever being found. Just look at the URL for one of your open jobs on your career site. It probably doesn't include any terms that would indicate it's a job posting. It's probably also designed within a frame that prevents standard search engines from finding it. Search-engine optimization techniques are being developed to help companies around this dilemma. Jobs2web.com and Careermetasearch.com do this by scrubbing your ads for keywords and then reposting them on a clonelike site so that they can be more easily found. There are new techniques being developed to push your jobs to where they can be found. This is important technology, so make sure you stay on top of these trends.

In the short-term, it's important to make sure your ads can be found using common keywords. To some degree, this is nothing more than making sure your ads are on the aggregator sites (Indeed.com, Jobster.com) or on the sites that do show up in the Google search listings. eQuest.com offers a process to broadcast your ads to the sites most used by people looking for the types of jobs you're offering. Then you'll need to figure out how to get them to the top of the listings using appropriate keywords or whatever techniques the site offers.

Over the long term, you'll want to redesign your career site so that your postings can be found directly by people looking for the jobs you're offering. Candidate tracking system vendors are now building this capability into their products. In the interim, you might want to create a separate splash page to act as a hub for a family of jobs. Have your marketing team design this site and optimize it using the same SEO techniques they use to make sure your customers can find your products. Top people will then be able to find this splash page directly from a search engine. The other advantage of this approach is that candidates are driven directly to your career site, bypassing the job boards. This way there won't be as much competition with jobs from other companies. You won't have to rewrite all of your job descriptions using this hub (splash page) and spoke concept.

■ MULTILEVEL SOURCING: USE A SERIES OF SOURCING CHANNELS TO ENSURE A CONSTANT FLOW OF GOOD CANDIDATES

The objective of a company's sourcing efforts should be to maximize candidate quality while reducing time to fill and cost per hire. To do this, use a variety of sourcing channels targeting top semi-active and semi-passive candidates. A sequenced sourcing process like this, if monitored on a weekly basis, also accommodates for cyclical economic changes mentioned earlier. Understanding this economic shift is important in designing multichannel sourcing programs. Include these sourcing channels in a multilevel sourcing strategy for a corporate recruiting department:

➤ Career web site and job boards
➤ Resume databases and CRM
➤ Internal transfers
➤ Employee referrals

- ➤ College recruiting
- ➤ Special campaigns
- ➤ Passive candidate name identification
- ➤ Cold-calling and networking

Done effectively, most companies should be able to fill 80 percent to 90 percent of their jobs with B+ or better candidates using the first five channels. This will also reduce the cost per hire and the time required to fill per hire. The key to effectiveness here is to monitor each channel using a variety of metrics involving candidate quality and recruiter productivity (e.g., quality or sendouts/per hire/per recruiter/per channel) to determine when one of the channels is becoming less effective. Revamp the channel and/or sequence up to a higher-cost channel to maintain a flow of good candidates.

It's well accepted that cost-per-hire and time-per-hire are not the best measures of sourcing, unless quality is embedded in the equation. Just because an A candidate is easily worth a 33 percent search fee from a return on investment standpoint, it doesn't mean you shouldn't seek to reduce costs and minimize time to fill while maintaining quality. In the past, the rush to reduce search fees and build internal corporate recruiters was the basic corporate recruiting department strategy. It wasn't too effective for a variety of reasons. In the end, candidate quality declined as corporate recruiters were given too many requisitions to fill.

A sequenced multichannel sourcing approach, as described here, provides corporate recruiting departments a strong foundation to handle any changes in workforce needs.

Monitoring channel performance is one critical component of this type of sequenced sourcing program. The other component is to make sure each channel is optimized. Since the career web site and job postings are critical to all of the channels, devote more time to getting this right. The following sections provide some basic ideas on how to optimize the effectiveness of the other sourcing channels.

➤ Resume Databases and Customer Relationship Management

Most candidate tracking system vendors now offer some type of customer relationship management (CRM) module built in. This is nothing more than a direct marketing email campaign manager. If you don't have this functionality available, you can use salesforce .com or some comparable low-cost system. Set it up with just a list of email addresses and the contact information and you can automatically pull off a resume. With this system in place, all you need to do is set up a series of email campaigns that are targeted to your specific candidate.

To get started, categorize all of the resumes in your database by job type. You'll be sending everyone in your database a monthly or semimonthly newsletter that consists of fresh, general company content in combination with some job-related information. Ask hiring managers who want to push their open jobs to prepare this. Ask them to describe some interesting things going on in their departments. Also, highlight a few key jobs with links directly to the splash page or the job opening. In the CRM system, prepare different email messages by job family, which will be automatically sent to the candidates in your resume database. While you might have 6 to 10 different emails going out at any one time, most of the content will be common. If you keep the content relevant, fresh, and exciting, you will get a number of good leads for current openings with this type of nurturing "drip marketing" system. The current CRM craze is just a variant of this highly effective process. Of course, ask for referrals and get people to opt-in to the newsletter. If your online job descriptions have been rewritten as described earlier, you should be able to fill 10 percent of your open jobs with this technique.

➤ Employee Referral Programs

As far as I'm concerned, a proactive company employee referral program should be at the core of every sourcing strategy. Most companies will tell you that their internal employee referral program has produced more top people than all other methods combined. In the past few years, we've heard this from representatives at Microsoft, AIG Insurance, Wells Fargo, Yahoo, Deloitte, Broadcom, SAIC, HealthEast Care System, Cognos Software, and scores of small- and midsize companies. Each indicated that their internal referral programs were by far their number-one source for top candidates. Your best employees know other great employees, so you need to tap into this network in an aggressive way. This should also be the primary means to accelerate your diversity hiring efforts. Your best diverse candidates know other diverse candidates.

Making your employee referral programs more proactive can yield even better results. A proactive employee referral involves an aggressive program of getting your employees to identify the best A-level people they have worked with in the past. As these names are being gathered, it's important to capture why they are being ranked as top performers. With this information, recruiters can recruit and network with these top people to develop an even bigger pool of top candidates.

To make an employee referral program more effective, use the following tips:

➤ *Make a formal, professional referral program that is heavily promoted throughout the organization.* This needs to be an ongoing activity, not just a sporadic event.

➤ *Make sure all new employees learn about the employee referral program during orientation.* Highlight the part about providing names of top performers with whom the person has worked in the past. Especially mention that you want to get names of top people who are not looking, and that the employee will get a referral fee even if the recruiter does all of the contacting. This alone will yield many more names of top performers.

➤ *Encourage current employees to only provide names of good people.* Let the staffing department call the candidate and do the recruiting.

➤ *Provide a bounty for referrals.* This can range from $500 to $3,000 for recommended candidates who ultimately get hired. Bounties seem to work better than some type of prize.

➤ *Follow up quickly with every referred person in a very professional manner.* The lack of proper backend administration can leave your employees with a bad impression of your company.

➤ Recruit Passive Candidates Using Networking and Cold-Calling Techniques

Calling passive candidates takes time, skills, and effort. There are techniques you can use to get better results, but before you start networking with passive candidates, ensure that you're doing everything else that's easier first. However, if you're still not getting enough strong candidates using the techniques described in this chapter, then you'll have to begin direct sourcing of passive candidates. The good news is that there are now some great ways to get names of passive candidates on the Internet. The best are Zoom-Info, JigSaw, and LinkedIn. While they differ in approach, these sites provide names of people with their titles, companies, and sometimes a quick blurb about their background. But the real skill here is how you call, recruit, and get more names from the original list of names.

First, act vague about the job when you first talk with the person. Provide few details about the job initially, with a goal of not asking questions that can be answered with a "no." Instead, when you get the person on the phone, ask, "Would you be open to explore a situation that's clearly superior to what you're doing today?" If the answer is yes (which it will be most of the time), tell the candidate you'd like to first obtain a quick overview of her background, and then you'll provide a quick summary of the job. This way, a quick phone screen can determine whether the candidate is even a possibility before the person has a chance to say she's not interested. This is a very critical step. Getting the candidate to respond first gives the recruiter an opportunity to develop a professional relationship. If the candidate is not a good fit, it's much easier to ask for referrals.

Conduct a quick work history review as part of your initial questioning. When it's appropriate to ask for referrals, ask the person for the name of the best person at her prior company. Getting names from prior companies like this is quite easy. You can also ask who the person's best boss was, or who mentored her, or who she mentored. Ask whether she knows somebody in the industry who might know somebody else. Make sure you don't ask for people who are now looking. State explicitly that you want to talk with people who are not looking. Try to get three names from each person you talk with who could be a potential candidate or someone else he or she knows in the same field.

Once you have the name, ask the candidate to describe the person. Find out why she considers the person highly qualified. Asking questions this way allows you to prequalify the candidate. When you do this consistently, you'll be able to develop a small pool of highly qualified candidates within days. You can save lots of time when you're only calling top people. If you can systematize this process, then you can maximize your candidate quality while dramatically reducing your cost and time to hire.

How to Work a Cold List

If you buy a list of names or use one of the name-generating tools noted earlier, don't even think about calling every person listed. This is too time-consuming. For one thing, many of the people listed are not top performers. For another, only a few will ever wind up being a candidate you'll present. However, the best people in this group probably know other great people who could wind up being candidates. The secret to maximizing the value of a cold list is to only network with the A players on the list, and get referrals of other A players from them.

To narrow your focus down to A players, start by calling the best 20 people on the list using some type of reasoned decision making (e.g., good title and respected company). When you call someone cold, there's only a 1 in 50 chance that the person is going to ultimately be a candidate for your job opening. However, there is a one in five chance this person knows someone else who is a good candidate. Your goal when making the first cold call is to get names of other good candidates. This is easier than it sounds. However, I've discovered that people will more likely give you names if you recruit the person first as described previously. If the person is not a good fit for your current opening, then begin the networking process. People are more likely to give you good names if you've spent 10 minutes or so getting to know them. That's why I suggest you recruit first and network second. If you tell him too much about the job before you get to know the person, he'll normally say he's not interested, eliminating the chance to develop the relationship needed to get some referrals. If you obtain his background first, you also can use this information to target specific companies and situations to get names. It's far better to say, "When you were at Motorola, who was the best coworker you'd like to work with again?" rather than "Who do you know?"

Recruit first, network second.

Once you've found three to four very good people from the original list of 20, only network with referrals these people have recommended. This way you'll only be calling top performers. Recruiting and networking with top performers is much more efficient than calling people at random. To be credible though, you must know real job needs, have a great elevator pitch, and become an expert at the "recruit first, network second" approach described earlier.

➤ Workforce Planning and Just-In-Time Sourcing

The key to developing a systematic process to hire top talent requires at least a six-month time horizon. This gives the sourcing group enough time to use all sourcing channels and build pipelines of talent. Most corporate sourcing programs are far too reactive. For many companies, new hiring requisitions are the result of someone quitting or the approval of a new project. The sourcing process then begins. This gives little time to source top talent and fewer options, generally job boards or third-party recruiters. Under this time-pressure scenario, standards fall since the need to fill the position overrides the desire for quality. The best people generally take more time to find, and when they're found, they take longer to decide. If your hiring process is primarily reactive, you have little chance to consistently hire top people. Forward-looking workforce planning can minimize these problems by providing the time to do sourcing properly.

A good workforce planning process consists of a rolling quarterly forecast of all hiring needs for the next year. This should be prepared by every hiring manager and it should tie into the company operating plan. It needs to take into account new programs, normal attrition, and changes in the company's business outlook. Every quarter, revise this forecast to maintain visibility over the next year. If the hiring forecast is done properly, changes for the upcoming quarter should be minimal. Changes in the forecast for the next two quarters provide an early indictor that business conditions are changing. A good workforce planning process, combined with realistic updated forecasts, is an invaluable tool for the sourcing group.

The essence of workforce planning is to forecast your hiring needs at least four to six months in advance. This provides you the time to implement all of the sourcing programs described in this chapter. Hiring the best requires preplanning. If you must hire people yesterday, you'll always compromise your standards. Planning ahead is important. If you need to hire 20 design engineers in six months, start the planning today. In six months, some top people will be waiting at your door.

➤ Sourcing—It's the Strategies, Not the Tactics, That Will Ultimately Determine Your Success

A number of sourcing tactics have been presented in this chapter, but it's the strategies that really matter. Most important is the need to create a proactive talent-driven culture. This mindset is essential to hire top people. If the senior management group doesn't buy into this concept, all of the best tactics in the world will have little impact. Jim Collins, in *Good to Great*, indicated that building a top team was the first step for every company that eventually became great.[*] In *Execution*, Larry Bossidy and Ram Charan clearly point out that an organization's people "are its most reliable resource for generating excellent results year after year."[†] It was clear in *Jack: Straight from the Gut* that setting up a methodology and culture that focused on hiring and developing outstanding managers was Jack Welch's true legacy at GE.[‡] These were three books that looked at the landscape of American business over the past 20 years. Although each took a different path, each came to the same conclusion—hiring the best is not some activity that can be talked about, ignored, or delegated to HR.

Aggressive and proactive sourcing is essential if you want to increase your share of top talent. This is more important today than ever before. Workforce mobility is increasing at a rapid rate. Everyone is visible. The winners in the new hunt for top talent will be those that have the most creative and aggressive sourcing and recruiting programs. Planning is a prerequisite and provides the time needed to do it right. If you treat candidates as potential customers, rather than future subordinates, a whole shift in attitude takes

---

[*] Jim Collins, *Good to Great: Why Some Companies Make the Leap . . . and Others Don't* (New York: HarperCollins, 2001).
[†] Larry Bossidy and Ram Charan, with Charles Burck, *Execution* (New York: Crown Business, 2002).
[‡] Jack Welch, with John Byrne, *Jack: Straight from the Gut* (New York: Warner Books, 2001).

place. This shift impacts advertising, priorities, the time spent on the process, the allocation of resources, and the quality of the interviewing and recruiting process. But if you want to hire great people, you have to find them first. That's why great sourcing is so important. Every company, big and small, has access to the same tools to find people. It's how they use these tools that make the difference in whether you hire great people or not.

HOT TIPS FOR TALENT-CENTRIC SOURCING

✔ *Implement a multichannel sourcing strategy.* You'll need this to counter the increase in workforce mobility and maximize candidate quality while reducing time-to-fill and cost-per-hire.

✔ *Use the hub and spoke concept to massively upgrade your career web site.* Your company career web site should be an inviting place where top people can find jobs quickly.

✔ *Make your advertising visible.* Work hard using search-engine optimization and reverse engineering techniques to make sure top people can find your jobs.

✔ *Offer careers, not jobs.* Don't post traditional job descriptions; these are boring and counterproductive.

✔ *You'll find your best candidates in the sourcing sweet spot.* Build your active and passive sourcing programs around how the best people in each group look for new opportunities.

✔ *Be fast. Be different.* To compete for the best, you must be different from your competitors. To hire the best, you must move fast. Redesign everything with these two ideas in mind.

✔ *Recruit first, network second.* The best people will give you the names of other good people if you build a personal relationship with them first. Recruiting them directly is the shortest way to build a relationship.

✔ *Implement a proactive employee referral program.* Your current employees know many great people who aren't looking. Ask them who they are and then recruit them.

✔ *Implement workforce planning.* Planning and forecasting resources and needs are at the core of good management. A workforce plan provides the time to find the best people available, not the best available people.

Chapter 4

The Two-Question Performance-Based Interview

Q: When you choose men and women to promote, to be a leader of the company, what qualities do you look for?

A: You clearly want somebody who can articulate a vision. They have to have enormous energy and the incredible ability to energize others. If you can't energize others, you can't be a leader.

—Jack Welch

■ THE FOUR CORE TRAITS OF UNIVERSAL SUCCESS

As you discover in this chapter, it only takes two questions to assess the 10 best predictors of on-the-job success. One of the questions involves understanding a candidate's past performance in great detail. The other question gets at the person's thinking, planning, and problem-solving abilities. The secret here is that you'll repeat the questions over and over again to see trends, links, and consistency. Before we get to the questions themselves, GE offers a slightly different view on assessing success that's worth evaluating.

In *Jack: Straight from the Gut,* Jack Welch discusses the importance of building outstanding teams, considering this to be his core legacy.* He also describes the four Es of GE leadership used to assess competency. The four Es are the ability to **e**nergize yourself, **e**nergize others, the **e**dge to make tough decisions, and the ability to **e**xecute.

I have been a headhunter since 1978, so I've had an opportunity to work with some great talent. I've tracked many of these top people over the course of their careers for 5, 10, some even as long as 15 to 20 years. It was clear to me that the best had four common characteristics that were observable in the initial interview: (1) self-motivation—everyone who achieved any level of success worked hard; (2) an ability to motivate others—inspiring others to work hard, including peers, superiors, as well as their own team; (3) achievement of results that were comparable to what needed to be achieved; and (4) an ability to solve comparable job problems in real time. While not identical to the GE four Es, they're certainly close. Collectively, my four became the Performance-based Hiring formula for predicting performance in a new job.

➤ Performance-based Hiring Formula for Predicting Performance

---

**Success = Talent × Energy² + Team Leadership
+ Comparable Past Performance
+ Job-Specific Problem Solving**

In this formula, energy^2 is by far the most important component. This is self-motivation, and identical to the first of GE's four Es. It's squared because it has enormous impact. We've all met people with great talent but little energy. Sadly, they never live up to their expectations. Others of average talent, but with extraordinary energy, often achieve success beyond all expectations. That's why self-motivation is so important. In over 25 years of dealing with

* Jack Welch, *Jack: Straight from the Gut* (New York: Warner, 2001).

some of the best people in the country, I've come to an obvious conclusion—the best work harder than everyone else. They make an impact (Talent × Energy^2 = Impact). The best people make things happen, do more than is required, and consistently deliver more results than expected, and they do it on time, all the time. This separates the best from everyone else.

The best people consistently deliver more results than expected, and they do it on time, all the time. This separates the best from everyone else.

Some call this quality initiative, or self-motivation, work ethic, drive, ambition, commitment, or anything else related to going the extra mile. Without it, even the most talented fail. With it, people with only average talent can become extremely successful. These people consistently exceed expectations, year in and year out. Don't be seduced by affability and social assertiveness. Assertiveness and positive energy demonstrated during the interview don't translate to on-the-job performance. Unfortunately, many interviewers falsely assume it does. If you've ever hired someone who is competent, but not motivated, this is probably the cause. This is a very common hiring error. Another common error is to eliminate quiet people assuming there is a lack of energy. Being quiet or outgoing in an interview does not predict personal energy, initiative, or work ethic. You can observe it, however, by getting detailed examples of accomplishments, and looking for a pattern of where the person went the extra mile. This is one of the core interviewing techniques described in this chapter.

The second component of the Performance-based Hiring success formula is team leadership. The ability to persuade and motivate others to achieve results is an essential component of long-term success. It allows a person to tap into the personal energy of others. This person could be a boss or subordinate, a peer, or an outside advisor. The ability to cooperate with others is a component of this team leadership. As Jack Welch said, "If you can't energize others, you can't be a leader." This is similar to the concept of emotional intelligence described in Daniel Goleman's book, *Emotional Intelligence: Why It Can Matter More Than IQ.** Here's the online Wikipedia definition: "an ability, capacity, or skill to perceive, assess, and manage the emotions of one's self, of others, and of groups." However it is defined, influencing and motivating others is a core attribute of success. It's often mistaken for affability during the interview.

Together, initiative and team skills are a winning combination. You won't find many successful people without them both. It doesn't matter if they're in accounting or sales, in a creative or technical position, the president or a clerk. It also isn't important if the person has 20 years of experience or is just starting out. Those who continually succeed have the core traits of personal energy and team leadership in abundance.

However, assess these traits in context. Just because someone has demonstrated drive and team leadership under one set of working conditions doesn't mean the person will perform at the same high level in all situations. A great boss, a flexible environment, and highly motivating work might not translate too well with a different manager, a different culture, and doing different things. That's why one of our core traits of success is measuring comparable past performance. The likelihood of success in a new job increases if the applicant has a track record of accomplishments that are similar to the performance objectives of the job described in the performance profile.

The fourth trait of success involves thinking, planning, and job-specific problem-solving skills. The best performers in any job, from entry-level accountant to company president, have the ability to solve problems related to the job. For the accountant, it might be how to reconcile an account. For the president, it might be to determine the cause of poor business performance or to develop a new product strategy. The best people know how to figure out job-related problems, or they can tell you how they'll go about solving these problems in real time. Asking them to solve a problem they'll encounter on the job is the fourth question.

---

* Daniel Goleman, *Emotional Intelligence: The 10th Anniversary Edition; Why It Can Matter More Than IQ* (New York: Bantam, 2005).

■ THE MOST IMPORTANT INTERVIEW QUESTION OF ALL TIME

If you want some quick insight into a candidate's technical competency, motivation level, and team leadership skills, start by asking this two-part question: "Of all of the things you've accomplished in your career, what stands out as most significant? Now could you go ahead and tell me all about it?"

Getting the correct answer to this question can tell you 65 percent to 75 percent of everything you need to make an accurate hiring decision. The correct answer comes by fact-finding and getting complete details of the accomplishment. As an example, let's try it out right now with you as the candidate. Write down a short description of your career-defining accomplishment in the space below. If you don't have a major accomplishment you can boast about quite yet, write down a project or an assignment you worked on that made you very proud:

My most significant accomplishment is . . . _____ .

Now imagine you're sitting across the desk from me and I ask you to tell me about this accomplishment. If, over the next 10 to 12 minutes, I asked you the following additional questions, how would you answer each one?

Fact-Finding Questions: Clarifying Major Accomplishments
➤ What were the three or four big challenges you had to overcome?
➤ What were the actual results obtained?
➤ When did this take place and at what company?
➤ How long did it take to complete the task?
➤ What was the situation you faced when you took on the project?
➤ Why were you chosen for this role? Did you volunteer? Why?
➤ What was your actual title? Who were the people on the team? What was your supervisor's title?
➤ What technical skills were needed to accomplish the task? What skills were learned?

➤ Describe the planning process, your role in it, and whether the plan was met. Provide details of what went wrong and how you overcame them.

➤ What was your actual role in this project?

➤ Give me three examples of where you took the initiative. Why?

➤ What were the biggest changes or improvements?

➤ What was the toughest decision you had to make? How did you make it? Was it the right decision? Would you make it differently if you could?

➤ Describe the environment—the pace, the resources available, your boss, and the level of professionalism.

➤ What was the biggest conflict you faced? Who was it with and how did you resolve it?

➤ Give me some examples of helping or coaching others.

➤ Give me some examples of where you really had to influence or persuade others to change their opinion.

➤ How did you personally grow or change as a result of this effort?

➤ What did you like the most and least?

➤ In retrospect, what would you do differently if you could?

➤ What type of recognition did you receive for this project? Was it appropriate in your mind? Why or why not?

Next write down just a few things I would have learned about you during this 15-minute interview.

It's pretty remarkable when you think about what an interviewer could learn about a candidate by just asking about his or her biggest accomplishment. It would include things like talent, motivation, critical thinking, personality, character, values, team or individual focus, self-awareness, communication skills, overall ability, cultural fit, and commitment, to name a few.

If I left it up to you to tell me about the accomplishment without the deliberate fact-finding, I would have been measuring presentation—what you wanted to tell me—not performance. This is a critical distinction. The interviewer needs to take responsibility to obtain this information from the candidate. It is not the candidate's responsibility to provide it to you. This is one of the basic rules of accurate interviewing. It's all about fact-finding, peeling the onion, and digging deep into an accomplishment, not asking a bunch of clever questions.

Accurate interviewing is about peeling the onion and digging deep into an accomplishment, not asking a bunch of clever questions.

All you need to do is ask the same question two or three more times to observe the trend of performance over the past 5 to 10 years. This way you determine consistency, growth, flexibility, adaptability, and impact in addition to all of the competencies, skills, behaviors, and traits noted earlier.

To balance things out, ask about major team or individual accomplishments if the candidate emphasizes one or the other. Then review the performance profile for the job to make sure you haven't missed something important. If the candidate for a sales manager job hasn't mentioned anything about taking the lead on opening up a new territory, ask the person what she's done that's most comparable to this type of task.

The key to using the most significant accomplishment (MSA) question is to ask it multiple times to observe long-term trends for individual, team, and job-related accomplishments. Some of these will overlap. For reference purposes, here's the basic form of the MSA question and three suggested variations:

1. *The standard MSA question*: "Can you please describe a major career accomplishment you believe represents your best work?"

2. *The MSA question for entry-level positions*: "Can you please describe a project or task you were involved in that made you quite proud, or where you really exceeded expectations?"

3. *The MSA question for team skills*: "Can you please describe a major team accomplishment you believe represents a great example of you leading, building, or working on a team?"

   4. The MSA *question for individual accomplishments*: "Can you please describe a significant individual accomplishment you believe best represents one of your individual strengths?" This could involve some technical project or where the candidate used his or her strategic or creative skills.

   5. The MSA *question for job-related accomplishments*: "One important project for us is _____. Can you please describe something you've been involved with that's most comparable?"

However, the subsequent fact-finding is the real skill. In just a few interviews, you'll get quite proficient at the MSA question, especially if you keep your emotions and biases in check. While the full 10-Factor Evidence-based Assessment process is explained in the next chapter, including how to increase your objectivity, it's relatively obvious that asking the MSA question provides great insight into the first four core traits of success—talent, motivation to do the work required, team leadership, and comparable past performance (see Figure 4.1).

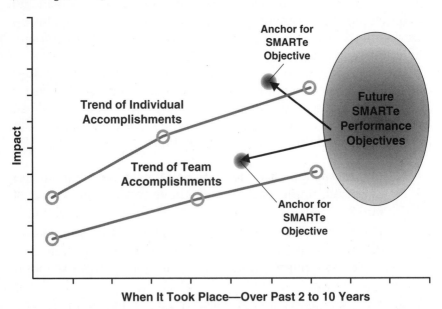

Figure 4.1   Develop a trend line of performance to
better predict success.

The trend lines in Figure 4.1 are quite revealing. An upward slope indicates that a candidate is still growing. A plateau or flattening out is not bad if the candidate is still highly motivated and continues to produce outstanding work. A decline or a roller-coaster trend is of concern. In each case, the interviewer needs to compare the candidate's accomplishments against the real needs of the job when assessing a candidate on the four core traits. The second question helps understand the fifth core trait of success—job-specific problem solving.

■ THE SECOND MOST IMPORTANT QUESTION: VISUALIZATION AND PROBLEM SOLVING

If you want to better understand a candidate's thinking, planning, and job-specific problem-solving skills, just ask this question: "If you were to get this job, how would you go about solving _____ [describe a typical problem]?"

Make sure you turn off the spotlights and talk about real work when you ask this question. The key here is to get into a give-and-take discussion about a realistic job problem. It's been my experience that top performers have the ability to discuss what's needed to solve typical problems. Even if the person can't provide the answer right away, she knows how to get to the answer.

A good discussion around this topic reveals problem solving, insight, intelligence, potential, vision, and leadership. If you're hiring a sales manager, you might ask, "How would you go about ensuring that the team met quota every month?" For an engineer, it might be, "How would you design and develop this product to ensure it's in production by next March?"

The best candidates I've met in my 25-plus years in executive search all have the ability to anticipate the needs of the job before starting. They can figure out very quickly what's wrong or what's necessary to accomplish a task, what they need to do to implement a solution, and what resources they need to do it. They also have a track record of implementing these changes. Success is about planning to accomplish a major task and delivering on these plans.

The "how would you" question gets at the planning and visualization aspect of every successful accomplishment. A lack of planning and visualization skills is one of the key reasons projects come up short, budgets are overrun, implementation is slow, or problems go unresolved. Allow the candidate to ask you questions to gain more insight into the specific problem or project under discussion. Asking, "What's the budget (time frame, staff, resources)?" are great questions and provide the interviewer another dimension to assess the candidate's competency and fit.

At the end of the interview, categorize the candidate's responses along four dimensions. First, determine whether the reasoning is complex, advanced, or superficial. The best candidates demonstrate a good understanding of the cause and effect of their actions. Superficial reasoning is evidenced by a bunch of seemingly unrelated ideas. Reasoning is more advanced if the ideas logically link together. Second, determine whether the focus of the response is technical, tactical, or strategic. Those with a tactical bent address more of the results than the process. Technical people provide too much detail. A strategic focus is represented by a longer time horizon, typically six months or more. Also consider whether the response emphasizes either team or individual factors. As part of this, consider if the candidate's ideas involve others. This is very revealing when compared to actual accomplishments. It's especially important if you're hiring a manager. Last, consider whether the discussion is multifunctional in perspective. The best candidates understand the implications of their job on other people and other functions. Listen for this as the candidate plans out a task and asks questions.

■ GAIN MORE INSIGHT USING THE TWO-QUESTION INTERVIEW

You'll need to practice asking these two questions to become proficient. In Chapter 5, we suggest using a group debriefing session using our 10-Factor Candidate Assessment template. This checklist provides guidance on how to rank the candidate's answers. One thing you'll learn in these sessions is that fact-finding is the key to an accurate assessment. This allows you to gather the evidence you need to make the correct decision. You quickly discover that many interviewers make these important hiring decisions based on generalities and intuition. Sometimes you need to push the candidate to get the information you want, rather than information the candidate wants to tell you about.

For one thing, don't accept generalities like "Created a new market," "Turned the department around," and "Developed a new procedure." Don't hesitate to ask for clarifying information. Many interviewers are reluctant to ask follow-up questions because they don't want the candidate to think they're confused. This is where good fact-finding comes into the picture. Probe deeply until you completely understand the true nature of the accomplishment and the applicant's role.

Use the following questions to get more insight if the candidate is somewhat vague or speaks in generalities:

➤ I'm a little unsure of what you've accomplished. Could you give me another example?

➤ What you described does not seem that significant. I must have missed something. Could you explain it with more details, or give me an example to demonstrate what you mean?

➤ I'm unclear of the challenges you faced in this job. What were they and why do you feel these were significant?

There is a natural tendency for candidates to generalize and give one-minute answers. It's important to get details; that's why getting examples is so important. Once you get candidates to speak freely you'll discover that they tend to give more information on subsequent questions.

One of my clients told me she uses this technique when she hires software developers. She has them clearly define their contribution made on each of their last few major projects. She wants to know what their impact has been and the specific role they played. She looks for a continuing and larger contribution in each successive position.

➤ Use Work Charts to Understand Team and Management Skills

Ask each candidate to draw a work or team chart, even if the person isn't a manager. A team chart can clarify accomplishments because it shows all the people the person is involved with on the job—peers, subordinates, boss, people in other departments, outside suppliers, and customers. If the candidate is a manager have the person draw an expanded team chart that includes all of his direct reports. Have the candidate rank the quality of the staff, how he developed the team, and how he improved the team's performance. Then find out who he hired, fired, and why. Do this for the past few jobs. If the candidate has developed a pattern of only building average teams, he's only an average manager.

Here are two additional MSA team-leadership questions you can ask:

1. *If the person isn't directly supervising others:* "Please draw an organization chart and tell me about a team project you were involved in, and describe your role."

2. *If the person is a manager:* "Please draw an organization chart and tell me how you built and developed this team, and describe the group's biggest accomplishment."

You don't have to be in a management position to exhibit team or leadership traits. We've discovered that people who aren't yet managers, but who will be soon, evidence strong team skills. The ability to motivate, work with, and persuade others is an important and recognizable talent. If the person is not a manager, or if you go back to a previous job when the candidate wasn't a manager, use the nonmanager version of this question. Ask for examples of team projects and be sure to explore the specific role the candidate played. Get specific. Get names, specific results, determine key obstacles, and find out how the candidate handled conflict and differences. Look for a pattern of implementing change, doing more than required, motivating and persuading others, and helping to define team objectives.

Drawing the organization chart provides a visual sense of the reporting relationships. Some important jobs often look less significant when shown on paper with only a few direct reports. A director of accounting and planning job can be equivalent to a vice president of finance and look very big when it covers responsibility for five countries, seven direct reports, and a staff of 100.

An East Coast distributor used this technique to hire an international manufacturing manager a few days after attending one of our seminars. The head of operations told me he truly understood the significance of the candidate's management skills when she described in detail how she developed an individual improvement program for each of her staff members. She was animated and involved during the exchange, presenting herself as she really was. The candidate described the strengths and weaknesses of each person and how he or she changed as a result of the program. The hiring manager felt this interviewing approach allowed the candidate to move away from the staged presentation of most interviews into a relaxed, more natural communicating style.

➤ Develop a Trend Line to Measure Long-Term Impact

The trend line is also important. By going back 5 to 10 years, you'll be able to observe the trend of these important traits over an extended period of time. This approach works for managers and non-managers alike, and entry-level or seasoned personnel. Students can demonstrate these traits early on, even in nonwork-related situations. You just have to look for them.

The trend line isn't always obvious, but getting major objectives this way will help determine whether the candidate's performance is on an upward trend, has flattened out, or is declining. A number of years ago one of my business associates asked me to interview a few candidates for his warehouse manager's position. All of the candidates were strong and held similar positions, but only one was on an upward growth path and I recommended him, even though he was a little quiet. The other two had significant success early in their careers, but for the past 10 years had settled into comfortable situations. While both of them could do the current job and professed a desire to grow, neither had taken any action to invest in themselves. The other candidate was taking night classes, learning advanced distribution techniques, and developing his staff. No matter what a candidate tells you, look for these signs of upward growth, even if they're not obvious in the candidate's titles.

There was an article in *Fortune* magazine by Geoffrey Colvin that represents the heart of what it takes to be great:

> *So greatness isn't handed to anyone; it requires a lot of hard work. Yet that isn't enough, since many people work hard for decades without*

approaching greatness or even getting significantly better. What's missing? The best people in any field are those who devote the most hours to what the researchers call "deliberate practice." It's activity that's explicitly intended to improve performance, that reaches for objectives just beyond one's level of competence, provides feedback on results and involves high levels of repetition.*

An upward trend line is one clue the person is getting better and working hard. If the person is excelling at the work described in the performance profile, it's highly likely you've found a top person for your open position.

Interestingly, the best candidates respond very favorably to this inquisitive approach. These people like to talk about their accomplishments. They also feel more positive about managers requesting this information. It tells the candidate that the manager has high standards, is thorough, and has probably built a team of other strong people. Good people want to work for these kinds of managers. They also feel very positive about the situation and the person conducting the interview. If every interviewer is this thorough, this approach demonstrates the professionalism of the whole company. Weaker candidates get put off and squirmy with this inquisitive style. Since they have less to show for their efforts, their answers are usually shorter, shallower, and more general. Don't settle for anything less than high energy, good team skills, and a good dose of talent or the ability to learn. These are the elements that stars are made from, but you sometimes have to look deep to find the sparkle, or to determine its real source.

➤ Anchor Every Performance Objective

Assessing comparable past performance is one of the five core traits of success. This is measured by getting examples of past accomplishments for each of the performance objectives on the performance profile. This is called an *anchor question* and it can be assigned to different members of the hiring team. Here's the basic form to use:

---

* Geoffrey Colvin, "What It Takes to Be Great," *Fortune*, October 30, 2006.

One of our key objectives for the person selected for this position is _____ [describe objective]. Can you please tell me about something you've accomplished that's most similar?

Combine this with the fact-finding techniques discussed earlier to paint a word picture of what the applicant actually accomplished. Look for comparable accomplishments. The process used to achieve the results and the environment in which they're achieved is more indicative of fit than identical accomplishments. Get details like staff size, comparable scope and complexity of the assignment, and similar company environments.

Comparability of accomplishments minimizes the need for industry fit and years of related experience. In our search practice, we place many salespeople all the way from reps to senior executives. We've discovered that the process used to achieve sales success is more important than a specific product or customer. People who have track records of selling complex technology to extremely discriminating customers can do this whether it's telecommunications gear, computers, or capital equipment used in manufacturing. The track record of sales success is most important. Next is comparability of the process including dollar volume, length of time, type and sophistication of the buyers, and the support services provided.

The performance profile lists different types of accomplishments. By anchoring every objective, you'll get a better picture of the candidate's ability to handle every critical facet of the job. This is also true for candidates who seem initially weak. Often other skills discovered later in the interview can more than compensate for an apparent weakness. If you exclude someone too soon, you could inadvertently miss a great candidate. The apparent weakness might not even be a real weakness. It could just be the result of an incomplete response.

A few years ago, I was evaluating a financial manager who had tremendous technical skills. He was personable, smart, and well educated. One of the major performance objectives of the position, but not the primary objective, was to work with other functions in setting up companywide performance reporting systems. He struggled coming up was a comparable example for this.

His answers were more general and shorter—two classic signs of lack of experience or interest. Even fact-finding didn't help. His best examples were superficial. The candidate's greatest successes were all individual projects. While a likable person, it wasn't clear he could work with manufacturing and operations people to meet the company's needs. We moved on to another candidate for the job.

The visualization question reinforces the anchor. It's especially useful in assessing a candidate's ability to handle significantly different accomplishments.

➤ Visualize the Two to Three Most Important Performance Objectives

The visualization process is less like an interview and more like a real working session. This is how and what you would talk about after the candidate starts. Sometime during the first week, you'll sit down with the new employee to discuss the objectives of the position. You'll normally get into a discussion on how these tasks would be handled. You'll outline strategies and tactics, talk about schedules and resources, allocate staff, and reprioritize. This is also your first chance to understand the candidate's planning ability and insight. Why wait? You can do the same thing with the visualization question before the candidate ever starts. This is a great way to transition the new employee into the job. Candidates know what's expected of them before they start, and you have a better sense of how they'll function in the new environment.

The best candidates for any position and any level have the ability to mentally organize the work before starting it. This is what good managers and leaders do on the job in planning out new tasks. They work with others in brainstorming the needs and challenges of the job before beginning. The visualization question is a way to test this ability during the interview. In the past 25 years, I haven't met one top-notch person who couldn't do this.

The questioning can take a variety of forms. One way is to allow the candidate to ask for more information. Another is to ask how the person would begin or organize an assignment. "As we've discussed [objective] is an important aspect of this position. If you were to get the job what additional information would you need to know, and how would you go about accomplishing this objective?" Good people know how to go from point A to point B and are not afraid to discuss how they'd do it, or to ask for more information. Some won't even take on an assignment until they're sure the resources are available or the company is committed to success. Allow this type of open discussion to take place. You'll see many thinking and planning skills emerge. You don't need to visualize all of the performance objectives, using just the top two to three will provide you with the insight you need.

In Steve Covey's best-selling business book, The 7 Habits of Highly Effective People, he urges people to "begin with the end in mind."* This concept is incorporated directly in the performance profile, requiring a manager to better understand real job needs before interviewing candidates. Not only is it an important trait for managers to have, it's an equally important trait for a successful candidate to possess. You directly test for it during the interview with the visualization question.

One of my clients used the visualization technique with great success to hire someone to head up a new business unit. My client told me they spent the whole second half of the first interview laying out the plan on a flip chart. Together he and the candidate developed the strategies, tactics, an organizational chart, and even prepared a preliminary budget. Both the candidate and my client believed this was one of the most revealing and insightful interview sessions either has ever had. A few months later, my client called to tell me how happy he was with the new employee. He indicated that the approach to problem solving and understanding shown during the interview was the same used by the candidate, now on the job. You don't have to go to this extreme to get similar results for yourself. Discuss a problem that has just come up, or an issue that needs to be resolved after the person comes on board. As long as the problem or issue is job related, the subsequent discussion is a great way to assess planning and thinking skills.

* Steve Covey, The 7 Habits of Highly Effective People (New York: Fireside, 1989).

➤ The Do—Do—Do—Think Interview Pattern: The Key to Interviewing Accuracy

Some caveats are appropriate as you begin using the two-question performance-based interview approach. It's the combination of the significant accomplishments and visualization questions that make them so powerful. There are some great communicators who can visualize, but who have never actually done anything comparable. Consultants or staff people fall into this category. They're often bright, persuasive, and self-confident. This is a great combo, but it is an incomplete mix. They can tell you how to do it but have never done it before.

We placed a very bright MBA who had just finished a two-year tour with one of the top consulting firms in an industry job. His caseload had been impressive, and he had conducted high-level cost studies for two Fortune 100 manufacturing companies. He struggled in this new position, though. In his new role as a planning manager, he had to do a lot of detailed, gritty analysis, wading through accounting detail. While important work, the lack of much conceptual planning combined with the monthly routine did him in. He was great at talking about and studying the problem, but not as effective at getting out with the functional departments and doing the real work. By combining the anchor and visualization questions, you'll be able to overcome this classic hiring problem.

Some behavioral interviewing experts don't like the situational nature of the visualization question. They contend that past behavior is the only accurate predictor of future behavior. In their mind, hypothetical questions are not valid. I agree with their concern when visualization questions are unrelated to the job. Job-related situational questions, however, are a great means to assess the required thinking skills used on the job. This type of situational question must be combined with a valid anchor to test complete competency.

The situational question minimizes the possibility of hiring someone who is not flexible, even though he has had some similar success in the past. I have met many apparently strong candidates who can effectively anchor performance objectives, but still sometimes fall short once on the job. No two jobs are identical. Some people don't have the ability to adapt their skills and experiences to new situations. They're more structured in their thinking, less adaptable, and often too analytical or rigid. By demonstrating an ability to apply knowledge in solving realistic job-specific problems, the visualization question minimizes this potential problem.

This approach works for all levels and different types of positions. If you are looking for a technical skill, some kind of test to demonstrate competency would be equivalent to an anchor. In a jewelry manufacturing company we've worked with, candidates were given pieces of jewelry to examine and asked to describe their quality level. The company was looking for people in the manufacturing area who have a good eye for detail and this was the way they tested for this ability.

One of our engineering candidates for a consumer products company was asked to examine a detailed engineering drawing for overall design effectiveness. He was then asked how he would have changed the design to function better. This was a combination of the anchor and visualization approach. At a retail pet-supply store, entry-level sales personnel, generally recent high school graduates, are asked how they would handle some typical customer complaints. Then they're asked to describe real examples of handling similar interpersonal conflicts. With this dual approach, the anchor and visualize pattern can be used to increase hiring accuracy for any type of position.

You'll never be able to complete all of your questioning during the first interview. I suggest you anchor the top two or three objectives and conduct one visualization exercise. Leave the remaining for a subsequent interview or another interviewer. Assign the assessment of specific performance objectives to the person most impacted by it. For example, have the manufacturing manager interview a cost manager who's required to improve the factory reporting system. While you won't be able to determine competency completely after one interview, the anchor and visualization questioning pattern enables you to see whether it's worth inviting the candidate back for another interview.

■ THE COMPLETE PERFORMANCE-BASED INTERVIEW: PUTTING IT ALL TOGETHER

While the two-question interview will give you a good understanding of candidate competency, there are a few other things you need to do to complete the assessment. The complete Performance-based Hiring interview combines the two core questions with a formal opening, a work history review, and a recruiting close. (Refer to the Appendix for a complete copy of this interview, or download it from the resources section on www.adlerconcepts .com.) The following eight steps provide a brief outline of the interviewing process:

Step 1: *Warm-up; do a quick overview and understand the candidate's motivation for looking.* Use the first 5 to 10 minutes to gain a quick sense of the candidate, overcome temporary nervousness, and find out why the person is looking for a job.

Step 2: *Wait 30 minutes and measure the impact of first impressions at the end of the interview.* Use the interview to collect information, not decide competency. Decide competency by carefully evaluating the candidate's responses against real job needs. It's best to do this at the end of the interview or during a group deliberation where everyone shares information.

Step 3: *Conduct a comprehensive work history review.* Go through every job and find out what the person accomplished, what the person didn't accomplish, the team the person worked with, why the person took the job, and any recognition they received. If you spend half of the opening interview on this, you'll know what you need to do in the second half.

Step 4: *Ask about major individual accomplishments.* This is the MSA question. During the work history review, ask about the highlights of major accomplishments, then select ones that best meet your job needs to learn more about.

Step 5: *Ask about a major team accomplishment.* This is the modification to the MSA question with the focus on team leadership. Spend a great deal of time on this, using specific team fact-finding follow-up questions.

Step 6: *Ask a problem-solving question.* During this visualization question, start a discussion about a realistic job problem, not some hypothetical situation.

Step 7: *Recruit and close.* Don't end the interview on a neutral note, but don't give the farm away either. Done properly, the close can be a useful way to begin the recruiting process without overselling.

Step 8: Measure first impressions again. You'll be dumbstruck when you measure first impressions at the end of the interview and compare them to your initial reaction. Many of the people you initially thought were great won't be, and many of the ones you thought were weak will turn into stars. That's why you need to measure first impressions at the end of the interview and ignore their impact—positive or negative—at the beginning of the interview. First impressions don't predict job performance.

➤ The Opening: Controlling the Jitters on Both Sides of the Desk

On a recent survey we conducted with over 500 candidates, 80 percent indicated they were somewhat or very nervous during the opening moments of the job interview. Even top performers and top salespeople fell into this group. So don't dismiss candidates for this during the first 30 minutes. If you conducted a phone interview, you've already established some rapport. Some people suggest a warm-up, or a get-acquainted period. I think this is unnecessary, although some casual conversation is appropriate. My approach is to get right into the interview. Accept the fact that some candidates will be nervous, and don't judge their early responses too harshly. Work with them in getting them to provide better or more examples. Once a "give and take" is established, I've found even nervous candidates open up.

I met with a very nervous manufacturing engineer a few years ago. He was so nervous I thought he would fall out of his chair. It took about 10 minutes for him to calm down, but the changeover took place when he told me the specifics of an automation project. I had asked him to draw a sketch of a high-speed assembly device he was working on. Once he got into it, he was a changed person. Getting him to stop talking was the new challenge. I told the hiring manager to conduct the interview on the factory floor and talk about specific projects and problems right away. In his element—which wasn't interviewing—all traces of nervousness were eliminated.

Accept the fact that nobody likes to interview and that a nervous candidate is just a nervous candidate. Don't assume this is related to performance. If you still have a problem after about a half-hour, move on to the next person on the list.

The most common opening question, "Tell me about yourself," is too big and broad. You give up too much, too soon, to the candidate. There are better approaches that establish the framework we need for both an effective performance-based interview and applicant control. We suggest the following opening question format:

As you know, we're looking for a _____ [position]. Let me give you a quick overview of the importance of this position. [Give a two-minute overview of the position and the company.] Tell me how your background has prepared you for this type of important position.

While this is a "Tell me about yourself" type of question, it narrows the focus down by requesting only relevant background information. Further, it establishes a recruiting opening by describing the importance of the job. When you make the job compelling, applicants tell you more about themselves. They sell you, rather than you having to sell them. This establishes the framework for good recruiting. Don't spend more than a few minutes on this pitch. There's a tendency to talk too much to open an interview. It's a waste of time. One or two minutes is all that's necessary to set the tone. Remember to listen four times more than you talk. A good interview is a fact-finding mission, not a sales pitch. The following example is a good opening:

We're looking for a product manager. This person will lead the implementation effort on much of our new product introduction program. This is a critical initiative for next year with new products representing 10 percent of new sales. We need someone who can coordinate the efforts of engineering, marketing, manufacturing, and sales to bring this new line out on time and within budget. Give me a quick overview of how your background has prepared you for this type of position.

The last request is a great warm-up. Don't forget the fact-finding, but don't start it too soon either. You want to establish a communication style that allows you to get enough information to validate the candidate's initial responses. Much of this will depend on the candidate's style of presenting information. Work with the candidate on this. I openly tell candidates that I'm more concerned with specific examples about a few major accomplishment than lots of broad generalities. Quiet candidates open up more when constantly asked for more examples, and louder candidates stop generalizing and start to focus.

➤ Modifying the Two-Question Interview to Assess All Traits and Behaviors

The 10-Factor Candidate Assessment template includes the evaluation of five other predictors of on-the-job performance in addition to the five core traits (i.e., talent, motivation, team leadership, comparable past performance, and job-specific problem solving). One predictor of on-the-job performance is the trend of growth over time, as described earlier, that reveals the candidate's consistency of performance. The remaining four factors are planning and executing comparable work, culture and environmental fit, character and values, and overall potential. While you'll still use the basic MSA question to get examples of accomplishments, you can change the type of fact-finding probes you use and the way you rephrase the question to better understand these other traits.

Alternate Forms of the Most Significant Accomplishment Question

In Chapter 7, you discover how to modify the MSA question to both excite and challenge the candidate. Other interviewers can also modify the question format to better understand other traits, skills, and competencies. Here are some examples:

> Do you have another major accomplishment that reveals your ability to persuade or influence people in other departments who might be peers or those who have more authority than you?

What accomplishment did you discuss with [prior inter-viewer]? Is there anything else about this accomplishment that you think was not fully discussed?

What was your absolute biggest failure?

What was your biggest accomplishment where you had the least amount of skills?

Do you have an accomplishment where you took a major risk?

Basically, these are variations on a theme, just modifying the MSA question to better understand what the candidate really brings to the table. Modifying the subsequent fact-finding also allows the interview to go down a different path. If you want more on team-related skills, follow-up with these types of probes:

➤ Did you mentor anyone on this project?

➤ Did anyone mentor you?

➤ Who was the toughest person to influence?

➤ Who was your best and worst supervisor? Why?

➤ What did you do when someone missed a deadline?

➤ Give me three examples of coaching others?

If you want to understand the candidate's technical ability, use these fact-finding probes:

➤ What was the toughest technical challenge you've ever faced?

➤ How did you solve the problem?

➤ What tools do you excel at?

➤ Give me some examples of where you've trained others?

➤ Where did you push the envelope on technology?

➤ What type of work gets you excited?

➤ Which parts of the job give you trouble? How do you handle this?

The key to this questioning pattern is to go to the edge of the person's current abilities. You do this by asking about the worst, the best, the most challenging, the biggest, the toughest, and the most challenging. By getting a good sample of the person's best and worst accomplishment and matching it to your needs, you'll be able to better predict on-the-job performance. Use the problem-solving question to gain a sense of how the person handles new situations and visualizes bigger tasks. This will give you real insight in potential and growth, especially when confirmed by the trend lines.

➤ Assessing Character and Values

If you want to assess character and values, ask, "Can you give me the best example of something you accomplished where you were totally committed to the task?" This quickly gets at the heart of character. The ability to persevere under difficult conditions is an essential trait of top performers. It's the character component of energy because it's easier to work hard under ideal conditions than difficult situations. Real character is better observed in less than ideal circumstances. Use fact-finding techniques to understand the true extent of the applicant's commitment to the task and the underlying environment. Determine the challenges faced and the results achieved. Listen to the response and determine whether the success was individual, team based, or companywide. Find out why the candidate felt strongly about the accomplishment. Look for a pattern of commitment in all of the examples of significant accomplishments. While this approach doesn't cover every aspect of character, it covers the most important.

A controller candidate told me about his role in rebuilding his manufacturing plant, which had been partially destroyed by the 1994 Northridge, California, earthquake. To get the plant up and running, he described two weeks of around-the-clock work and another few months of extended hours. He said the process was the most satisfying experience he had ever had. The camaraderie and team spirit kept him and the others going through some very difficult times. Although he was a strong financial type, it was this team orientation and sense of commitment that made him exceptional.

You also might use the character question if you're unsure about a candidate or have a candidate you think might be weak. Often the response to this will eliminate a marginal candidate or revive one you thought lost. Use this question in the later part of the interview when candidates are likely to be more candid. You have to stay open-minded, though. If you've already made a decision, the answer will have little value. Although it's very difficult to override your own internal decision once made, always use this question on commitment to validate your judgment. The answer can sometimes be powerful enough to overcome even the most strongly held beliefs.

➤ Measuring Personality and Cultural Fit

By the time you measure personality and cultural fit—at the end of the interview—you pretty much know the answer. By the time the interview ends, you'll have explored at least five or six different accomplishments in-depth. Personality, interpersonal skills, and management style will come out of this assessment. Personality in an absolute sense is unimportant. How candidates have used their personality and style to achieve results is what's really important. You'll discover this by using the impact, leadership, anchor, and visualization questioning patterns and the fact-finding techniques we've suggested. Use this question as part of your probing to confirm your insight and add a few more specifics:

> As part of this project, what three or four aspects of your personality would have been observed? Give me actual examples of when these traits have aided you in the performance of your job and when they have hurt.

A candidate who knows himself will be able to quickly list a few critical traits and provide some good examples. Many of them should have been previously discussed. If they seem inconsistent with your own evaluation, do some probing to uncover the differences. Raise the caution flag if the candidate seems evasive or if you notice extremes of behavior. Also look for flexibility. If the person appears overly dominant, ask for examples of coaching, patience, and team skills. For the overly analytical person, probe for examples of team skills and the ability to persuade others. People who are the supportive type often have difficulty making tough decisions. Explore for this. The outgoing salesperson is often weak on details. Don't reach this conclusion without getting some examples of analytical work. Good candidates are sometimes excluded because they don't seem to fit the required personality profile. You'll get at flexibility in personality by looking for the candidate's apparently missing parts.

Look for personal development. I often ask candidates to describe how their personality has changed over the years. This gets at maturity. A former arrogant MBA from one of the nation's top business schools told me how he became more sensitive to others after working with a tight team on an extended crash project. Of course, I got the specific details of the project to confirm his makeover. It's best to be a bit of a cynic, especially when interviewing a smooth-talking professional.

Look for candor. It might be time to raise the caution flag if the candidate can't openly describe some failures. The second part of the question is revealing: "Give me examples of when your personality has hurt your performance." Don't ignore this part. Continue probing. Be concerned if you get a run-around or some vague response. Good answers here are also a sign of character.

A few years ago, a sales manager told me he was sometimes too rough on his team, particularly when they were falling short of quota. He told me his New York personality sometimes got the best of him. He knew this was a weakness, but he said he hadn't lost any good people as a result. His solution was to work more closely with his people in developing monthly objectives, so that they were both equally committed to the results. Previously, he didn't get into the details as much so he didn't understand their specific strengths and weakness. Getting this close to the process was unnatural for him, since he was more the entrepreneur, but it was helping him become a better manager, and less confrontational. He became more proactive than reactive as a result. I'm sure the hard-driving personality is still there, but by adapting to a more analytical style, this person was able to compensate for a potentially fatal flaw.

You can't really separate personality from performance. Personality is naturally revealed with the fact-finding and probing techniques discussed earlier. You might want to add more emphasis to personality if this is a major area of concern. You can even make it a performance objective. One of my clients was looking for a property manager with good interpersonal skills. It turned out that the real problem was with a very demanding owner who required 100 percent attention to his every whim. We created a performance objective that stated, "Set up a quick response, support program to deal with a very aggressive and demanding property owner." The candidate had to have the personality to deal with these kinds of people, but it was more than just having good interpersonal skills.

The ability to handle and resolve conflict with other departments or with difficult people is the most common type of issue and requires a real attention on personality. During the interview, get some examples of how the candidate handled similar interpersonal problems. This gets at a specific area of personality. Personality is important, but by measuring it through performance and again at the end of the interview, you'll be in a better position to understand its importance in getting the job done.

■ THE CLOSE: USE RECRUITING TO END ROUND ONE

You can use the following classic ending to the first interview for all candidates, but it's essential for those who you think will make the initial cut. This statement starts the formal recruiting process:

> Although we're seeing some other fine candidates, I personally think you have a very strong background. We'll get back to you in a few days, but what are your thoughts now about this position?

Three important things occurred with this close.

First, you created supply. Good jobs are more attractive when other good people are being considered. Jobs are not only less desirable when no one else is being considered, but you also lose control of the interview, since the candidate now knows he is the only one in the loop. This is a sure-fire way to pay more than you need to, or lose the only candidate you have.

I remember an engineering vice president telling a manufacturing manager candidate that she was the only good candidate he had seen. When we tried to close the candidate, she demanded, and got, another 15 percent. Everyone else on the interviewing committee knew what to say, but we forgot to give this one person the guidelines.

The second point in this closing question is that you created demand by expressing sincere interest in the candidate. A compliment goes a long way. Candidates think more about why they want a job when told they are well liked and qualified. They think about why they're not going to get it when the ending is left neutral or flat. By itself, "We'll get back to you in a few days," is the classic kiss of death, so never use it alone, particularly for candidates who you like.

The third point, asking the candidate for a response to the job, is to gauge true interest level. The supply and demand prefaces are used as set-ups to obtain this in an unbiased fashion. This is important. You want candidates to openly discuss their thoughts, feelings, and concerns. Suggest they call you back with other questions after they've thought the situation over. It's important to establish this open dialogue as soon as possible with all of the potential finalists. As you see in Chapter 7, this is the key to smoother negotiations and closing.

If a candidate you like is not interested, it's important to understand her concerns. Most often good candidates don't initially see the merits of a job. Perhaps they need more strategic information or time to digest what they've heard. Don't push it. Take the time to explore their issues, but don't attempt to resolve them right away. Tell the candidate you'd like to get back to her in a few days for further discussion. Suggest that at that time, you'll be able to give her a different perspective on the job, but first you want to finish interviewing all the candidates. Indicate that if the candidate does want to come back for a second interview there will be another series of interviews. State that it really won't be until after the complete assessment that the candidate will truly understand the scope and importance of the position. Your objective with reluctant candidates is to get them to stay open-minded and come back for another series of interviews.

■ FACT-FINDING: THE MOST IMPORTANT INTERVIEWING TECHNIQUE

The interviewing approach we recommend is more a methodology than a list of clever questions. We've discovered that the questions themselves are less important than the quality of the information obtained. Get lots of information about the candidate's top five or six major accomplishments. This is all that's necessary to make an accurate hiring decision. The key for each accomplishment is to understand the results achieved, the process used to achieve the results, and the environment in which these results took place.

One of my candidates told me her greatest accomplishment was in never making a hiring mistake. She told me she clearly understood the work that needed to get done, she didn't initially care whether she liked or disliked the candidate, and she spent the first interview only getting examples, facts, and figures to verify a candidate's past performance. This is the way interviewing and hiring needs to be done.

To reinforce the point, I turned the tables on her and asked her how many people she hired, their positions, their names, how they performed after starting, the impact they made, and specifics regarding her role in their personal development. She got a laugh from this, but it became clear that her hiring accomplishments were real and worthy of note.

The difference between good answers and bad hiring decisions lies with fact-finding.

The difference between good answers and bad hiring decisions lies with fact-finding. The MSA question is simple to ask. Fact-finding is what makes the answer meaningful. As an added benefit, fact-finding naturally minimizes exaggeration. There is a tendency on the part of candidates to overstate or mislead, either through outright fraud or generalizations. Fact-finding peels away the onion to get at reality. By asking for specific examples to support any generalization, you force the candidate to justify a response. Remember to ask the five Ws (i.e., who, what, when, where, and why) to paint a clearer picture of the applicant's actual involvement in the task. Find out critical decision points, what went wrong, the resources available and how they were allocated, the strategies, the tactics, and who made the decisions. Be inquisitive, not inquisitorial. Most interviewers ask too many general questions. A few questions with lots of fact-finding is a better approach.

Turn generalities into specifics by getting examples of everything.

Always convert generalities into specifics by using this basic question to start the fact-finding process: "Can you give me a specific example describing what you mean?" This should be the most important question in your interviewing tool kit. Use it to get behind any generality or statement. If someone says she has great technical skills, is very creative, or is a real team player, ask for examples. If she says she is a problem solver, ask for an example of a problem. Use this technique often. It will be the key to real understanding. While certain candidates generalize to cloud reality, some do so as a result of upbringing. Some cultures minimize the role of the individual and have been instructed not to talk about themselves. Fact-finding will help clarify this.

Fact-finding can be the bridge that improves communication and understanding. I recently met an articulate, professional woman seeking an HR management position. She said her greatest accomplishment was establishing a framework and direction for the department. After asking for a clarifying example, it turned out she based this conclusion on updating the policy and procedures manual for her company. This important (but not glorious) task took about three months of part-time work. In another example, a financial manager who stated he was a great manager was somewhat sheepish when asked to name the five best people he has ever hired and describe why. He could only come up with one over five years. During another interview, a soft-spoken engineering manager whom I was about to exclude because he did not seem assertive enough eventually told me about a crash program he had led to commercial success. He described the late nights and motivational talks to his engineering team. I can still hear his enthusiasm and energy.

In the words of Sergeant Joe Friday on *Dragnet*, "Just the facts, ma'am."

■ PREPARATION IS THE KEY

A good part of interviewing has to do with avoiding dumb mistakes. The other part has to do with determining whether the candidate can do the work. If you understand the job and can control the urge to decide too soon, the candidate assessment part is straightforward. Preparation is the key. Don't wait until the candidate is in the lobby.

Re-read the resume before an interview, even if you have already conducted a phone interview. If you haven't conducted a phone interview, going over the resume is even more important. Somebody has already made the decision for you to talk to or meet this candidate. Figure out why. Circle the strengths and put big plus marks next to them. Asterisks and minus signs also help. During the interview, ask for specific examples to validate strengths and clarify concerns. Don't forget that a great deal of work has already gone into the effort to arrange this first interview. It can all be lost in the first few moments if you don't carry the momentum.

Re-read the performance profile and review the performance objectives. These performance objectives cover every aspect of the job—major objectives, interim objectives, problems that need to be solved, changes to be made, team issues, management and organizational issues, and technical needs. You'll be benchmarking candidate competency against these top six to eight deliverables.

During the interview, the candidate will sense your preparation. Always assume that you'll be meeting a top candidate and that top people want to work for professionals with high standards of performance, job know-how, and a balanced, attentive demeanor. Floundering interviewers turn off the best candidates.

Here's an example of how I lost a great candidate for a director-level position because of this. The candidate made a great first impression and had strong credentials. In my mind, this was an instant placement. As soon as the interview started, the vice president of operations, who was clearly unprepared, began talking too much, asking a bunch of meaningless questions, and selling too soon. Right after the interview, I got a call from the candidate. She was pulling herself out of contention. She felt that the hiring manager made too quick of an assessment based on a few superficial facts. She told me his understanding of the job was vague and shallow, and she didn't want to work for someone who could make an important decision so quickly. The rule here is to listen four times more than you talk. Don't oversell or underlisten. Ask questions instead.

The interview process we're proposing and the preparation needed to pull it off increases objectivity and validates competency. In addition, it gains candidate interest. All three are critical if you want to improve your hiring effectiveness.

■ THE TELEPHONE INTERVIEW SETS THE STAGE FOR THE CANDIDATE AND THE INTERVIEWER

To minimize the impact of first impressions, conduct a quick phone interview before you meet the candidate. The phone interview decreases the visual aspects of the first impression before you personally meet in a one-on-one session. On the phone, spend half of the time reviewing the candidate's work history and the balance on one or two major accomplishments. In about 20 minutes, you'll know if the candidate is a definite no, and in about 30 minutes, you'll know if the person is worthy to bring in for a more intensive interview.

If the candidate passes this screen, I always ask him to be prepared to discuss his most important team and individual accomplishments, suggesting a written summary as an addendum to the resume. A half-page for each accomplishment is enough. This helps the candidate respond to your questions. In addition the effort put into writing the accomplishments provides some insight into interest and writing skills. This performance-based phone screen by itself will diminish the impact of first impressions when you meet. The accomplishment write-up is an added touch that will speed the assessment process along.

■ WHAT NOT TO ASK: THE INAPPROPRIATE AND ILLEGAL QUESTIONS

At the beginning of one of our hiring training workshops a few years ago, one of the attendees complained that one of the causes of hiring problems was an inability to ask personal questions. Another person affirmed this and in rapid-fire sequence asked what questions were off limits. My response to both was that you don't ever need to ask a personal, compromising, or illegal question to conduct a great assessment. I further went on to say that if a question doesn't pertain to job performance, don't ever ask it. You won't gain any more insight. In my mind, performance is all that matters.

While this is a good general rule to follow, knowing what's illegal and what's not can keep you out of trouble. Here are some guidelines that cover most of the basic issues, but contact your HR or legal advisor for more details.

Things You Must Never Ask About

➤ *Age or anything related that can determine age*: Like asking, "When were you in the army?"

➤ *Race, nationality, or related issues, or anything that can determine it*: Something like, "Where do you live?" is an inappropriate question that could be perceived as addressing this.

➤ *Clubs, social groups, sexual preference, or religion*: Avoid questions like, "How do you spend your spare time?" or similar questions that pry at a candidate's personal life. It's okay if the candidate volunteers the information, but don't solicit it.

➤ *Anything about the candidate's arrest record*: Being arrested is not the same as being convicted for a crime, so avoid this line of questioning. You can ask about a candidate's felony convictions and the details.

➤ *Children or family issues, now or in the future*: Don't even attempt to bring this up. If the candidate begins talking about his or her family, it's okay to respond, but don't pry.

This is a sample of illegal and inappropriate questions. There are others, but they're all in the same family. Get legal advice if you're unsure, but the key is to avoid all personal questions. There are plenty of performance-based questions to ask that will give you valuable insight into a candidate's ability to perform the work. Personal questions won't give you a clue, and asking them could compromise your whole hiring program.

Don't be afraid to ask questions if they relate to the needs of the job. You're certainly allowed to ask about the candidate's academic background, if it's job related, just don't ask for the graduation date. If travel or extended hours are important, ask the candidate directly if she can travel or work unusual hours, don't go around this by asking about her family. You can inquire about professional groups and certifications. These relate to specific job qualifications and they're appropriate.

➤ Complying with the Americans with Disabilities Act

The Americans with Disabilities Act (ADA) prohibits discriminating against an applicant with a disability who is otherwise able to perform the essential job requirements. The employer might need to make some modifications to the workplace to address some of the candidate's needs, if the person is otherwise capable, but there is no need to lower the performance standards of the job. You may ask a candidate with a disability how he or she would meet these performance needs of the job given the disability. Asking a person who is using a wheelchair how he would conduct an operational audit of a manufacturing plant is appropriate only if this is a critical part of the job.

Make sure these performance objectives are essential and then don't generalize the physical requirements. This is something I see often happen. If the performance objective requires the employee to work with personal computers, don't require that she lift one. This has nothing to do with job performance.

■ THE PERFORMANCE-BASED INTERVIEW: PUTTING IT ALL TOGETHER

Good interviewing skills are only one part of an effective hiring process. You need to know the work, control your emotions, have enough good candidates to interview, and be a great recruiter. All of these factors are integrated into the performance-based interview. The performance objectives define the work in a compelling manner. This reinforces the recruiting aspect of the closing question. The structured questions when combined with good fact-finding increase objectivity. Peeling away the onion, taking notes, and listening are all essential to an accurate assessment. Practice these skills on all candidates. This is the only way you'll become proficient. The process itself will impact sourcing. You may find some great candidates you would have eliminated and some weak candidates you initially thought were stars. This is what the learning process is all about.

At some point along the way, you'll recognize that the questions are not the important part of the interview. Objectivity, probing, fact-finding, and skepticism combined with a thorough knowledge of the performance needs of the job are all it really takes.

HOT TIPS FOR PERFORMANCE-BASED INTERVIEWING

✔ Review the performance profile and the top performance objectives before the interview. Use these performance objectives to guide your fact-finding.

✔ Read and annotate the candidate's resume. Know the candidate's strengths and weaknesses before the interview, then use fact-finding to validate them.

✔ Conduct a 20-minute preliminary phone interview before meeting the candidate. Focus on the work history review and one or two major accomplishments. This will eliminate unqualified applicants sooner and minimize emotions for those you meet.

✔ Ask the candidate to submit a short addendum to his or her resume describing one team and one individual accomplishment. This quickly establishes the performance-based nature of the interview.

✔ Measure first impressions at the end of the interview. Put your emotions in the parking lot. Sometimes even top salespeople make average first impressions, so don't exclude anyone too soon.

✔ It's the answers, not the questions that count. Turn generalities into specifics. Get examples and quantify everything. Ask for facts, figures, dates, names, and measurements. This will reduce exaggeration and validate responses. It will also quickly minimize candidate nervousness.

✔ Be skeptical. Interviewing is a fact-finding mission, not a popularity contest. As long as you know what you're looking for, don't give up until you find it. As long as the job is great, great candidates won't mind.

✔ The Formula for Success = Talent*Energy^2 + Team Leadership + Comparable Past Performance + Job-Specific Problem Solving

✔ Anchor and visualize each performance objective in the performance profile to determine job-specific competency. This directly measures the candidate's ability to apply past performance and talent to meet future objectives.

✔ Use the interview to recruit the candidate. State your sincere interest, create competition, and then ask the candidate to state his or her interest.

Chapter 5

The Evidence-Based Assessment

Did you ever have to make up your mind
Pick up on one and leave the other behind
Did you ever have to finally decide

—Lovin' Spoonful*

■ IMPLEMENT AN EVIDENCE-BASED ASSESSMENT PROCESS TO IMPROVE SELECTION ACCURACY

The January 2006 edition of the *Harvard Business Review* (HBR) is devoted entirely to the decision-making process. It's a great edition and provides a wealth of information for revamping the hiring decision-making process. Here are just a few key points HBR makes about the causes of bad decision making:

* Lovin' Spoonful, "Did You Ever Have to Make Up Your Mind," 1965.

➤ *Most decisions are made with little evidence.* Managers tend to have preconceived biases, beliefs, and perceptions. Facts are then collected to support these preconceived ideas and contrary information is avoided, ignored, or dismissed as irrelevant.

➤ *Consensus is good—unless it's reached too easily.* In other words, it's okay to argue and disagree about a point of view: this way, more information is considered analytically. Subordinates should be encouraged to disagree, not be chastised for it.

➤ *The only time you should make a gut decision is when you don't have any.* Time, that is. "Gut decisions are made in moments of crisis when there is no time to weigh arguments and calculate the probability of every outcome," HBR points out.

The previous classic decision-making errors translate into the following common hiring mistakes. How many have you observed in your company?

➤ *Too many managers overvalue presentation skills and/or their intuition or gut when judging candidates.* Anybody can determine in 30 minutes to an hour whether a person is a complete dud or a superstar. It takes much more time, insight, and skill to figure out the ability of those in between.

➤ *Most managers overvalue a narrow range of technical skills or related experiences and then assume global competence or incompetence.* This approach ignores critical traits like motivation to do the work, organizational and planning skills, team leadership, and cultural fit.

➤ *The up-down voting process precludes a balanced assessment across those job factors that best predict job success.* For one thing, a "no" vote is more highly valued than a "yes," and little substantive information is used to determine either. The real critical issue is that it's too easy to reach consensus when no one is allowed to present a contrary point of view. As a result, good people are excluded for the wrong reasons.

➤ Balance across Critical Job Factors Is a Prerequisite to an Accurate Assessment

Accurately assessing candidate competency is the key to better hiring decisions. Unfortunately, given everything else going on, there is a natural tendency to short-circuit the hiring process. In the rush to decide, managers often overvalue one piece of data or the input of one influential person. We assume a candidate we initially like with a few good traits can do it all. This is how the partially competent get hired. A somewhat nervous candidate who is apparently missing something may be improperly assessed and excluded. This is how great people often get overlooked.

Do not base the hiring decision on a few narrow traits. It must cover all job-related performance factors. Here's an example that best demonstrates this point. A number of years ago, I started working with a new client in the food industry leading a search for a director of quality. One of the candidates had a low-key personality, and I was concerned about her ability to lead change. While otherwise qualified, during our interview process she just didn't seem dominant enough for me. We didn't have many candidates, so we reluctantly sent her to meet the client.

A phone interview with the CEO and HR vice president overcame my initial concerns. Their first interview was a combined three hours. They got detailed examples of complex quality improvements the candidate instituted, team-building efforts, and projects she led when working with government agencies in developing industry standards. Her values and character were explored at subsequent meetings, as well as technical competency, motivation, and critical-thinking skills. This was a superb well-rounded candidate with tremendous upside potential. She ultimately became a senior vice-president with this company and a recognized industry expert. This was our first of many searches with this company and this person established the ongoing standard of quality for top candidates. Without the company's thoroughness in seeking balance across all factors of job performance, it is unlikely this person would have been hired. It's an important lesson we can all learn from.

In the big scheme of things, hiring a top person does not take that much more time. It's the rush to decide that causes most of the problems. The evidence-based assessment and formal debriefing process described in this chapter should not be considered an impingement on time. It takes much more time to correct a bad hiring decision. In the process, you'll discover some great people you might previously have inadvertently excluded. Here's a great example:

> Many years ago a vice president of finance at one of the major entertainment companies let a top-notch candidate slip away. The vice president was an intuitive interviewer and liked applicants who were smart, socially confident, and assertive. We sent in a great candidate who had all three traits in spades and more, yet tended to be a little tongue-tied early in the interview. I knew this and suggested to the vice president that he wait at least 30 minutes before making any judgment. Unfortunately, the advice was ignored, and within 15 minutes this very promising young man was eliminated from consideration. This candidate subsequently took a job at one of the competing entertainment companies and within a few years became one of their senior financial executives. Making the story even better is that this overlooked person negotiated the purchase of a major asset with the same vice president of finance who initially overlooked him, for a significant "stick-it-to-you" premium.

This "decide and collect" approach to assessing competency needs to be eliminated from the hiring decision-making process. The best way to do this is to "systematize it out." In previous editions to this book, I spent a great deal of effort presenting the case that interviewers should wait 30 minutes before making a hiring decision. This is still important. By consciously putting emotional biases in the parking lot, objectivity is increased. By measuring first impressions at the end of the interview, the interviewer better understands his or her own biases. However, this is not enough to eliminate biases and emotional decision making from the hiring process.

By setting a few rules and procedures, a company can proactively systematize these bias-causing errors out of the process. Here are five key steps involved in implementing this type of evidence-based assessment process:

1. *Evaluate all candidates for every position in comparison to the real job needs.* The performance profile sets the standard here.

2. *Don't give any interviewers other than the hiring manager complete yes/no voting rights.* Instead, assign each interviewer a subset of factors to evaluate.

3. *Assess all candidates using a formal assessment tool across the best predictors of job success using a clear ranking system.* In this chapter, we introduce the 10-Factor Candidate Assessment template, which serves this purpose.

4. *Conduct a formal debriefing session with all members of the hiring team actively participating.* Submitting written notes is not as effective as a conference call or meeting.

5. *Generalities, gut feelings, and intuition are unacceptable inputs for ranking a candidate.* Facts, dates, details, and specific examples must justify the ranking for each factor.

Using an evidence-based assessment process will go a long way toward eliminating the following common hiring problems:

➤ *Bad hires*: People who can't or won't do the work, don't fit your culture, or can't get along with others. This problem is usually caused by overvaluing presentation skills and making a hasty decision.

➤ *Mismatched hires*: People who are competent to do the work, but don't want to do it. This problem is caused by lack of understanding of real job needs and overvaluing the depth of technical competency during the interview.

➤ *Incomplete hires*: People who can do parts of the work well, but not everything. This problem is caused by interviewers who overvalue a few traits and then assume global competency across all job needs. This is also referred to as "bad intuition."

➤ *Nonhires*: The great people we didn't hire. Sometimes good people get nervous during the interview and give dumb or short answers. Some great people, even top salespeople, don't make good first impressions. Sometimes great people are unimpressed by an unprofessional interviewing process and shut down.

■ ORGANIZING THE INTERVIEW

Although all interviewers will use the same performance-based interview and complete the 10-Factor assessment, this doesn't mean that everyone will ask the same questions. Even if an interviewer asked about the same accomplishment, fact-finding would take the person down a different path, uncovering different issues. To get the most out of performance-based interviewing, it's best to organize it ahead of time. The "Organizing the Performance-Based Interview" form in Appendix C can be used to organize roles and assign tasks to each of the interviewers on the hiring team. (Download this form from www.adlerconcepts.com.) Here's a short version of the form:

Interview Step	Hiring Manager	Interviewer 1	Interviewer 2
Work History			
10-Factor Assessment			
1. Overall Technical Competency			
2. Motivation for Required Work			
3. Overall Team Skills			
4. Problem Solving			
5. Achieve Comparable Results			
6. Planning & Organization			
7. Environment/Culture			
8. Trend of Growth			
9. Character & Values			
10. Potential			
Team Projects, Tasks			
Tech Projects, Key Tasks			
Problem Questions:			
Recruit/Close			
Interest Level			

This form lists the 10 core factors of success with space to write down the major performance objectives and the problems to be discussed. This form should be filled out and handed to everyone on the team along with the candidate's resume and a copy of the performance profile for the position. Just put a checkmark indicating each interviewer's area of responsibility. This ensures every key topic is covered.

In general, the hiring manager should conduct an in-depth work history review, ask two to three major accomplishment questions, and ask at least one problem-solving question. This should be sufficient to gain a strong understanding of the first five core traits of success (technical competency, motivation to do the work, team skills, problem solving, and achievement of comparable results).

The other interviewers on the team should be each assigned a few of the other traits so that all are covered. Some overlap is appropriate. Everyone should also review the candidate's resume before the interview and ask a few questions about work history. This provides all interviewers some sense of the candidate's general background. This approach naturally overcomes the problem of giving each interviewer complete yes/no voting rights. When assigning roles, suggest that the person focus on collecting information to determine the person's competency on just the areas assigned. By narrowing the focus this way, overall interviewing accuracy is improved since each interviewer has more time to assess fewer traits. Finally, share this information with the whole interviewing team in a formal debriefing session as explained in the following.

■ CONDUCTING THE EVIDENCE-BASED ASSESSMENT PROCESS

A short version of the 10-Factor Candidate Assessment template is shown in Table 5.1. A complete version is included in the Appendix. You can also download a copy of this form from our web site, www.adlerconcepts.com. The objective of the performance-based interviewing process is to accurately assess each of the 10 factors on a 1 to 5 scale. The differences in ranking are important and lead to five levels as shown in the following list:

Table 5.1 The 10-Factor Candidate Assessment Template

Factor	Level 1 Unqualified	Level 2 Less Qualified	Level 3 Fully Qualified	Level 4 Highly Qualified	Level 5 Super Star
General Evaluation Summary	Incompetent Unmotivated Uncooperative Distracted Demotivating Reactive No potential to grow	Needs extra training Needs extra pushing Needs urging Avoids Neutral Passive Not promotable	Meets high standards Self-motivated Fully cooperative A contributor An asset On top of issues Promotable	Does it better Does more, faster Initiates helping Trains, sought-out Influences others Anticipates issues Quickly promotable	Sets standards 120% committed Proactively coaches Is asked to lead Motivates others Forward looking Double promotable
1 Technical	Can't do the work. Incompetent. Below minimum standards.	Can do the work, but needs added training, and supervision.	Can perform all required work very well. An asset.	Does more than required; does it better, does it faster.	Leader in the field. Sets the bar. More creative and insightful.
2 Motivated to Do the Work	Lazy, passive, doesn't want to do the work.	Will do the work if urged or pushed. Not a good fit for work.	Motivated to do this type of work with little supervision.	Takes initiative to do more, faster, better. Looks for work.	Totally committed to do whatever it takes to get the job done.
3 Team Skills in Similar Groups	Uncooperative, bad attitude, negative. Hides problems.	Will cooperate if asked. Needs urging to be involved.	Fully cooperates with others without urging. Deals with conflict.	Takes initiative to help others. Persuades, motivates.	Inspires, coaches. Minimizes conflict. Is asked to lead.
4 Problem Solving, Thinking	Doesn't understand any key issues or develop any solutions.	Needs support. Understands basic issues. Weak solutions.	Clearly understands all key issues, develops good solutions.	Quickly understands all issues. Develops multiple solutions.	Understands all issues. Optimizes results. Sees impact.

5 Achieves Similar Results				
Experience and accomplishments are totally mismatched.	Some comparable accomplishments. Needs extra training.	Has handled similar projects with very good results.	Environment and projects match with better results.	Scope, span, scale, and culture match for exceptional results.
6 Planning and Executing				
Unorganized. Weak planner. Very reactive. Wastes time.	Reactive. Misses deadlines. Plans when pushed.	Consistent planner. Meets deadlines. Organizes and prioritizes.	Always plans, anticipates, prioritizes, and beats deadlines.	Superb. Anticipates everything. Sees big picture and all issues.
7 Environment and Cultural Fit				
Complete mismatch of culture and/or environment.	Reasonable match on culture and environment; not a perfect fit.	Close match on people, pace, approach, and organizational structure.	Has been successful in this type of culture and environment.	Thrives in this type of environment and culture. Great success.
8 Trend of Growth				
No personal or business growth noted. Makes excuses.	Flat trend. Capable, but needs to be pushed to grow.	Job growth trend shows consistent positive pattern.	Strong upward growth trend. Consistently does more.	Great upward trend. Great progress supported by results.
9 Character and Values				
Questionable character. Job does not fit with values.	Job somewhat fits values and needs. Will be a distraction.	Job is a strong fit with values and motivating needs.	Job clearly meets values and motivating needs. Principled.	Strongly committed person of great character. Role model.
10 Potential and Summary				
This job is over the person's head. Not a candidate.	Can handle this job, but not likely to grow beyond job.	Can handle all key aspects of job plus has upside potential.	Will make quick positive impact and has near-term upside.	Will make great impact with potential to move up two levels.

Level 1: Doesn't want to do the work and/or can't do the work. This is easy to figure out usually within 30 minutes.

Level 2: Competent to do the work, says he or she will do the work, but won't do it. This is the most common hiring mistake. It's caused by judging people on their skills, technical depth, and/or presentation, but not their motivation to do the work.

Level 3: Competent and motivated to do most, if not all, of the work described in the Performance Profile. This is a top employee and should be hired unless a stronger person is available. The person is clearly promotable in a normal time frame. The major difference between a Level 2 and a Level 3 is largely motivation to do the work.

Level 4: A great hire. Look for an upward trend line and examples of consistently exceeding expectations in comparable types of work. This person is quickly promotable in a short period of time. This person does more, does it better, or does it faster. This person typically invests significant time in personal development.

Level 5: A super hire. This person has a track record of doing excellent work in comparable situations and has a pattern of consistently receiving recognition for doing remarkable work. This person is promotable at least two levels in a short period of time. This person not only puts effort into self-improvement, but also improves the company and the team.

➤ No Level 2s!

Most hiring mistakes occur in determining the difference between a Level 2, 3, and 4 ranking. The Level 1s and Level 5s are easy to assess using just about any interviewing methodology. One of the primary goals of the Performance-based Hiring interviewing process is to prevent Level 2s from being hired. These are people who seem pretty good during the interview, they might even make a great presentation, but once on the job they fall short. Some of these Level 2s are the people you hire who aren't motivated to do the work, even though they might be competent. Some are those who say they'll do the work, but once they're on the job, their attitudes change. Regardless, they need too much urging, coaching, training, or supervision just to become average. These are the people who shouldn't have been hired in the first place. If you go out of your way never to hire another Level 2 again, you'll eliminate all of your hiring mistakes forever.

A Level 3 is a fully qualified candidate. This is the person who will meet most of the performance objectives of the position very quickly. This is also a person who is promotable, or one who can take on a bigger job in a normal period of time. Be ready to move fast when you meet a Level 3 because they are not that common. Move immediately if you meet a Level 4 or Level 5. The real objective of interviewing is to not hire Level 2s. This ensures you hire Level 3s, or better. In the long run, this means you'll have built a team of high performers with few, if any, laggards. Every now and then, you'll hire a few future leaders who will eventually be playing a significant role in managing your company.

➤ Conducting the Formal Debriefing Session

All members of the hiring team need to meet either in person or on a conference call to debrief. This is better than submitting comments without discussion. Often these comments are changed when information is shared in a formal and deliberative manner. One person, typically the hiring manager or the primary recruiter, should formally lead this session. You can either do this for each candidate or for multiple candidates. Here's a checklist to follow when conducting the debriefing process:

- [ ] *Tell each member of the hiring team to bring a completed 10-Factor Candidate Assessment template for each candidate being discussed.* Each member's evaluation notes are a part of the 10-Factor Candidate Assessment form. Each interviewer must rank his or her assigned factors, although he or she should provide input on any factors where he or she has some insight.

- [ ] *Draw a matrix on a whiteboard or flipchart to keep track of everyone's ranking.* You can also compare rankings of multiple candidates this way.

☐ *Begin the debriefing process by soliciting only positive information.* This is important. Start this initial discussion with the lowest-ranking member of the hiring team. Delay any negative discussion until each factor is discussed.

☐ *Go through each factor one by one, going around the room and writing down each person's ranking.* As you do this, have each person share his or her rationale for the ranking. Use details, examples, and facts to justify any ranking. Generalities and gut feelings are not permitted. These superficial rankings *must* be ignored and should not be included in the overall scoring. If there are too many superficial rankings, interview the candidate again. This process increases the probability that the interviewer will conduct a more thorough fact-finding the next time. Enforcing this rule is an important part of the evidence-based assessment process.

☐ *Ignore a "no" vote based on superficial information.* The difference between Level 2s, 3s, and 4s can sometimes be very subtle. Hiring a Level 2 is a mistake, while a Level 3 or better is a great decision. In each of the 10 factors, the difference is usually motivation to excel or the depth of personal commitment. The primary purpose of this debriefing process is to share information. Sometimes this is by challenging each other. It's easier to say no, but this is often the incorrect decision. While you want to stop hiring Level 2s, you don't want to incorrectly eliminate a good person because someone conducted a superficial interview.

☐ *Allow people to justify an alternative point of view, both positive and negative.* Seek this out. This ensures that all information is heard. This is an important part of the debriefing and clarification process and often will alter someone's initial evaluation.

☐ *As you debrief on each factor, read the 10-Factor guidance for each of the 1 to 5 scores on the form.* There are important clues here on how to rank the person for each of the factors. Reading these aloud helps the interviewers focus their justification for their score.

☐ *Prohibit team members who have conducted only a personality or cultural fit interview from participating in the discussion, unless the person has factual information to share.* These interviews, often conducted by senior-level executives, are always useless. Worse, they can poison the work of the hiring team by over-riding everyone's hard work. To be a member of the hiring team, each person must conduct a performance-based interview.

➤ How to Minimize All Common Interviewing Mistakes

Here are five additional points to consider for improving your interviewing accuracy:

1. *Don't make a yes/no decision during the one-on-one interview.* Instead, use the interview to collect information on the assigned areas, not to vote. By narrowing the focus, objectivity naturally increases, ensuring all of the information colleted is of equal value. Too many interviewers go out of their way to use the interview to collect information that confirms their initial assessment. This is called the *decide and collect* approach, and it's the primary cause of hiring mistakes.

2. *Don't let anyone have full voting rights.* Most hiring errors are caused by making yes/no hiring decisions too quickly based on a narrow range of factors. To obtain a balanced viewpoint, solicit the collective advice of the hiring team, then discuss each of the 10 factors.

3. *Disallow gut feelings and intuition.* To obtain unbiased information, each interviewer must justify his 1 to 5 ranking with facts, examples, and details, good or bad. "I don't think the person would fit," is inappropriate. However, a comment like "the environment, pace, available resources, and the lack of a formal decision-making process at the person's past two companies is a clear indication that the person would not survive here," is certainly sufficient.

4. *Encourage alternative points of view.* Force controversy and disagreement during the debriefing session. You don't need to force consensus. Support people who have evidence that is contrary to most people's assessments. Make this a formal

part of the process. Good or bad, this will allow all view-points to be heard.

5. *Make a "no" harder to justify than a "yes."* A "no" is safe and easy. It encourages laziness, and it rewards interviewers who are weak or unprepared. To eliminate this potential problem, demand more detailed information and evidence from those invoking the "no." A "no" is okay as long as it's based on factual information. Too often, it's based on weak interviewing.

➤ Assess Each of the 10 Best Predictors of On-the-Job Success

Keeping detailed, specific notes can help the hiring team accurately describe whether a candidate is particularly strong or weak in each category. These notes will help you make the necessary trade-offs later on when you begin comparing candidates. Sometimes there are some major strengths that can offset what initially appears like a deal-breaking weakness. Sometimes major strengths don't appear as important in the face of a critical void. Try not to make the final decision until each factor has been considered. With the rush to hire, there is always a tendency to make premature decisions without all of the facts.

The following sections provide some additional guidelines to better understand how to measure each of the 10 traits during the interview. Notice that each factor is measured in comparison to the real job needs described in the performance profile. This way the 10-Factor form can be used to assess candidates for all jobs with only minor modifications.

1. *Talent to Do the Work*

This factor focuses on the person's current technical level of competency and potential to learn. Many technical managers miss the mark here by overvaluing the absolute level of technical skills, rather than their practical application. Here's an example illustrating this point. A number of years ago we had a search for a CFO for a Fortune 100 company. The CEO insisted that the candidate must have strong hands-on experience as a cost accountant. This was his number-one priority. I asked how the skill would be used on the job. The CEO said the person needed to set up a multiplant perfor-mance reporting system, evaluate each manufacturing plant's oper-ating results, and hire good plant controllers. As he wrote these down, he recognized it wasn't the cost accounting skills that were important, but their application in preparing and evaluating re-ports, and in hiring people with those skills.

When evaluating the talent needed to do the work, don't look just for technical brilliance. Instead, look at how a candidate will use his technical ability in achieving practical results. A Level 3 ranking in this category indicates that the person has all of the technical skills to handle the current needs of the job. A Level 4 or 5 indicates that the person has the demonstrated capacity to better use these skills in some important way (i.e., doing the work much faster, im-proving a process by simplifying something, or being a great re-source as a trainer).

2. *Motivation to Do the Work*

This is energy[2] and without it you're hiring a dud. On the job, moti-vation shows up as passion, desire, self-motivation, commitment, work ethic, and persistence. Don't ever compromise on this factor. It's the universal trait of success. Look for it in every job. During the fact-finding, get examples of initiative and extra effort. Find out where the person went the extra mile. Get specific examples and understand the circumstances behind the extra effort. Look for pat-terns here. Don't make the leap that a highly motivated person is always highly motivated. Most people work hard doing work they like to do. Sometimes it's due to working for a great manager or in a perfect environment. Be extra diligent trying to find the circum-stances underlying the motivation.

An extroverted personality is neither proof of, nor a prerequi-site for, self-motivation on the job. Nor does a low-key person indi-cate an inability to work hard on the job. Have all candidates provide examples of where they have exceeded expectations with specific facts, dates, and quantities. You'll be able to eliminate a number of candidates this way who are socially assertive, but not necessarily motivated on the job.

Look for special projects, extra effort, and major accomplish-ments for recent graduates and for anyone in an entry-level job.

This could be in the form of school work, extracurricular activities, or in part-time jobs. Highly motivated people always do more than required, and this trait is evident early. If the candidate has no big projects, look for a series of small successes. In this case, always ask for three—three examples of initiative, three examples of exceeding expectations, or three examples of where the candidate did more than required. Everyone can come up with one or two. Few people can come up with three good examples. Those who can are the ones you want to hire. Be concerned if the second or third example is weak.

For example, during her initial job interview, I asked a candidate for our office manager position to describe three things she did on her previous job that she started on her own. She promptly told me about learning and writing a number of complex Word macros, setting up an open-invoice tracking system on Excel, and reorganizing large mailings with an outside production company. This is the type of performance that indicates a strong work ethic. We hired that candidate in the mid-1990s, and she is still as energetic today.

On the 1 to 5 ranking of the 10 factors, a Level 3 person works hard to get the job done regardless of the challenges faced. A Level 2 person makes excuses about why the work couldn't be done on time. A Level 4 candidate not only gets the job done on time, but constantly improves the situation or does far more than required. A Level 5 is totally committed and will not fail regardless of the challenges or situation. A consistent pattern of exceeding expectations is the key to a high ranking on motivation.

3. Team Leadership: The Ability to Persuade, Motivate, and Cooperate with Others

Team leadership, the third core trait of success, involves working with others in a positive and sustainable way to improve overall team performance. Team leadership is very similar to the concept of Emotional Quotient (EQ) as described in Daniel Goleman's must-read book Emotional Intelligence: Why It Can Matter More Than IQ.* Here's what he had to say about the importance of EQ:

---

* Daniel Goleman, Emotional Intelligence: The 10th Anniversary Edition; Why It Can Matter More Than IQ (New York: Bantam, 2005, p. 80).

Emotional Intelligence is a master aptitude, a capacity that profoundly affects all other abilities, either facilitating or interfering with them.

Here's the Wikipedia definition:

Emotional Intelligence, *also called* EI *and often measured as an* Emotional Intelligence *Quotient or* EQ, *describes an ability, capacity, or skill to perceive, assess, and manage the emotions of one's self, of others, and of groups.* *

Team leadership has two dimensions: one organized around the subordinate team, the other involving coworkers. Whenever a person has some degree of power over another, the team-leadership component gets clouded. Motivating a subordinate is easier than motivating someone who doesn't work for you. For management positions, look for those who have a track record of developing their team. They can usually name a number of people who they have personally helped become successful. They are proactive with respect to this staff-development issue and take great pride in it. As a result of this, they have the ability to inspire their own staff to exceed expectations. When you ask about these issues, get names and examples of how they helped them become better. Give high rankings to those who consistently go out of their way to hire superior people, and then help upgrade the skills of each team member.

Team leadership is also important in dealing with people outside of a person's own department. The ability to persuade and motivate people who don't work for you is a critical component of leadership. Examine this area for managers and nonmanagers alike. Get examples of major team projects and use fact-finding to uncover the candidate's true role. Get examples of dealing with conflict or persuading others to change their position and determine how compromises were made. Ask about dealing with difficult people in other functions and find out how this was handled. People who rank high in this aspect of team leadership are often selected to lead groups, always do more than they're required to do within the group, and understand how to develop real win-win situations.

* http://en.wikipedia.org/wiki/Emotional_intelligence.

They are sensitive to the needs of others and they can describe numerous examples of similar team-leadership roles.

Don't assume all extroverted people are strong at team leadership. Those who are too individualistic or have overblown egos create more problems than solutions. Introverted people can also be great team leaders. Don't make any instant judgments based on affability.

Rank candidates a Level 3 if they can provide numerous examples of cooperating with others, developing their teams, and working effectively with people of all levels in a variety of functions. Remember our "No Level 2s" caveat: a Level 2 ranking on team leadership is deserved if a person has few good examples of working with people in other departments, can't provide names of people they've helped, is vague about cooperating with people in teams, or is reluctant to describe situations where they've been helped by their peers to get better at something.

Rank the person as a Level 4 if the person can provide numerous examples of persuading and motivating others, especially if these people are peers and outside the department. Taking on leadership roles is a good clue for a Level 4, and if the person is often asked to lead, you might have a Level 5. Inspiring others is common for Level 5 team leadership, so look for this, too.

4. Problem-Solving and Critical-Thinking Skills

A strong candidate needs to have the ability to solve job-related problems and anticipate what needs to get done. Collecting and processing information in order to make appropriate decisions is part of it. So is the ability to apply previous knowledge and experiences in solving new problems. You're directly testing for problem-solving and critical-thinking skills using the problem-solving question.

How the candidate organizes a major task or evaluates a current problem requires insight and understanding. The quality of the questions asked by the candidate are a strong indicator of the candidate's thinking and reasoning skills, adaptability, communication skills, logic, decision making, knowledge, and problem-solving ability. This is great insight.

To gain more insight, ask the candidate what kinds of questions he or she would ask to get the information needed when starting one of the major projects described in the performance profile. Many great questions, but limited experience, are a good sign of a high-potential person. Raise the caution flag if the candidate's experience is strong but the questioning is weak. These people have difficulty adapting to new situations. When selecting candidates, it often becomes a trade-off between experience and potential. My favorite mix includes lots of potential, just enough comparable experience, and a track record of being able to learn quickly. To better understand these traits, ask candidates to describe their greatest accomplishment with the least amount of experience.

On an assignment a few years ago when searching for a marketing director for a direct-mail company, I asked each of the candidates to describe how he would re-layout the company's catalog. Two of the candidates knew exactly what to do. They spent a few minutes reviewing the catalog, asked me some insightful questions, described what additional information they needed, and then suggested a number of courses of action based on different alternatives. This is consistent with a Level 3 or Level 4 ranking. Two of the candidates asked some good questions, but their ideas regarding what to do were vague and too general. This is consistent with a Level 2 or 2.5 answer. The remaining person didn't even ask relevant questions. The person was clueless as to what to do. This is a Level 1 ranking. A Level 5 would have not only answered the question well, but would have asked more in-depth questions and then would have provided a series of realistic alternatives never before considered.

5. Comparability of Past Accomplishments

Getting detailed examples of past accomplishments allows the interviewer to compare the candidate's past performance with the required performance objectives described in the performance profile. When the interview is conducted this way, past performance is a great predictor of future performance. But don't be myopic here. To expand the pool of highly qualified candidates, look for comparable performance in comparable environments rather than identical performance, in identical companies in identical industries. An example will help illustrate this point.

Recently, I was helping a Fortune 100 company prepare a performance profile for a director of workforce planning. This was a person who had to lead the effort to implement a very comprehensive forecast of all hiring needs for all positions within the company for the next five years. The company was planning to add 50,000 people over this time frame to meet some very aggressive global expansion plans. One of the demands of the vice president of HR was that this person currently hold a similar position with a major company. Since very few people have done this type of work, I suggested that instead they look for someone who has done comparable work like planning for the expansion of complex facilities on an international level. This could be someone at a major distribution or transportation company leading the effort to forecast and organize people, resources, buildings, and equipment.

The key here is to find people who have successfully handled the complexities of the required tasks, rather than the exact tasks. Not only does this open the job to other top performers, these other top people often find the challenge of working in different industries and on different challenges more exciting and motivating.

When ranking someone on this category, look at the breadth and scope of the person's accomplishments in comparison to real job needs. The size of the teams managed, the type of people on the team, and budget are all clues. Review the types of decisions made and the complexity of the issues the person had to deal with. When you ask about accomplishments, make sure you also understand the environment surrounding these accomplishments. This includes the pace, the types of resources available, the level of professionalism, and the types of systems the person used.

A Level 3 ranking would be deserved if the person has been successful achieving comparable success in comparable environments for most of the performance objectives in the recent past. A Level 4 ranking is appropriate if you have examples of a person exceeding expectations for all of the major performance objectives. A Level 5 ranking is deserved on this category if the person thrives in your type of environment and has demonstrated not only great success for each major performance objective, but also takes this performance to a totally unexpected level. A Level 2 ranking is appropriate if the person's past accomplishments don't compare too well to the real job needs.

6. *Planning, Management, and Organization*

Most interviewers focus too much on individual skills and technical competency. Only good interviewers focus on the planning and organization aspects of completing projects on time and on budget under different types of challenges. Recovering from setbacks is one aspect of this. Just getting your own work completed in an organized and logical fashion is an important part of success, so don't ignore this factor for individual contributor roles. Being part of, or leading, a small cross-functional team requires solid planning, organization, and management skills.

If the person is a manager, another component of this factor involves building and developing the team as well as managing it to achieve results. When assessing managers, make the comparison based on comparable teams of similar size composed of similar types of people.

Use projects to understand organizational skills when the candidate doesn't have a big staff. A few years ago, I was interviewing a candidate for an operations position requiring someone to organize a number of small teams over many facilities. At first I didn't think the candidate possessed the necessary management skills to handle the job since he seemed too technical. To better understand his organization skills I asked him to describe the most complex project team he had led. He told me about an eight-month crash project getting a very sophisticated piece of automation equipment debugged, installed, and operational. He took over when the project was severely behind schedule. The successful completion of the task required the coordinated efforts of a dozen engineering and manufacturing personnel, plus balancing the competing needs of his own company, the customer, and two other major vendors. Budgets were tight, tempers were on edge, and the credibility of his company was on the line. He won an award for his efforts and the appropriate kudos. There was no doubt he could handle, what now appeared to be, my client's pretty tame management need.

During the interview, ask the candidates to prepare a work chart for their last few positions listing all the people working on the team and their relationship to the candidate. Include other departments, vendors, customers, and outside consultants to better understand the types of people your candidate has worked with and influenced. This type of chart is very revealing as you get examples of where the candidate influenced others and where the candidate had to deal with conflict. Make sure you understand the candidate's actual role on the team.

A Level 3 ranking means the person is very strong at planning, organizing, and managing teams of similar size and composition in comparison to real job needs. Someone could score as a Level 3 here whether the person was an individual contributor or managed a department of a 1,000 people. Good planning and organizational skills are an important trait for those who get promoted. A Level 2 ranking means the person is very unorganized. This would be revealed by a pattern of excuses for failing to meet deadlines, reacting to problems rather than anticipating them, and an approach to planning that does not seem to improve over time.

From a management perspective, be concerned if the candidate has lots of turnover within the group, complains about his or her staff, and seems to talk less, or in more general terms, about management successes. Get references from subordinates to validate any of your concerns. They have the best perspective on someone's management skills.

To score as a Level 4 on this factor, the candidate would need to demonstrate superior management skills that involve anticipating problems before they occur, a track record of rarely missing deadlines, overcoming unexpected problems, and having handled big projects typically beyond the scope of the job. A Level 5 would encompass these same things plus a demonstrated pattern of completely rethinking and reorganizing comparable projects in some unusual way to dramatically improve performance.

7. Environmental and Cultural Fit

This is a critical factor for job success that's often overlooked during the interviewing process. To increase the accuracy of the assessment, compare a candidate's accomplishments and the environment where they took place to the performance objectives listed in the performance profile and the environment at your company. In this case, environment means the pace and pressure, the degree of autonomy, how decisions are made, the bureaucracy, the level of sophistication, the hiring manager's style, and the resources available, among others. In many cases, this is also referred to as the culture. Also, consider the candidate's personality when assessing environmental and cultural fit.

When assessing cultural fit, don't overvalue the candidate's use of "I" or "we" when answering questions. Instead, consider the project described using the ABC method of tracking responses. To do this, make tick marks based on how often the person mentions working alone (A), being part of a team (B, or belonging), or in charge of the team (C). For example, you might get too many "we did this or that," for an individual project, or a lot of "I did this or that" regarding team projects, so listen carefully. At the end of the interview, the collection of tick marks will provide some real insight into the candidate's preferred way of working. Lots of As means an individual contributor; a team player would have a majority of Bs; and a manager inclination would have more Cs. How someone scores depends on the needs of the job. If the job is an individual contributor role (e.g., salesperson, technician, analyst, or consultant), make sure you hire someone who likes to work independently.

A Level 3 on environmental and cultural fit would be justified if the person's accomplishments took place in an environment that was very comparable to your company's. A Level 4 or 5 is appropriate if the person thrives in an environment like your company's. As part of this ranking, consider the style of the person's previous managers, the degree of autonomy needed, and the types of people the person works best with.

8. *Trend of Performance over Time*

When assessing this factor, evaluate the candidate's team and individual accomplishments over time. From this, it's easy to see how the candidate has grown and impacted the organization. A Level 3 ranking requires an upward pattern including significant self-improvement, or a pattern of doing great work, even if the person has plateaued. Jobs don't need to be identical to get a high ranking here. Consider instead staff size, complexity of the issues, standards of performance, pace, environment, and level of sophistication. Combine these factors when evaluating comparability.

During the dot-com era, we conducted an engineering management search in the telecommunications industry. One of the final candidates was a close match on staff size, company environment, the product-development process, and the level of systems support and sophistication. The candidate was pretty far off on the technology side, though. He compensated for this by demonstrating an ability to learn new technology very quickly and hiring great people. By taking a balanced look at strengths and weaknesses, we looked for engineering managers who demonstrated an upward trend of management growth, independent from the technology. This allowed us to find a great candidate who otherwise might have been overlooked.

If the growth pattern had been flat for this candidate, we would have required him to be stronger on the technology side. Give a 2 to 2.5 if the trend is flat and the comparability is a little weak. Use your judgment, since a pattern of upward growth is always more important than experience. These are the people who get promoted, so look for this in the people you hire.

I recently met a vice president of finance candidate who had a strong work ethic, was highly energetic, and always seemed to be taking on new projects. I ranked him a Level 5 in energy,[2] but only a Level 3 in the trend of performance category. While he was a very self-motivated person, he had been at the same management level for the past 10 years, an indication that he had plateaued careerwise. I still recommended that the company consider him for the position, since his skills were consistent with the needs of the job, but I didn't expect him to ever take on a significantly bigger job.

A steeper growth trend line would justify a Level 4 or 5 ranking if the person demonstrated real impact in each job and an ability to take on more complex challenges. Don't ignore time-in-grade here, though. I recently met a CFO candidate who received a number of quick promotions based less on performance and more on being at the right place at the right time. This person had a very steep growth curve, but only scored a Level 3 on this factor since performance wasn't consistent with the title.

9. *Character*: *Values, Commitment, and Goals*

Character is a deep-rooted trait that summarizes a person's integrity, honesty, responsibility, openness, fairness in dealing with others, and personal values. Observe these traits by asking the right questions and applying appropriate fact-finding.

Ask the candidate why he or she wants to change jobs and what aspects of work the person finds important. Also have the person explain each past job change. This will help determine both fit and satisfaction. If the basic needs of the job are incompatible with the candidate's motivational needs, you'll only create problems later on. Understanding a person's value system allows you to predict how he'll react under various work-related circumstances. If work is a secondary priority in the person's life, you could be in trouble if you need to rely on him for a crash project coming up, even if he agrees to it.

Having goals is an important part of character and personal motivation, but the typical "what are your goals" question can be misleading. Everyone has goals, many of them very lofty, but few are actually achieved. As part of your fact-finding, ask the candidate if the accomplishments were related to some major personal goal. During the interview, look for a pattern of goal setting and achievement. It's easy to talk about future goals, but it means little if nothing has ever been achieved. Compare the size of the goals already achieved to any future goals and to the needs of the job. Ask if the goals are in writing. This helps validate the candidate's real, versus stated, philosophy. Goals always require a series of substeps before they're completed. Ask about this progress.

If a candidate wants to be promoted, ask her what she's doing to improve herself to get ready. Only a few people spend time at personal development. This could be in the form of continuous outside education, volunteering for new work, or taking the initiative of expanding the role of their current job without any expectations of a reward.

Commitment is a critical component of character that complements energy[2] and potential. Ask the candidate to give you an example of when he or she was totally committed to a task. Some high-energy people are great starters but poor finishers. Look for a pattern of meeting deadlines. Get related examples. Find out when the candidate missed an important target and then determine the recovery response. A one-time commitment is less meaningful than a consistent pattern.

When assessing character, look for frank and open responses, especially regarding failures. Determine whether the candidate takes responsibility for both the successes and the failures. Be concerned if this is one-sided. Also be concerned if the answers become vague, too short, or too general. This is a sign of misleading or avoidance.

Rank the candidate a Level 3 or 4 in character/values when you observe the combination of sincerity with a sense of commitment, strong values, and a pattern of goal setting and achievement. Look for honesty, actions, and decisions based on right and wrong, and an ability to openly express a point of view. A Level 5 ranking is appropriate if the person is a role model and sets the standards of character and values for the group. Rank the person a Level 2 if you have no strong sense about character and values, or if there is a lack of congruity between the candidate's answers and track record. Lots of excuses are pretty much the norm for Level 2 performance.

10. *Potential*

When ranking potential, consider all of the other nine factors described earlier in combination. Consistency is a big part of this ranking. Review trend lines, critical-thinking skills, team leadership skills, and personal commitment to grow and develop. The capacity to take on bigger roles is largely intellectual. As part of this, consider the person's ability to think technically, tactically, and strategically. You'll also need to understand how business-savvy the person is and the ability to think across functions. But capacity to grow is only one dimension. Desire to take on bigger roles is, in many ways, a more critical factor to consider. This is evidenced by the extra effort put into every job; a pattern of personal development, goal setting and achievement; and a competitive "won't lose" spirit. It would be hard to rank a person too high on potential if he didn't have a bunch of Level 4s and 5s in the other nine critical factors. However, don't hesitate to rank a person high in potential if the person is a little light for the specific job at hand. It's often better to hire someone who has more upside even if he requires more short-term support.

Here's a good example. I remember a great financial analyst I met in the late 1980s. He was very technically competent, and even though he was only a few years out of school at the time, he was already managing small groups. In addition, he really understood the strategic impact of all the financial advice he was providing. He was insightful, a great problem solver, and also clearly understood the role that finance could play in helping each function operate more effectively together. I lost track of him for almost 10 years, but was not surprised to discover that he became the president of a mid-size, fast-growing medical products company in his early 30s. He demonstrated all the traits of high-potential thinking and competency long before they were to come into play. At our luncheon meeting, I could tell he still had the capacity to continue his rise up the corporate ladder.

Ranking someone a Level 3 in potential means the person has the capacity to get promoted or take on a bigger job in a normal period of time. A Level 4 ranking means the person could be quickly promoted, and a Level 5 means the person could be promotable at least two management levels within a relatively short period of time. If the person is more interested in a technical rather than a managerial track, then a Level 3 ranking means the person has the capacity and desire to take on more advanced technical responsibility within a normal period. A Level 4 ranking means the person has the capability and desire to push the technology envelope to a major degree, and a Level 5 ranking means the person is pushing the state-of-the-art.

The 10-Factor Candidate Assessment is as much a checklist of what a good interview needs to address as it is an evaluation tool. Don't exclude or include candidates too soon. The "collect information before deciding" approach will lead you to a balanced assessment, considering strengths and weaknesses in an objective manner across all of the critical 10 factors.

While you should complete the 10-Factor Candidate Assessment template right after you meet the candidate, consider it a work in progress. Update your evaluation of the candidate based on reference checks, subsequent interviews and phone conversations, testing, and the inputs of other interviewers. Consider all of these factors before the final hiring decision is made.

■ SPOTTING FATAL FLAWS

Don't overlook the fatal flaws. These are the less-obvious traits that can cause an apparently great person to fail once on the job. An abusive personality, intolerance in some form, or an inability to make critical decisions under pressure are some common fatal flaws. These sometimes go unrecognized during the interview, either because they were overlooked or they were masked by an offsetting strength. Clues abound, but you must be observant and vigilant. Raise the caution flag if you discover one of the following tendencies or traits:

Clues to Some Fatal Flaws

➤ Great communicator, with lots of self-confidence, but the person's management role doesn't seem to be growing. You might have found a great individual contributor or a consultant-type person, but a weak manager.

➤ Vague, superficial, or short answers when explaining critical issues, especially gaps in employment and why the person changed jobs, or failed to get the recognition deserved.

➤ Inconsistent track record—flat, down, roller coaster—that is always blamed on external circumstances.

➤ Lots of drive and ambition, but maybe too assertive. This could relate to ego problems, immaturity, or an inability to work in cross-functional teams.

➤ Too fast of a track record. The person might have been promoted beyond his capability.

➤ Extremes in any behavior—too analytical, too assertive, too friendly, or too persuasive. Usually this leads to problems regarding lack of flexibility or balance.

➤ Lots of energy, great personality, but answers are too general. This is the classic—lots of sizzle, but little substance.

➤ Lots of excuses about why things didn't happen, results weren't achieved, or why recognition didn't occur. A pattern of excuse making is the biggest clue that you're hiring the wrong person.

If you observe any of these signs, you must get proof to overcome the potential concern. The best way is to get an example of a significant example that disproves the potential fatal flaw. If lack of team or management ability is the concern, get the candidate to describe his most significant management or team project. Get more than one example and make sure you get lots of facts, figures, dates, and names to substantiate the example.

For extremes in behavior, get examples of the opposite trait. Someone who is too friendly might not be strong-willed enough, and vice-versa. Likewise, someone who is always selling might not be detailed enough. Have these people describe a project involving details or analytical work. Get the overzealous analyst or individual contributor to describe some important team projects. Then get specific examples of how she persuaded or motivated others to take actions against their better judgment. Reference checks and testing can help here. Do not ignore these caution flags. They can mean the difference between a great hire or a big problem.

During the dot-com boom, we placed a candidate who was very bright, assertive, and a great communicator. His references confirmed this, but they also indicated that he was only an adequate manager. He indicated to us that his style was to hire strong people and then let them manage themselves. However, he overstated his capability on this trait. Once on the job, this person didn't even want to spend the management time necessary to build the team. We were so excited about getting a candidate who was superb in all but one critical dimension that we ignored a fatal flaw. He was asked to leave within four months.

■ THE PROFESSIONALISM AND QUALITY OF THE INTERVIEW COUNTS

Sometimes a weak assessment is due more to poor interviewing skills than a weak candidate. You need to be a good interviewer to evaluate the candidate properly. In the process, you'll attract a better class of candidates. Here's why. The best candidates want to work for great managers, and good interviewing skills, especially knowledge of the job, demonstrate this. Candidates judge the quality of the company and the quality of their potential supervisor by the quality of the interviewing process.

The quality of the assessment process is only as good as its weakest interviewer. This is especially true if every person has an equal vote. If you rely on the weak assessment skills of others, the whole process is compromised. I've seen many strong candidates lose out, because one or two interviewers missed the mark. The hiring manager must be confident enough to override these flawed inputs. That's why giving partial voting rights is so important.

On a search for a vice president of HR, the CEO of a large financial organization wanted to reduce the scope of the inputs of a few members of the interviewing team, while still giving them the courtesy of having an input. We told these interviewers that the CEO and CFO thought that one candidate was the best candidate of the five presented. Their only role was to determine whether there were any fatal flaws in the candidate that had not yet been detected. By limiting the authority of other interviewers this way, you can minimize the problems associated with weaker interviewers.

A different tactic is required if the problem is the hiring manager's boss. This is a problem if the boss is a weak interviewer, or just wants to conduct a personality and fit interview. In this case, it's best to write up the reasons why you want to hire the candidate beforehand, and ask the boss to validate one specific area only. The primary performance objective is a good choice for this. By narrowing the scope of a less reliable interviewer, you can easily turn a personality contest into a short performance-based interview.

If the weak interviewer is the hiring manager, it's best to conduct a panel interview with some good interviewers taking the lead. This allows the hiring manager to participate. Lots of time is wasted, and bad hiring decisions are made, when incompetent interviewers influence the final decision. Identify these "problem people" and establish alternative procedures ahead of time. There is too much riding on every hiring decision to allow controllable error to affect the outcome.

HOT TIPS FOR IMPLEMENTING AN EVIDENCE-BASED ASSESSMENT PROCESS

The likelihood that every individual hiring manager in your company will prepare a performance profile, wait 30 minutes, conduct the two-question performance-based interview, complete the 10-Factor Candidate Assessment template, and then share information before voting yes or no is remote. It takes a disciplined person to pull this off. Yet, that's all there is to increasing hiring accuracy into the 70 percent to 80 percent range. (Note: References checks, testing, and background verification can boost it even higher.) Enacting a few rules will instill this type of discipline throughout your company's entire management team. The following checklist reinforces the necessary guidelines:

✔ Only give the hiring manager full voting rights. Assign everyone else a narrow range of traits to evaluate instead.

✔ Make sure everyone uses the 10-Factor Candidate Assessment template to evaluate the candidate, including the hiring manager. Use detailed examples of past performance to rank each factor, not intuition or gut feelings.

✔ Every interviewer must be prepared before the interview. This includes reviewing the resume, reading the performance profile, knowing his or her assigned roles, and how to conduct the two-question interview.

✔ Invoke the "collect information before deciding" method of interviewing. This means everyone must put his emotional biases in the parking lot the moment he meets the candidate.

✔ Look for an upward pattern of personal growth and development. Be concerned if growth has flattened or is declining, along with motivation.

✔ Debrief formally using the 10-Factor template as a guide. Share information on each factor before deciding. Start with the positives, and make sure the lowest-ranking person speaks first.

✔ No Level 2s! Go out of your way to not hire people who are unmotivated to do the exact work you require.

✔ Compare the environment (complexity, growth, standards, pace, level of bureaucracy) of the candidate's prior companies to your needs to determine real compatibility.

✔ Watch out for the fatal flaws—too bright, too dominant, too analytical, too clever, or too many excuses. Too much of anything can be a clue to a problem.

✔ A professional, well-run interview is as important to you as it is to the candidate. Strong candidates judge companies and managers based on the quality of the interviewing process. Unless the interview is thorough, the conclusions obtained will be less reliable.

Chapter 6

Everything Else after the First Interview: Completing the Assignment

Far more crucial than what we know or do not know is what we do not want to know.

—Eric Hoffer

■ STAY OBJECTIVE: THE FIRST INTERVIEW REPRESENTS LESS THAN HALF OF THE TOTAL ASSESSMENT

Additional interviews, reference checks, and testing are all invaluable. Frequently, these important steps are ignored or minimized. Once a candidate is on the short list, most managers use the added time to look for information to confirm a "yes" decision. By this point, so much time has been invested in the candidate, and momentum is building for an offer, that a "no" possibility is only passively being considered. In my experience, once someone passes muster during the first round of interviews, there's better than a 50

167

percent chance an offer will be made. Positive data is magnified and negative data rationalized away. This is a major cause of bad hiring decisions. Objectivity must prevail throughout the assessment. Negative information must still be sought as aggressively as positive data.

There are some great tools available to increase the accuracy of the assessment. They're especially valuable when used in conjunction with the Performance-based Hiring interviewing process. As mentioned earlier, an unstructured interview is only 57 percent accurate in predicting subsequent performance. This improves to about 75 percent using a performance profile and the structured performance-based interview. When combined with some of the other tools suggested in this chapter, accuracy can increase to 80 percent or 90 percent. It takes some work to pull this off, but not nearly as much work as managing and firing someone you should never have hired in the first place.

Some of the things you must do after the first interview include reference checking, background verification, drug testing, assessment testing, and more interviews. These are all critical to making the process of hiring a professional and effective business process.

■ THE IMPORTANCE OF REFERENCE CHECKING

If you're serious about a candidate, you need to conduct reference checks. Here's a basic rule about reference checking that's probably not 100 percent true, but you should follow it 100 percent of the time. Strong candidates have strong references who will openly tell you about them. Lack of good references is a sign of a potential problem.

Strong candidates have strong references who will openly tell you about them. Lack of good references is a sign of a potential problem.

There are very few exceptions to this rule. Here's one: Once in awhile, a candidate's job search is extremely confidential. Under these circumstances, it's sometimes hard to find a colleague willing to vouch for the candidate if he's been there for a long time. In this case, look for someone who has recently left the company. Since 1978, when I became a headhunter, I've never had a problem getting a reference from a good candidate. Once a candidate is serious about a job, a reference check is in order. Good candidates expect it, and they will find some good references for you. This is a great sign. It means the candidate is serious about the position. I become anxious if a candidate can't give me a few people to call.

A few years ago at one of our training sessions for hiring managers, a buttoned-down vice president of HR vehemently disagreed with my contention about references. First, she told all of the managers attending not to provide references for anyone. She then said they should only give the bare minimum of information about an employee who had left the firm in order to avoid any liability. I then asked her about one of her coworkers we both knew very well, and asked whether she would give me a complete and positive reference about her. She said, "Of course, but that's different, I know her." And that's why there are no exceptions to the basic rule. Good people know other good people who will tell you openly about them. Weaker people come up with excuses about why they can't give you references.

Corporations restrict references in order to protect employers from lawsuits from their former employees if the references are negative or less than stellar. Some companies are now stating that employees can give open references if it's clearly stated that the reference is personal. In September 2005, the U.S. government issued a pamphlet, entitled "Reference Checking in Federal Hiring: Making the Call." While it primarily covers how to check references when hiring government employees, it addresses many issues faced in private industry. Here's one point that suggests why you must conduct reference checks: "An additional concern is the possibility of negligent hiring accusations when employers do not take sufficient care to check an applicant's background." The main issue is if someone you hire causes your company to be sued, then you could be considered negligent because you didn't conduct a proper reference check. As far as I'm concerned, you're negligent if you don't conduct a battery of checks and tests after the first interview, whether you get sued or not.

➤ How to Really Conduct a Reference Check

Conduct the reference check just like the interview by getting specific examples to prove a generality and then by fact-finding. Even those people who do give you a reference may talk in glowing terms or generalities. Don't buy into this. Instead, dig deep and get facts and details to support the overall statement. If someone says the candidate has great team skills, ask for specific examples.

It's important for the hiring manager to personally check at least one or two references. It doesn't matter when you conduct the reference check, although sometime after you've established intent and before the last round of interviews is best. Don't quickly delegate this important task. The HR department or the recruiter has a vested interest in placing the candidate, so they won't be as inquisitive as the hiring manager. Plan on at least 20 to 30 minutes for each reference, because this gives you time to do some fact-finding. The key to good interviewing and good reference checking is to ask many questions and get examples. Use peers, subordinates, and supervisors as references. Subordinates are sometimes the best references, so don't ignore these people.

Although not getting a reference is a sign of a weak candidate, getting flowery, glowing comments is not the sign of a good candidate. References, even from strong candidates, need to be validated. First, determine the quality of the reference, then get the reference to give specific examples to validate the hyperbole and generalities.

1. Qualifying the Reference

The following reference check checklist is divided into two distinct parts. First, qualifying the reference and, second, qualifying the candidate. The quality of the reference is as important as what the reference tells you about the candidate. Let's address this first.

All of the information in the checklist will allow you to place the reference's subsequent comments in context. If the reference is personal, ignore it. If you decide to use it, get great examples of exceptional, above-the-call-of-duty activities. From nonwork-related references, determine why the candidate is special and how this relates to on-the-job performance. Volunteer work, of some sort, would apply here. This is especially useful for candidates just starting their careers when there's not a great deal of work history.

REFERENCE CHECKING CHECKLIST

Part 1—Qualifying the Reference

☐ Determine the relationship to the candidate. Find out the titles of both the reference and the candidate, how long the working relationship lasted, and their most recent contact.

☐ Obtain the reference's current title, company, and the scope of the job in comparison to the job when the reference knew the candidate.

☐ Determine the reference's scope of responsibility by asking about the size of his or her organization and the number and types of people on the staff.

☐ Determine what the company environment was like—pace, standards of performance, quality of the people, and the quality of the processes and systems.

Knowing what criteria a reference uses to rank performance provides additional insight into the quality of the reference, and also a means to validate the reference's comments. The reference might value traits differently than you do, so this could be important. Some of the more common value systems include teamwork, interpersonal skills, results independent of methods, intelligence, commitment, character, and loyalty. You can get many different answers about accomplishments depending on the rating system used.

2. Qualifying the Candidate

Use the checklist on page 173 to qualify the candidate. You will rarely obtain all of this information, but this will help guide your thinking when you're on the phone. The key to good reference checking is to get details and examples to back up general statements about the candidate's competency. If the reference states that the candidate was really committed, ask the reference to give you an example that best demonstrates this trait. If you probe like this a few times, the reference will realize you're serious. Most reference checkers just want to check boxes. By showing your professionalism this way, the reference will be more open and frank.

The key to good reference checking is to get details and examples to back up general statements about the candidate's competency.

Start the second part of the reference check by asking for an overall summary of strengths and weaknesses. From this, you can cherry-pick your way through the balance of the reference items. The key is to ask for a specific example demonstrating the skill or behavior the reference mentioned. If initiative was mentioned as a key strength, ask for a specific accomplishment demonstrating initiative. Do the same thing for weaknesses. Don't form judgments about the candidate based on generalities from a reference. Get proof with good examples. This is the most important aspect of good reference checking.

Get proof with good examples. This is the most important aspect of good reference checking.

Ask the reference to compare the candidate to others at the same level. "How would you rank this person among other people you know at this level?" is a good opener. Ask how many are in the group and what percentile the candidate falls within (i.e., top 10 percent, top 25 percent, or top 50 percent). Then find out the basis for this ranking, like team skills, energy, or technical competence. Ask what it would take for the candidate to move into the top 10 percent or top 5 percent. This will get at weaknesses. Also ask where this person excelled, and again get an example for proof.

Here are a few other good ways to uncover weaknesses. Ask the reference to describe the one single thing the candidate could do or change in order to be more effective. Then find out how the lack of this affected performance. At the end of the interview, ask the reference to summarize the candidate's overall performance on a scale of 1 to 10. Usually, you'll get a number anywhere from 6 to 9. Then ask what it would take for the candidate to move up 1 point. Asking whether the reference would rehire or work with the candidate again and under what circumstance is also revealing. Probe this to confirm previous statements.

REFERENCE CHECKING CHECKLIST

Part 2—Qualifying the Candidate

☐ Please give me a summary of (candidate)'s strengths and weaknesses. Get examples of accomplishments to support major strengths and weaknesses.

☐ How did the weaknesses affect job performance?

☐ Can you give me some examples of where the candidate took the initiative?

☐ How would you rank this person as a manager? Get an example to prove it.

☐ How strong was this person in building/developing teams or working on teams? Get examples and note the types of people the person worked with.

☐ How would you rank this person's overall technical competence in [job-specific] area? Get specific examples.

☐ Is technical competence a real strength? Why?

☐ Determine timeliness and reliability—get examples of meeting deadlines under pressure.

☐ Find out ability to handle pressure or criticism. Ask about the company and environment. Get examples.

☐ How strong a decision-maker is the person? Can you give me some examples and how they were made?

☐ Would you rehire the candidate? Would you want to work with this person again? Would you work for this person again? Why or why not?

☐ How would you rank this person's character and personal values system? Why?

☐ How would you compare this candidate to others at the same level you know? Why is the candidate stronger (or weaker)?

☐ How would you rank the person's overall performance on a scale of 1 to 10? What would it take to move up 1 point?

☐ What advice would you give this person on how he could be more effective in his next job?

Use the reference to confirm the information obtained during your actual interview with the candidate. Throughout the interview, you should have obtained numerous examples of the candidate's greatest accomplishments. Ask the reference to validate this information. Get examples of core success traits and see whether the traits and examples are the same as the candidate described. If different, find out why. Ask the reference about the candidate's actual involvement in the major accomplishments. Compare this to what the candidate has stated. It's easier to correlate information if you focus on the most exceptional work the candidate has done in each job.

Conduct the reference check with an open mind. If you really want to hire the candidate, you might unintentionally avoid asking the tough questions. Many years ago, a senior executive at a large health care company told me he was asked to provide a reference for a candidate we both knew. The candidate was solid, but not a star, more an individual contributor than a manager. The senior executive told the person conducting the reference that the candidate was a superb analyst, but only an average manager. He said that once he mentioned this, the HR person conducting the reference did not ask any further questions about management and tried only to reinforce the strengths.

You can get any answer you want by conducting a reference check the wrong way. If you are not objective and are unwilling to change your opinion, it's a waste of time to even conduct the reference check. It's embarrassing to admit you've made a mistake in judgment and eliminate a candidate at the last moment. It's a much bigger mistake to go forward and hire someone you shouldn't have, no matter how important it seems at the time.

Reference checking allows you to validate the candidate's true role in each major accomplishment. Concerns about style can also be addressed. Weaknesses can be validated with other references. As the hiring manager, you'll also get some great tips on how to better manage or motivate the candidate if hired. You can prevent more hiring mistakes with a good reference check than any other method. But we've seen hiring managers ignore negative data because they were too sold on the candidate. This is another important reason to stay objective until completing the whole evaluation process.

■ WHAT TO DO IN THE SECOND ROUND
OF INTERVIEWS

One interview will never give you enough information to make a foolproof hiring decision. Use a second interview to confirm core issues and explore new ones. Make use of other interviewers the same way. Tell them what you want them to look for. By itself, this will make their interviews more meaningful. Do whatever you can to eliminate courtesy interviews or to see whether the person "fits with the culture." These are no more than popularity contests, whose only purpose is to eliminate a good person for bad reasons, since little real investigating goes on. Conduct a reference check or have the candidate take some type of assessment test prior to the second interview to validate any of the concerns raised by these checks.

➤ Conducting the Second Interview

For any staff or management position, the hiring manager needs to interview the candidate at least twice formally. A third interview involving a lunch or dinner is also appropriate. While part of this is social, treat each time you meet with the candidate as an opportunity to better assess job fit. Focus less on chitchatting and more on asking questions. As you discover in Chapter 7, you can ask questions to recruit the candidate, but this is less about selling and more about career counseling. In Appendix C, there is a second-round interview form that can be used to supplement what's presented in this chapter. The primary emphasis of a second interview is to validate both concerns and perceived strengths. To start, write down everything you still have questions about using the 10-Factor Candidate Assessment template as a guideline (see Chapter 5).

Use the performance-based interviewing techniques for all subsequent interviews. The key is to dig into accomplishments and failures to understand true performance. If you have a question about management style, dig into the candidate's best and worst management accomplishments and figure out what happened. Look at all of these management accomplishments over an extended period of time to observe growth or change. You can do the same thing for any trait, skill, behavior, or competency. Spend more time in the second interview on management, team, and organizational skills. Typically, the focus of much of the first interview is on individual contributor traits, so use later interviews to restore some balance here.

Anchoring and visualizing all of the performance objectives is best done over two or more sessions. Format the second interview around some of the performance objectives in the performance profile that you haven't yet discussed. Assign some performance objectives to other interviewers. If the hiring manager's supervisor is involved in the interview, make sure she anchors and visualizes at least the most important performance objective. This will go a long way to ensure that the boss's boss doesn't conduct a superficial personality and fit interview.

Have peers anchor and visualize the performance objective most relevant to their work. We had an engineering manager ask a potential marketing manager about the development of product requirement documents* as the main focus of his interview. This tightened the focus of the interview.

Candidates don't mind this line of questioning, even though it appears that you're asking similar questions over again. The process of anchoring performance objectives and fact-finding always results in a different line of questioning because the trail followed is always different. As a result, you'll always get different answers and somewhat different conclusions. By controlling the breadth of the interview this way, you can obtain useful, objective information. Don't ignore the need for facts to justify the assessment as described in Chapter 5 on conducting an evidence-based assessment.

Subsequent interviews are extremely useful to conduct the deep job-matching process recommended. This ensures a strong match between real job needs and a candidate's abilities and true interests. To get at this, find examples of where the candidate excelled at doing work comparable to what you need done. During the interview, candidates will often tell you that they have no problem doing portions of the work that aren't too exciting. Be skeptical here. Once on the job, these parts of the job are often ignored or done poorly. If a candidate needs a job, he will say anything. This is how competent but unmotivated people are hired. To overcome this, obtain recent examples of the candidate going the extra mile to complete the type of work required. Raise the caution flag if you don't find some reasonable evidence. Check this out during the reference checking.

---

*These documents describe in detail the performance and design requirements of a product.

■ THE PANEL INTERVIEW: A GREAT WAY TO SAVE TIME AND INCREASE ACCURACY

If you want to increase assessment accuracy and save time, conduct more panel interviews. These are much better than an all-day series of one-on-one 45- to 60-minute interviews. When organized properly, panel interviews help everybody involved learn more about the candidate. Even weaker interviewers learn something, if they just observe. Panel interviews also provide a great means for subordinates to get involved in the hiring process. Note: Subordinates should never conduct one-on-one interviews. Since they usually prefer to work for someone they like, they focus on the wrong issues. For another, they're rarely objective, and worse, many of them are weak interviewers. A panel interview overcomes all of these problems.

However, I didn't always believe that panel interviews were that good of an idea. In the early 1990s, the CEO of In-N-Out Burger, a potential client, asked me about panel interviews. "They're intimidating, cold, a poor recruiting tool, and unwieldy," was my instant reply. The CEO looked at me and said, "That's too bad, because that's all we use here, and if you want the CFO search, you'll have to use them." Without hesitation, and because at the time this would have been our biggest assignment, I indicated that I was willing to try. You should, too. They're a great tool. I was totally wrong. We went on to place about six executives with this company over the next few years using panel interviews as the standard.

As long as they're organized well, panel interviews provide a truer picture of a candidate than the one-on-one interview because:

➤ *Panel interviews are more objective.* There is less personal interaction, and it's hard to chitchat, which is a good thing, since chitchatting is a waste of time.

➤ *There is a chance to think more about the candidate's responses.* You're not the only one asking questions, which increases the validity of the assessment. In most one-on-one interviews, you're often thinking about what you're going to ask next, rather than listening to the candidate's answer.

➤ *You don't make instant judgments about the quality of an answer while the candidate is answering because others are clarifying information.*

This is one of the reasons one-on-one interviews aren't too effective. More in-depth responses are possible when others are helping with the fact-finding.

➤ *It's a great way for subordinates to meet the candidate without the typical awkwardness.* Since it's less of a personality-based interview, the subordinate's hidden agendas stay hidden.

➤ *Strong candidates like panel interviews if they're well organized and if the candidate is not put into an intimidating situation.* You'll also see more of the candidate's true personality, especially if most of the follow-up questions are about how accomplishments were achieved.

➤ *It saves time.* It only takes three or four people one to two hours to conduct a complete interview versus a whole day.

➤ *Weaker interviewers can be involved.* This is especially important if the weaker interviewer is the hiring manager. I often lead the panel interview for my clients if the hiring manager isn't a strong interviewer.

➤ *The assessment is more accurate and consistent.* Since everyone is using the same information to make an assessment, consistency is achieved. If the lead interviewer conducts a comprehensive performance-based interview, the information obtained is extremely insightful. This is something the other interviewers couldn't have obtained on their own.

➤ How to Organize and Conduct a Panel Interview

The panel should include no more than three or four people, otherwise it can be both intimidating and unwieldy. One interviewer should be the leader, and everyone else should be in a support position. This is critical. Too many panel interviews go awry because everyone competes to ask his or her own questions. While all of the interviewers need to be involved throughout the interview, the difference in the two roles needs to be very clear.

Primary Interviewer

One interviewer leads the panel session, acting as the host and describing to the candidate how the interview will be conducted. During the actual panel interview, the primary interviewer will ask the basic questions and follow up with some fact-finding. Only the primary interviewer can change the topic or the focus of the question.

Secondary Interviewers

Every other member of the panel interviewing team is in a support role. However, each person should be active during the interviewing, asking for examples and clarifying information. These people help the primary interviewer peel the onion by following up the main questions with questions like, "Can you give me an example of what you mean?" "When did that happen?" and "What were the results?" Organized properly, this type of panel interview follows a very natural flow and reveals a great deal of useful information.

It's okay if one of the secondary interviewers becomes a primary interviewer for a different question or for a different section of the interview. Someone can take on the primary responsibility for a question addressing a job-related technical accomplishment while someone else can be the primary interviewer for a different accomplishment, like team or management focus. If this type of shift is made, plan ahead of time to minimize any confusion and make sure that everyone else takes a support role asking for clarifying information.

Make sure all interviewers have read the performance profile for the job before convening. Make the thrust of the interview a discussion of the candidate's major accomplishments. It's okay to ask the candidate to come prepared to discuss a few of her most relevant major accomplishments. This will improve the information exchange. As part of this, ask the candidate to be prepared to cover individual contributor, team, and management projects. You should conduct a 10-Factor Candidate Assessment right after this interview to capture everyone's comments.

During the dot-com boom, one of my manufacturing clients excluded a great candidate for an operations management position because he was too chatty during the first interview. My client got put off by this superficial banter, most likely caused by initial nervousness. Our client was a typical entrepreneur—bright, fast-paced, prone to making instant decisions, and strong-willed. These are not the traits of good interviewers. The candidate was top-notch, though; a perfect match for the entrepreneur to build the solid infrastructure to maintain his fast-growing import and distribution company.

We didn't want to let this candidate go, so we arranged a panel interview with one of my associates leading the session. There were about four people in the room, but we orchestrated the questioning. It lasted about 90 minutes and covered everything, focusing largely on comparable past accomplishments dealing with rapidly changing environments. The candidate passed this more grueling session with flying colors. After a subsequent three-hour one-on-one interview with the CEO, the candidate was offered the position and accepted. During this interview, they created the operations plan and budget for the next 12 months. A few months after the person started, our client called to thank us for intervening and indicated that the candidate's job performance was top-notch, as expected.

One potential problem with panel interviews is that they can be intimidating to the candidate. Describe the format of the session a few days beforehand to ease the candidate's fears. During the interview, use a round table or seat the candidate in the middle of a long table. The candidate will feel like one of the team this way. Don't make it seem like an interrogation. It's better to sound low key by requesting more information in a neutral tone of voice.

➤ Take-Home Case Study: Don't Just Talk about the Job, Have the Candidate Do It

You'll see instant positive results with a panel interview, leading to more agreement and fewer hiring errors. The process can be made even stronger if you give the candidate a take-home problem to present in the panel session.

The take-home project is something the candidate does outside of the interview that's discussed at a subsequent meeting. Topics for this can include reviewing reports, solving real job-related problems, evaluating new products, assessing tactical or strategic plans, and providing consulting advice on a mini-project. The take-home project is effective because the candidate is required to do real work, not just talk about it.

The take-home case-study approach has a number of tangible benefits. For one, it reveals true motivation and desire. Candidates won't spend much time preparing if they're not truly interested in the job. This approach does a better job of revealing competency through direct observation compared to opinion or gut feelings. The spontaneity of the session allows true character and personality to come out.

A few years ago, a CEO called me about three months after we placed a vice president/controller at his company. He wanted to tell me how pleased he was with the candidate. He said the candidate's performance, sense of humor, and interpersonal skills were exactly as demonstrated in the panel interview. However, this did not match his initial assessment. After the first interview, the CEO thought the candidate was not confident enough for the job, that he had some quirky mannerisms, and that he was unsure of the candidate's technical competence. He thought the two other contenders were far stronger.

I knew all three candidates very well and knew that this person was the best of the three, although he was nervous in the interview. I suggested that the CEO conduct a panel interview coupled with a take-home problem. Each candidate was asked to assess a potential acquisition. After reviewing the financial reports, the candidates were told to make a 15-minute presentation about the merits of the opportunity. This would be followed by a 45-minute open discussion. During the panel session, this candidate wowed everyone. He explored the financial impact on taxes and earnings. He raised serious questions about costing and financing. He was confident, funny, and insightful. In this element, which was much more natural for the candidate than the interview, he had a chance to demonstrate his true capabilities.

Unfortunately, the best candidate is often eliminated too soon for the wrong reasons. In the previous example, I personally intervened to bring a dead situation back to life, but that is rare. You can preclude the possibility of missing a great candidate by exploring accomplishments in greater depth, rather than assuming competency based on presentation skills.

One of our clients in catalog distribution went a bit overboard with the panel interview idea. The day after the first interview, our candidate for a marketing manager position was asked to come in for a panel interview. The candidate was not 100 percent sold on the job, so this type of panel session was premature. After arriving, she was told that there would be six people in the panel and she had to present her solutions to three marketing problems. She was given 25 minutes to prepare an evaluation of these problems, which weren't truly relevant to the job.

Although the candidate handled it well, the problems could have been avoided. If you use take-home projects, give the candidate a few days to prepare, and then only if the candidate has expressed a desire to be considered as a finalist. Make sure the issues explored are relevant and job specific.

You don't need to have a panel session to review take-home projects, but if you do, you get the benefit of both assessment techniques. Here are seven ideas for take-home projects:

1. Review reports, financial statements, studies, or plans.

2. Give the candidate a performance objective to study. Have the candidate describe a significant anchor and then tell you how he would accomplish the task (visualize). Use a flip chart and get into a serious give-and-take discussion. This is what you would discuss after the candidate starts, so why wait?

3. Give a loan officer a credit application to assess.

4. Have an engineer assess a design and present some alternative solutions or approaches.

5. Describe a problem in a process (e.g., order entry, logistics, manufacturing, accounting) and have the candidate describe how she would come up with a solution.

6. Have a salesperson tell you how he would attempt to secure a big account.

7. Have a product manager describe how she would develop and launch a new product.

The types of issues are endless. The key is to make them job specific. Situational questions that don't directly relate to real job needs are a waste of time and give misleading results. Always get examples of comparable accomplishments during the panel interview; this way, the take-home project is actually an expanded anchor-and-visualize exercise. It reveals true job competency by applying the candidate's knowledge in solving job-specific problems. In addition, the amount of time spent on the assignment directly reveals true interest.

■ BACKGROUND VERIFICATIONS: CHEAP INSURANCE YOU MUST HAVE

You must conduct a background check on every candidate including degree verification, employment history, credit review, driving record, and criminal background. The cost is low and the protection is high. According to Rob Bekken, a partner with Musick, Peeler and Garrett, and a former partner with Fisher and Phillips, the third-largest employment law firm in the United States, most labor-related lawsuits are brought by those who should never have been hired in the first place. A standard background check can eliminate most of these types of hires.

Eric Boden, the CEO of Hire Right (www.hireright.com), a highly regarded firm that specializes in background checking for large corporations, told me that 85 percent of large multinational firms and 50 percent of small firms now conduct background verifications.* He also told me that companies without a formal background verification process in place will likely lose a negligent hiring lawsuit. This is the same issue faced if you don't conduct reference checks. Background verifications need to be part of the hiring process. For about $100, you can conduct a background verification for every finalist. This is cheap insurance. Not only will it help ensure that you don't hire the wrong person, it will minimize your legal liability. Boden also indicated that firms that don't conduct background verifications are magnets for people with problems, since these are the only places they'll possibly be able to get jobs. Be careful here because you don't want to be known as the company where "problem people" can get jobs.

Misleading resumes are also a problem that companies need to deal with. While most resumes describe the basic truth, many do a great job of camouflaging the sand traps. The background verification testing will help sort this out, especially unexplained gaps in employment. Boden told me that 44 percent of the

---

* Personal interview with Eric Boden, CEO of Hire Right. November, 2006 (www.hireright.com).

resumes his firm checks have some discrepancy. Generally, I'm a real cynic with respect to trusting resume content. This sad story makes the point. Many years ago, we were looking through our resume database for candidates for a material control manager's position. We found some strong candidates, and we called them personally to determine their current level of interest. Three were interested and sent in their current resumes. They must have forgotten we had earlier versions. One candidate was identical, other than updated for the current period. Another candidate falsely added a Master's degree in an earlier time period. The other candidate eliminated a job from the earlier resume to minimize turnover. The latter candidates were eliminated from contention, without further contact.

This is disturbing, but it reveals a trend of candidates falsifying resumes. In general, don't trust resumes. Remember Michael Brown, the former Federal Emergency Management Agency (FEMA) director, who was fired for his mishandling of the Hurricane Katrina disaster? His resume indicated he was the assistant city manager for Edmond, Oklahoma. It turns out he was an assistant to the city manager. In February 2006, Dave Edmondson had to step down as the CEO of Radio Shack when it was discovered that his two college degrees were phony. From the candidate's perspective, the resume is a marketing tool, not an historical document. While a clever layout is okay, fraud is not. Spend the money and wait the two days it takes to conduct a background check to separate fact from fiction.

On your applications, state that you'll be conducting a background check and then require the candidate to validate the truthfulness of the information, affirmed by his or her signature. This will reduce some fraud. You can also use the background check as part of the close to test both interest and truthfulness. Before the second or third interview, tell the candidate you'll be conducting a rigorous background check. Ask the candidate to reconfirm that everything on the resume and application is 100 percent consistent with the facts. If the candidate says yes and agrees to come in for another interview, he's demonstrating sincere interest and honesty. A few will opt out at this time. You can learn a great deal about the candidate by using this conditional approach to moving forward.

■ ASSESSMENT TESTING TO CONFIRM, NOT PREDICT, COMPETENCY

I've been interviewing candidates since 1978 and have been using tests for almost as long, yet I'm still not sure about their validity or value. Don't get me wrong, some tests are better than others and, in certain instances, they're appropriate. In this section, we review different types of tests and name a few names. The purpose of this section is to provide guidance on how to use assessment tests in general, not to recommend any specific tests. I've collaborated with Charles Handler* over the past five years on a number of projects, including asking him to validate the usefulness of the Performance-based Hiring interviewing and selection process recommended in this book. His white paper is included in Appendix B. Charles is a well-known authority on how to best use assessment testing. We tend to see eye-to-eye on the use of assessments, and in this section, I've summarized my experiences tempered with his wisdom.

Divide assessment tests into four broad categories:

1. *Assessing skills*: Determining whether the person can, for example, use Excel, run the call center system, or program in C++.

2. *Assessing personality*: The Myers-Briggs and DISC assessment instruments are examples.

3. *Measuring cognitive ability*: Testing, for example, the use of verbal and numeric reasoning.

4. *Measuring competencies*: Watching for patterns showing factors like drive, honesty, and dependability.

Personality-related tests are pretty useless, whereas a test that accurately measures a specific job-related skill is a useful indicator of subsequent performance. Some of these include testing software knowledge, equipment usage, computer skills, solving job-specific problems, and manual dexterity. If the job is narrowly confined to this specific area, weigh the test more heavily in the hiring decision. For most jobs, it's the application of these skills that ultimately determines success and, in these cases, the testing will give the wrong

* Charles Handler PhD, CEO of Rocket Hire (www.rocket-hire.com).

conclusions. But it's not because the testing is invalid. The real problem is that the true job was poorly defined. That's why the most important component of good hiring is the performance profile.

Despite these drawbacks, some tests are useful tools if used to confirm a strong performance-based interview. In a general sense, preinterview assessment tests are more useful for hourly positions when you need to quickly select from a large pool of candidates. Preinterview assessment tests are less useful for staff and management positions and useless when you want to hire an A-level passive candidate. The problem here is that the best people won't spend the time to take the test. Despite this caveat, some tests are useful and appropriate, and I recommend them for everyone on the short list of final candidates, even for executives.

The following sections summarize the most common tests, with tips to maximize your time.

➤ Cognitive Ability Tests

Cognitive ability tests measure intelligence. Intelligence is a good predictor of ability to learn, so this type of test is frequently used to screen candidates. The ones I've used are the Wonderlic Personnel Test and Profiles International's Profiles XT. There are other tests like these available, and there is definite value in using them. According to John Hunter (Michigan State University) and Frank Schmidt (University of Iowa), there is a strong correlation between the ability to learn and on-the-job competence. In their landmark study, they conclude that 25 percent of a candidate's subsequent performance can be measured with this type of test.* This is significant, and the same study concluded that a test of mental ability along with structured interviews and some type of work sampling are the top three predictors of on-the-job-performance. Based on this, it's easy to recommend the use of some type of test for every final candidate. It's especially valuable when combined with the performance-based two-question structured interview. The second question on job-related problem solving is quite similar to a work sampling or job simulation test.

---

* John Hunter and Frank Schmidt, "The Validity and Utility of Selection Methods in Personal Psychology" *Psychology Bulletin*, 1998, vol. 124.

However, I strongly recommend that you use a cognitive test to confirm performance, not to predict it. The smartest people don't always deliver the results you want. However, people who deliver the results you want are usually smart enough to do the job. And that is what you really want to confirm.

In the late 1990s, a candidate for a police officer position in Rhode Island was denied the opportunity to join the force because he scored too high on the Wonderlic test. The community leaders felt he would have been bored by police work because his score exceeded their norms. This is where I think this type of test is wrongly used. My suggestion would have been to get examples of work the candidate had recently done that best duplicated the routine nature of police work. If the work was similar and the candidate was motivated by it, then I would discount the high Wonderlic score. However, if the past work required a higher degree of intellect than police work, then the high Wonderlic score would confirm this concern. This is how this type of test should be used during the assessment process. It shouldn't be used as a stand-alone measure, but rather in the context of the real job. Most tests try to eliminate the need to understand real job needs to simplify the hiring process. In my opinion, this is why they are less effective.

Here's an example of a potential problem that can occur when using these tests as filters to eliminate weaker candidates. Many years ago, I was working with a top-notch candidate for an HR manager's job. She seemed great, but she scored very low on the Wonderlic test. The score was totally inconsistent with her track record of success based on our personal interviews and her reference checks. Checking further, we found out that English was her third language. She grew up in Italy, lived in Quebec as a young adult, and went to school in the United States. Surprisingly, she had no noticeable accent. Many of these tests rely on knowledge of the idiomatic expressions of the language and others are timed. If English isn't the candidate's primary language, the tests can give flawed results. The woman was ideally suited for the job and was subsequently promoted to an executive position. If we relied on the test for guidance, we could have eliminated a top-notch candidate from consideration. This is an example of adverse impact—potentially eliminating a group of people since the test was poorly designed.

There are new tests that correct for such biases. Some are ethnic- or gender-related. If you over-rely on these tests to eliminate candidates or predict performance, you might miss some fine candidates. That's why they should not be used as a substitute for a good performance-based interview. Someone who scores lower on the test might be a top producer, substituting work ethic for talent. Someone very bright might get bored with the job or try to get by without working hard enough. However, these tests are very useful when you use them as guides for further evaluation if the results are inconsistent with your expectations.

➤ Personality, Style, and Behavioral Assessment Tests

Personality-style tests like the DISC and the Myers-Briggs broadly measure traits like extroversion, methods of processing information, and how people influence others. There is very little correlation between these tests and subsequent performance. One problem is that these tests measure preferences, not competencies. This is an important distinction. If you prefer to be at a party rather than read a book of poetry, you will be classified in a certain way, yet you might not be competent at either. The party-goer might be able to offer more insight into Frost, and the poetry reader might be a more effective leader. Another problem is that most of these tests present an "either/or" choice. You might like to read poetry and go to parties, but the test only allows you to select one. This forced-choice distinction doesn't give a true reading of personality balance.

For these reasons, never use personality tests to predict performance. If the test indicates an inconsistency with the performance-based interview, further investigation is mandatory. Use panel interviews, take-home tests, and additional reference checks to validate your findings and figure out the discrepancies. The best means to predict future performance is based on past performance, and if a specific test raises concerns, use examples of past performance to figure out why there's a difference.

Never use personality tests to predict performance.

A recent situation illustrates this point. One of our candidates for a marketing position did well on the creative portion of a personality-style test, but scored quite low on detail-orientation. Our client was justifiably concerned. On further investigation, the problem was in the way the test was used and interpreted, not the candidate. The client's test forced the candidate to indicate a preference for the creative over the analytical work, since this is what she preferred. The job required solid database marketing skills to supplement the creative aspects of the job, and our client was correct in raising this issue. To address the concern, we gave the candidate the Wonderlic Personnel Test for intelligence and she did well on the math component. In addition, we conducted a number of reference checks to confirm her analytical abilities by getting specific examples of some of her analytical projects. Finally, the client had the candidate interpret some of their database reports and present her findings at a panel interview. With this added insight, it was clear the candidate had the ability to handle the analytical aspects of the job. In this case, the personality testing was used correctly—only to raise the concern, not to predict performance.

The Predictive Index (PI), DISC instrument, and Myers-Briggs Test are based on the early work of Hippocrates regarding the four temperaments. In the first part of the twentieth century, Carl Jung developed this concept into a theory of human nature based on four personality types. This led to the Myers-Briggs Test. The DISC and PI instruments arose out of the style and behavior analysis work conducted shortly thereafter by William Marston. Both of these tests are quantitative and describe the degree to which a person is **D**ominant, **I**nfluencing, **S**teady, and **C**ompliant. Figure 6.1 provides a quick overview of the four types.

The primary style is determined by a person's tendency to be active or passive (the horizontal axis of the graph), combined with his thinking or feeling orientation (the vertical axis). Plot yourself to get a quick sense of your primary style. Through word choices, the tests quantify how strong you are in each of the four styles. These tests have value in team building and improving communications within a group. They do not predict job competency. Despite this caveat, if the test results are inconsistent with past performance, conduct more reference checking or have another round of interviewing. As a checkpoint and a feedback tool used

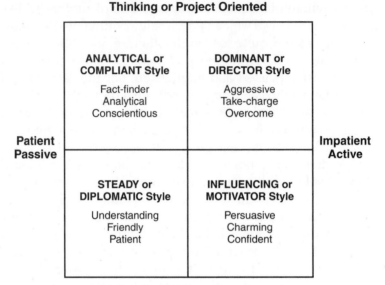

Thinking or Project Oriented

ANALYTICAL or COMPLIANT Style Fact-finder Analytical Conscientious	**DOMINANT or DIRECTOR Style** Aggressive Take-charge Overcome
STEADY or DIPLOMATIC Style Understanding Friendly Patient	**INFLUENCING or MOTIVATOR Style** Persuasive Charming Confident

Patient Passive (left) **Impatient Active** (right)

Feelings or Relationship Oriented

Figure 6.1 Use this chart to quickly assess the four dominant personality styles.

this way, the tests are useful in improving the accuracy of the overall assessment.

Myers-Briggs is based on similar behavioral theory, but the output is more qualitative than quantitative and results in 16 different personality types, classifying people as Introverted or Extroverted, Sensing or iNtuitive, Feeling or Thinking, and Judging or Perceiving. By mixing and matching the four fundamental behavioral traits, you can wind up at one extreme being an ENTJ, the "natural leader," or at the other end of the spectrum as one of "nature's observers," the ISFP. This is a useful tool to understand people better, but it doesn't add much to the hiring process. I've met many supposed ENTJ leaders who are incompetent, and some great leaders who are introverted and quiet. I interviewed one candidate who told me his greatest strength was that he was an ENTJ. When I asked him to describe his most significant leadership accomplishment (this is a variation of the core MSA question), he couldn't come up with much substance, just excuses.

There's a classic logic argument, *asserting the consequent*, which addresses this inconsistency. The phrase itself means that specific truths are often incorrectly generalized for all conditions. The result is bad guidance. For instance, assume that a test of a group of successful managers revealed that 7 out of 10 were extroverted. From this, some people would conclude two things: First, you probably need to be extroverted to be a successful manager. Second, all extroverts are managers. Both generalizations are untrue, but somehow these underlying details get lost as people start believing and applying the concept. This is why I think all of these personality-style tests are flawed. It's my opinion that you should look for the manager first. Then find out whether the person is introverted or extroverted and how the person uses this trait to be successful. It might turn out that the trait is completely irrelevant.

The Profile XT from Profiles International is a combination of personal style and cognitive tests. I use it 100 percent of the time before making a final hiring decision either for my company or for one of our search clients. While not foolproof, it offers great value. It's longer than most, with additional questions that increase reliability. The Profile XT also measures what they call Thinking Style, a form of general mental ability. The Profile also adds in a measure of occupational interests, which most assessment tools ignore. This has some value when comparing these results to the deep job-matching process aspects of the performance-based interview. The personality section is comparable to the other tests, but the report itself is very useful, especially the comparative graphs and charts. The Profile XT can be taken online, so it's easy to send a link to the candidate. It takes about an hour to complete and is worth the added time since it covers additional material.

This test is also part of our recruiting and closing process. When a candidate is clearly on the short list, I tell the person that the next step is to go online and complete the Profile questionnaire. Those who readily comply are far more interested in the job than those I have to persuade to take it. This helps in putting together the offer package. The candidates also find the test somewhat strenuous, adding credibility and professionalism to the whole process. This is important as candidates compare one company to another. Overall, I recommend the Profile XT as a useful preemployment hiring tool because it covers both cognitive ability and personality style.

If you use the Performance-based Hiring interview methodology, you'll soon discover that your assessments and the tests you use will yield similar results. Over the past 20 years, 80 percent to 90 percent of these types of tests generally confirmed what I observed during the interview. When the tests don't match up with the interview results, it's important to conduct more in-depth probing to better understand why the two differ. It could be attributed to a problem with the test, a problem with your interviewing methods, or a clue to a flaw in the candidate, possibly a fatal flaw. These typically include extremes in behavior—too smart, too aggressive, too warm, or too intense.

While these and related testing instruments offer insight into personality, mental ability, and skills, none are substitutes for a detailed and structured performance-based interview. Conducted properly, the two core questions reveal all of the traits as they relate to the candidate's actual on-the-job performance. If you dig deep into a candidate's accomplishments over an extended period of time, you'll observe leadership, initiative, team skills, motivation to succeed, dependability, cultural fit, and character, as well as every other important behavior and competency. Better yet, you'll be able to observe how these traits and behaviors have changed and developed over time. Testing can then be used to confirm this.

In the case of hourly or entry-level positions, tests that address reliability and basic skills are very useful in separating qualified and unqualified candidates if the candidate pool is large. There are also tests available that assess drive, the need for achievement, honesty, dependability, the ability to influence others, team skills, selling skills, and other important core competencies. As long as they don't cause adverse impact, these tests are worth considering, with one big caveat. You don't want to use them too early in the hiring process when good people aren't convinced it's worth their time. This unintended consequence means the only people who take the test are the ones you don't want to hire. A little up-front marketing regarding the positive aspects of the job and the career opportunities available can minimize these problems. For experienced staff and management positions, tests like these are less useful when they're conducted before the initial interview, but they're very useful when a candidate is sold on the job. There are many changes going on in how these tests are delivered and when, to make them more palatable to top performers. However, the information derived from these tests has not changed much over the years, nor have they improved the predictability of the hiring decision.

■ PERFORMANCE-BASED INTERVIEW: PUTTING IT ALL TOGETHER

While the performance-based interview should represent the heart of the hiring decision, it needs to be supplemented with the other tools described in this chapter. If you prepare a performance profile, conduct a performance-based interview, and conduct a formal, deliberative debriefing session, you'll be about 75 percent accurate in predicting on-the-job performance. Better yet, if you go out of your way to avoid hiring Level 2s (see Chapter 5 on using the 10-Factor Candidate Assessment template), you'll stop hiring underperformers. You'll be able to push overall predictability and job fit into the 80 percent to 85 percent range if you add the reference checking, background verification, take-home problem, and a cognitive skills assessment into your hiring process. If you do this consistently, you will never be accused of negligent hiring. You might want to add some type of personality-style test into the mix. This might help you avoid some mistakes, particularly if it indicates some extreme in behavior, but be careful here. You might inadvertently eliminate a good person for bad reasons.

Table 6.1 provides a summary of the interviewing and assessment techniques described throughout this book. Implementing all of these steps will minimize the two big classes of hiring mistakes—hiring someone you shouldn't have and not hiring someone you should have. Avoiding both problems will make a huge impact on your overall hiring effectiveness.

Of all of the techniques suggested here, the most important is the preparation of a performance profile before interviewing any candidates. When everyone on the hiring team knows what they're looking for, there is a natural tendency to ask the right questions. The other half of this is the implementation of a formal debriefing session where all interviewers share the information gathered during the interview. The 10-Factor Candidate Assessment template is a great tool to collect this information. Most people learn how to interview properly after they have been through a few sessions, when their inputs

Table 6.1 Interviewing and Assessment Checklist

Tool, Technique, or Test	Impact and Comments
Prepare performance profile	Real job needs must drive the assessment process, not behaviors, skills, and competencies.
Increase objectivity—wait 30 minutes	Put the impact of first impressions in the parking lot in order to increase objectivity.
Performance-based interview	A structured interview digging deep into a person's accomplishments is the foundation of an accurate assessment. Use the interview to collect information, not to decide yes or no.
10-Factor Candidate Assessment	This form integrates competencies, behaviors, and skills in a logical way to assess the candidate's match with the job needs described in the performance profile
Implement formal debriefing—No 2s!	Require evidence, not feelings, to reject or move ahead with every candidate.
Panel interviews	Weaker interviewers can be involved as observers, while automatically increasing everyone's objectivity.
Reference checking	To make reference checking worthwhile, get details to justify generalities and glowing statements.
Take-home problem solving	A great job simulation technique that also gets at thinking, visualization, and teamwork.
Cognitive skills test	Intelligence is a good predictor of job success, but don't put in some arbitrary cutoff. Also, be sure it doesn't cause adverse impact.
Personality assessment	Use it to confirm everything else. Never use it to exclude people from consideration.
Skills testing	This is a valid indicator of job success as long as the skills tested are required for on-the-job performance.
Drug testing and background verification	Cheap insurance to avoid hiring the walking lawsuit. You'll also be able to validate the info on the application and the resume.
Behavioral assessments	Tests that measure achievement and dependability are useful for hourly and entry-level positions.

have been challenged by the better interviewers. A panel interview can help accelerate this on-the-job training. However, without an understanding of real job needs, all of these tools and techniques won't help all that much. Too many people use these tests as substitutes for conducting a thorough performance-based interview. They are not replacements; they are supplements.

My philosophy is that you should try anything and everything to increase your assessment accuracy. The additional few hours to get it right are worth the investment. Just conducting the performance-based interview with the candidate at different times of the day in different situations will help. I know one CEO who conducts three different interviews—one in the office, one during a meal, and one in a social gathering. He gains something from each change in setting. Personality and style are revealed in a natural fashion this way. I learn a great deal about my candidates during casual phone conversations scheduling meetings and negotiating offers, even when talking with a spouse or children. Don't base the hiring decision on one interview by one person. Use the combination of all of the techniques presented in this chapter to increase the accuracy of the assessment.

HOT TIPS FOR MAKING AN ACCURATE HIRING DECISION

✔ The one-on-one interview is not a complete means to get all the information you need to make an objective hiring decision. Use reference checks, panel interviews, take-home projects, and tests to understand competencies, motivation, and preferences.

✔ Always conduct reference checks. Do not accept any excuses from candidates who don't have any. Good candidates always have good references who will talk openly about them.

✔ Make sure references give many examples to prove every positive statement. Also, ask references to describe the candidate's biggest accomplishments, providing details and examples.

✔ Get at weaknesses by asking references how the candidate can improve in the technical, management, and decision-making areas.

✔ Use second interviews and other interviewers to gain more facts about past performance. Get additional examples to support

(continued)

the critical performance objectives. Forget courtesy interviews. Have other interviewers get useful examples of past performance as it relates to their specific function and need.

✔ Use panel interviews for every candidate on the short list. They minimize emotions, allow you to think rather than judge, save time, and give subordinates and weaker interviewers a chance to participate. Candidates like them since they rely on performance and less on personality.

✔ Take-home case studies are useful job simulations. One flaw with the typical interview is overreliance on spontaneous responses. The take-home project taps into reasoning, judgment, and motivation for the job. The quality of the take-home presentation case study is a better indicator of ability because it demonstrates real work, not just a discussion about it.

✔ Background verifications and drug testing are required components of any professional hiring process. Resumes are prone to misrepresentation. The background check will uncover this.

✔ Cognitive and skills testing are very useful predictors of performance, but they're not foolproof. There are some people without all of the skills who are top performers. Think about top internal candidates who are promoted into bigger jobs. Skills tests would have knocked some of them out.

✔ Personality tests are not reliable. They can be used to confirm performance, but not predict it. These tests sometimes indicate areas for additional performance-based interviewing questions or reference checking.

✔ Use a combination of interviewing and tests as part of an overall assessment process. The more tools you use, the more accurate the whole system will become. Make sure you don't lose any good candidates in the process of implementing too many tests too soon in the process.

Chapter 7

Recruiting, Negotiating, and Closing Offers

Sure, luck means a lot in football. Not having a good quarterback is bad luck.

—Don Shula

■ RECRUITING IS NOT SELLING AND OTHER MISCONCEPTIONS ABOUT THE MOST IMPORTANT PART OF HIRING

After you've made an offer, but before accepting it, your candidate is probably shopping it around, hoping to get something better. As soon as a candidate accepts your offer, she gets buyer's remorse, wondering whether she made the right decision or left something on the table. Even if the candidate doesn't have a better offer, lack of conviction when resigning sets the stage for a counteroffer. Effective recruiting makes the difference when you want to ensure that more offers get accepted and stay closed.

Here are two fundamental recruiting principles. Violate them at your peril. First, never make a formal offer until it's accepted. This way, there's no time for the candidate to shop it around. Second, provide your candidate a compelling future vision that overwhelms the past. This way, there's no chance of the person taking a counteroffer.

First, never make an offer until it's accepted.

Second, provide your candidate a compelling future vision that overwhelms the past.

Implementing these rules is what recruiting is all about. As far as I'm concerned, recruiting is the most important part of the hiring process. Everything is a wasted effort if a top candidate doesn't accept a reasonable offer. However, don't worry, if you've followed the advice in this book so far—especially the preparation of a performance profile—you've set the foundation for getting recruiting right.

Let's start this chapter with some fresh ideas about what recruiting is, and what it isn't:

➤ Recruiting is not something you do at the end of the interview. It starts at the beginning of the hiring process, when you write the performance profile and post the compelling ad.

➤ Recruiting is more about buying than selling. If you sell too soon, you stop evaluating. If the job is compelling, candidates will sell you as they attempt to convince you why they're qualified.

➤ Recruiting is more about consultative needs analysis than transactional selling. For the candidate, accepting an offer is a long-term strategic career decision based on opportunity, not a short-term tactical decision based on compensation. So don't rush it.

➤ Recruiting and closing are not about compensation, it's about opportunity. If your job is not different from the competition's, then all you have left is the money. So if you want to hire more top people, make the job bigger, not the compensation.

➤ The best candidates will never make the decision alone. Part of the recruiting process is to provide the right information for the candidate to use to persuade others.

➤ The role of the hiring manager is more important than ever. This is your ace in the hole. Use it wisely and often. Managers must be totally committed to hiring top talent and be involved from beginning to end.

➤ In the Beginning

Recruiting starts when you first contact the candidate, whether it's a compelling written ad or verbal pitch. Recruiting then continues throughout the interviewing process from the first phone screen to the final interview. It does not begin after you've assessed the candidate and decided that you want to move forward. This is too late. Interviewing and recruiting must take place in tandem. Present the compelling nature of the opportunity up front. This way, the best candidates join the initial pool of applicants hoping to be selected. If you wait, the best will either not apply or they will filter themselves out during the course of the assessment.

While you need to start at the beginning, don't rush it. Just because you think you've found a hot candidate, don't start selling within 15 minutes. Some managers think they can sell or charm a candidate into taking a job. This is not recruiting. This is selling in its worst form (e.g., think about the pushy car salesperson). It not only demeans the job and the hiring manager, but it also drives the best candidates away. And if they do stick around, you'll wind up paying unnecessary premiums. Recruiting is more about career counseling and solution selling. The key to recruiting: Create a compelling opportunity, present it early and often, and make the candidate earn the right to have it.

The key to recruiting: Create a compelling opportunity, present it early and often, and make the candidate earn the right to have it.

To do this right, the hiring manager needs a complete understanding of the job, a thorough knowledge of the candidate's competency, the person's short- and long-term career needs, and the compensation requirements. A balance among these competing issues is the key in bringing a fair deal together. This takes time and strong recruiting skills. Open and honest communication is a pre-requisite. None of this happens when you're selling. Listening is more important than talking. Listen four times more than you talk to get recruiting right.

Listen four times more than you talk to get recruiting right.

Think about the hiring and recruiting process this way. When you're sourcing, you want to put candidates in the driver's seat to get their attention. This encompasses all of the items we discussed in Chapter 3. Once you begin the screening and evaluation process, you'll put the candidates in the passenger seat, ensuring their interest and moving the process forward together. When you decide a candidate is worth pursuing, put him in the back seat. You do this by making the job so compelling and conducting the interview in such a way that your candidate can't wait to drive.

It's never about the money. It's always about the opportunity. I've been recruiting for over 25 years and training recruiters and hiring managers for over 15 years, and I've learned a few lessons along the way. One of them is that the best people rarely take the job for the money; they take it for the opportunity to meet their personal life plans, ambitions, and goals. Another lesson learned is that there is never enough money in the budget. Someone can always pay more. So never make it about the money, make it about the opportunity to become better. Great recruiting skills enable you to pull this off.

Many years ago, I worked with a very strong candidate on an as-signment with a company that had a very rigorous selection pro-cess. The candidate was excited about the prospects and went to each interview ready to sell himself on why he was the best person for the position. He didn't get it, but he tried like heck. The job be-came more appealing the more difficult it was to obtain. This same candidate was turned off by another client who started selling him within 15 minutes of the first interview. On a recent training event, one of the best recruiters in the country told me about his world-class Oracle developer who was offered a huge increase to do basi-cally the same job. He was wooed throughout the selection process, given the red-carpet treatment every step of the way. He turned the job down for far less money to do something more compelling.

Effective recruiting involves a fundamental principle of human nature that most people ignore: When you give someone the job, he doesn't want it. When you make it hard to get, he wants it more. The bottom line is that a job has more value when it has to be earned. It has less value if it's too easy to get, and you have to pay more, too. Top candidates are excited by competition, real challenges, and an opportunity to grow. Candidates sell you when they see an opportunity worth pursuing. Strong candidates are proud of their accomplishments and want their potential new boss to know all about them. This is the concept you need to use to attract top people without selling them.

If you make it too easy for someone to get the job, he or she doesn't want it as much. If you make it challenging and difficult to get, he or she wants it more.

A job is never perfect. You never have enough money, the location is never great, the best candidates generally have multiple opportunities, and there's always a chance of a counteroffer. A good recruiter or hiring manager can level the playing field. Attractive opportunities need to be presented in an open, give-and-take manner. Every step of the way requires persuasion and understanding to overcome the natural resistance to move forward. At the same time, you need to collect additional information about the candidate's competency. The first step is to position the opportunity as a strategic career move, not just another job. This shift will increase the likelihood of getting a top person to consider the idea of joining your team despite the typical problems, issues, and hurdles always prevalent.

■ WHY CANDIDATES TAKE JOBS: UNDERSTANDING AND MANAGING MOTIVATION

Understanding candidate motivation is the first step in implementing an appropriate recruiting strategy. On a very simple level, there are only two reasons why candidates look for new jobs and ultimately accept offers. One reason is a "going-away" strategy. This usually has to do with leaving a bad job situation. This could be the result of a layoff or a spouse's relocation. Recruiting is relatively easy if the candidate's current situation is weak and future options are limited. Standards are lowered based on these personal circumstances. If you find strong candidates in this position, move fast. You have a good, but temporary, advantage. Their future opportunities will change for the better very quickly.

A "going-toward" strategy is the other side of the coin and the more common reason good candidates take other positions. These people need some very compelling reasons to leave an already solid position, or to compete with other opportunities that are very attractive. It takes more effort to find, recruit, and close these candidates, but you have more time, since these people will rarely make a quick decision. This is both good and bad.

For most candidates, the underlying motivation to change jobs is usually a combination of these two strategies. It's the interviewer's job to determine the degree of both and which one is most important. Early in the interview, ask why the candidate is considering a move at this time. This gets at the going-away strategy. Then ask what the person's looking for in a new job. This gets at the going-toward strategy. The candidate typically says something like, "Looking for a better opportunity and more challenge." Then ask him or her why having these conditions met is important. This requires an applicant to think at a deeper level and often reveals true motivation. Remember what the person says here. You'll be able to use this during the closing process as you present the merits of your job.

Compare the consistency between the going-away reasons with the going-toward strategy. It makes sense if a person wants to leave a chaotic situation for more security. It doesn't seem logical though, if someone is leaving this same chaotic situation for more growth opportunity. Look for congruity at every level.

If the candidate is currently in a good situation, or has multiple opportunities, you'll need to work harder and offer more to pull the person away. This is when strong recruiting can win the hiring game for you. It starts by understanding why top candidates who have a going-toward motivating strategy decide to accept one job over another. It's usually based on these five key reasons in the order shown:

1. *The quality of the job*: This includes the short-term challenges and the long-term growth opportunities. Top people take jobs primarily to meet their needs for growth, challenge, and learning.

2. *The quality of the hiring manager*: Top people are looking for leaders and mentors. A professional interview with high standards establishes this foundation.

3. *The quality of the team*: Top people want to work with other top people. Everyone who interviews the candidate must conduct a thorough assessment based on a clear understanding of real job needs. I recently visited a major engineering and construction company that lost a number of great recent college graduates because the interviewers were superficial and "chatty."

4. *The quality of the company, especially the relationship of the job to the company's growth plans*: This is why the concept of job branding is important as described in Chapter 3. By tying the job to a major company initiative, you establish an important link.

5. *The compensation package*: As long as the compensation is competitive, you have a good chance to consistently hire top people, assuming the other factors are positive. If the compensation is too low, it's very difficult to consistently hire top people. If it's very high in comparison to the competition, then it makes the other factors less important.

➤ The 30% PLUS Solution

To get a top person to accept an offer, you will need to offer at least a 30 percent increase, but it doesn't need to all be in compensation. The biggest part of the 30 percent should be in job stretch (a bigger job now) and part can be in job growth (potential for a bigger job in the future). If the job is 15 percent bigger, you are halfway to the 30 percent objective. You can get another 5 percent to 10 percent in long-term job growth by demonstrating realistic future opportunities. That leaves 5 percent to 10 percent, which can be in the form of compensation increase. This is quite reasonable. The PLUS factor represents the hiring manager's total commitment and involvement in the hiring and recruiting process. This is critical. Top people want to work for a strong leader who can help employees grow and become better. This requires managers to personally commit to the process, staying involved from beginning to end. Managers must not delegate the recruiting and hiring process to HR. This is a strategy doomed to failure. Hiring managers must take personal responsibility for hiring the best people, involving HR, but not ceding the task to them. Collectively, this is what I call the 30% PLUS Solution. Here's the formula:

30% PLUS Solution = Job Stretch + Job Growth
+ $$ Increase
+ Manager's Total Involvement

Without the hiring manager personally describing the job stretch and job growth—which are the primary reasons the candidate accepts the offer—there is little believability or substance to the offer. That's why the performance profile is so important. The performance profile, in combination with good interviewing skills, allows the interviewer to demonstrate the opportunity gap between the candidate's current and competing positions and your open job.

Shifting the decision to accept an offer based on opportunity needs to start early in the hiring process. Suggest to your candidates that the decision to take an offer with your company should not be based on the money. It should be based on the opportunity represented by the job, primarily the job stretch and the job growth components. Back this by saying that these two pieces need to be at least 20 percent better than where the person is today in order for the candidate to stay on an upward career path. Typically, people will sacrifice this career path for money, which in the long-term is a bad decision. Go on to say that the person should turn this or any offer down, regardless of the compensation increase, if the job growth piece is not obvious. This is how you have to posture the hiring and recruiting process at your company if you want to hire more top people and minimize counteroffers and competitive offers.

The 30% PLUS Solution is not just words. You must prove it to the candidate during the interview process. This requires the recruiter, the hiring manager, and everyone on the hiring team to be fully prepared and onboard. Here's how. First, review the performance profile as part of this to extract the employee value proposition (EVP). An EVP is a clearly defined summary of the reasons a top person would want your job irrespective of the compensation. Consider why the job is important; describe some of the big challenges; link the job to some major company initiative or as part of a long-term career development plan. Also think about any new products, new strategies, or new markets as you create this EVP. Forget, "this is a great place to work." Be specific and say, "The person taking this job will lead the sales effort to open the Northeast territory, a critical part of the company's growth strategy." Your hot candidate needs ammunition to convince her circle of advisors why the job represents a great career move, even though the compensation increase might be modest.

During the interview, play it cool. Present this EVP in one-minute sound bites, using them carefully throughout the interview as you frame some of your questions. This creates interest and allows you to get the candidate excited about the opportunity as you ask the candidate about related accomplishments. Done properly, candidates will then attempt to convince you why they're qualified for your unique opportunity. You can't tell a person how great a job is. The person needs to learn it on his own. Internalizing the job this way is how you create a vision of the job based on substance, not compensation.

Telling a candidate how you're planning to grow in a certain area has great appeal if you relate it directly to the importance of the job. Statements like this establish the foundation for long-term growth and opportunity. By creating excitement, they challenge the candidate to rise to the occasion. Well-written performance objectives are sufficient to address the position needs. For example, "The new IS system will help us get control of our rapid overseas expansion programs. Can you give me some examples of when you took the lead in setting up new complex systems like this?" This type of question makes the job more important and more interesting. Follow this up with the detailed fact-finding described Chapter 4.

Emphasize the PLUS factor. Strong candidates want to work for stronger managers. This increases the likelihood that they'll grow, develop, and improve themselves if they take the job. The best evidence of this is the quality of the hiring manager's interviewing skills. Knowing the job, having high standards, asking tough questions, and openly listening to the responses in a nonjudgmental way provides insight into the manager's leadership qualities. As part of this, the manager must understand what motivates the candidate, and suggest how this job will help her grow in this area. Managers need to give specific examples of how they've helped other people in a similar way. Provide real names and describe how they have advanced within the company. Then allow the candidate to talk to them. Recruiting is much easier if the candidate has a strong desire to work for the hiring manager. This is a surefire way to overcome just about every potential recruiting problem. It is almost impossible to hire a top person to work for a weak manager, unless the manager's boss intervenes.

If done right, this multilevel recruiting approach will overwhelm all competing opportunities. It needs to be planned out beforehand and integrated into the performance-based interviewing process. While there's a tendency and a need to attract and pursue great candidates, going overboard will usually misfire. Good recruiting provides the balance by making the job worth having and worth earning.

Before you start meeting candidates, prepare a table like Table 7.1, which we did for a marketing manager for a software company. This sets the stage for the multilevel recruiting process we recommend.

Differentiating the job is how you beat out the competition. Someone else will always be able to offer more money.

Present this information in pieces throughout the course of the interviewing process. Some of it can be told directly while asking questions. Some of it can be included in the performance profile given to the candidate, or it can be in the form of literature, an informative web site, conversations with others who have worked for the hiring manager, or during a tour. Surprisingly, most companies do a very poor job with this. If you don't constantly build up the im-

Table 7.1 Creating the Employee Value
Proposition—Software Manager

The Job	The Hiring Manager	The Company	The Hiring Team
Critical game-breaker position—owns the product line	Strong leader and background with one of top software companies in the United States	Financially sound company, creating new vision to move into new market space	Top software developer from primary competitor has recently started
Establish product road map using latest technical advances	Great leadership style, allows subordinates to take on new challenges and grow fast	Has publicly committed resources to grow market share in this segment	The product marketing team is strong and looking for an outstanding team leader
Push the envelope from a product usage and application standpoint	A real team player, has demonstrated ability to build great teams everywhere	Strong executive team with relevant experience	Manager's staff largely in place with a few key openings
High visibility position working closely with progressive marketing team	Has been promoted based on successfully developing the company's core line	Solid compensation plan; bonus and equity based on performance	New software group recently established with key managers supporting this new project

portance of the job, the quality of the company, the quality of the hiring team, and the strength of the hiring manager, all you have left is the compensation package. Differentiating the job is how you beat the competition. Someone else will always be able to offer more money. Very few can offer a better job without a great deal of deliberative thought.

■ CREATE THE OPPORTUNITY GAP BY ASKING CHALLENGING QUESTIONS

The opportunity gap is the difference between your opportunity and the candidate's current job and competing offers. It's the combination of job stretch and job growth. Your goal is to use the interview to create this opportunity by asking questions, not by talking. One way to do this is by prefacing your questions with a set-up using some of the information from the EVP. For example, "We're creating an advanced line of industrial lubricants that will dramatically reduce machine maintenance costs. This will be backed by an extensive advertising campaign. We're looking for some top industrial salespeople to handle the Fortune 100 market. Can you give me some examples of your most comparable sales accomplishments?" This type of opening allows the interviewer to describe the strategic or tactical importance of a task before asking the candidate to describe a related accomplishment. Recruiting questions like this are effective because they create interest by demonstrating the importance of the job. Candidates then go out of their way to demonstrate their competency and interest. This is how you put the candidate into the passenger seat. They want to go along for the ride.

Challenging questions are another way to create interest by pushing the candidate away to see whether the candidate pushes back. This is how you put candidates in the back seat. For example, "While I like your background, I'm concerned you don't have enough experience in developing international accounting systems. Have I missed something? If not, can you describe something you've accomplished that you feel is most related to our needs?" This slight challenge increases the importance of this skill and requires the candidate to sell the interviewer. This approach, used judiciously throughout the interview, can increase a candidate's interest in a job. If the concern is valid, it demonstrates areas where the candidate can learn and grow if she were to get the job. This is how you use the interview questions to establish the opportunity gap.

Often applicants self-select under this type of questioning pattern. If the job represents a clear career move, you'll sense the candidate's excitement and tenacity by how hard she pushes back. If the job is too challenging, she'll exclude herself from consideration.

Use caution with challenging questions, which may be perceived as abrasive when carried to an extreme. The goal is to be inquisitive, not inquisitorial. A compliment can offset the concern. "While you have great experience in consumer marketing, it appears you haven't been exposed to industrial products. Can you describe some comparable task where you believe your marketing expertise can be transferred to our industry?"

Recruiting and challenging questions can also be combined by mentioning the importance of a task and raising a concern about the candidate's apparent lack of skills in this area. For example, "Developing the international market is essential for us in achieving our three-year plan. From your resume, I'm concerned you don't have enough European experience to handle this. Describe some of your international background so I can better understand how it might fit."

The recruiting and challenging questioning techniques are essential tools if you want to attract the best. Candidates need to learn for themselves why your opportunity is more than just another job. You can't talk them into a job; they must own it for themselves. They do this as they attempt to convince you their skills are adequate. In the process, they are also convincing themselves about the true merits of the job. This will be a vital factor when the candidate has to decide which offer to take or to ignore the temptation of a big counteroffer. When they own the opportunity gap, they can provide evidence to their circle of advisors, their boss, their current associates, and other recruiters as to why they choose your job over everything else available. If the opportunity gap is big enough, the compensation only needs to be fair.

■ END THE INTERVIEW ON A POSITIVE NOTE

As described in Chapter 4, the hiring manager should use the following as the last question at the end of the first interview. It's a must for all strong candidates:

> "Although we're seeing some other fine candidates, I'm very impressed with your background. What are your thoughts now about this position?"

For those candidates you like, this is a good way to test their interest at the end of the first interview. By stating that you have other strong candidates, you create supply and make the job more desirable. Candidates believe the job is less valuable if there are no other candidates. By creating competition, you also have more leverage as you negotiate offers. For example, if you decide to discuss salary as a precondition to coming in for a second interview, you can suggest that the person is a bit lighter than others you're considering. Despite this, you want the person to come back in with the proviso that the salary increase might be modest when taking into account the difference in experience.

The positive affirmation in the closing statement is also important. This feedback tells the candidate she's in contention. She'll think more about why she wants the job this way, not why she's not going to get it. This supply-demand implication is the set-up for asking about interest, which is what you really want to know. You want to understand their true interest level and uncover any possible concerns. If any concerns are voiced, acknowledge them and suggest that they will be discussed at a later meeting or discuss them briefly at this point. Also suggest that the candidate call you back if she has any questions or needs more information. This is a good way to put the PLUS into the 30% Solution. This open two-way exchange of information will become more important as you move the hiring process forward.

If a candidate balks at some point and does not want to move forward, it's okay to try to convince the candidate, but don't push it too hard. Tell the candidate that while you want to convince her that this is a great opportunity, you'll still need to complete your assessment. This approach allows you to strongly present your position, while maintaining underlying control. Often, an interviewer will move too fast after a candidate has been persuaded in the traditional way, forgetting that the evaluation process is not yet completed.

■ HOW TO NEGOTIATE AND CLOSE OFFERS

We're now ready for the second interview. One of the short-listed candidates will ultimately be getting an offer, so you have to be careful here. The techniques in the following section have been designed to make sure that the closing process moves along as smoothly as possible.

Don't start too soon or wait too long to talk about salary. The best time is when both parties are somewhat serious, but well before completing the assessment. A preliminary discussion can take place after a good 30-minute phone screen, but it's even better to wait until the end of the first interview. In fact, if you can, wait until you're scheduling the second interview to begin a discussion about salary in vague terms. If you don't have much room, then you might want to say that the person is close to the top of your range, and then introduce the 30% PLUS Solution concept. Your goal here is to put compensation aside and present the idea that it's still worth moving forward to determine whether this is a true career opportunity. Explain that it makes sense to at least evaluate it, especially if it could be demonstrated that the job is 20 percent bigger. Don't waste your time if the phone-screen results indicate that the job represents a lateral move.

The financial considerations are rarely the reason why a deal falls apart. In the past 20 years in my search firm, with over 1,000 different salary negotiations under our belts, less than 5 percent fell apart because of compensation. This was the basis for one of our primary recruiting rules: keep the person focused on the importance of the job even if the salary demands seem out of whack. Candidates are always more realistic after they understand the opportunity, and companies are always more flexible when they meet a strong candidate. I had one candidate for a COO position for a $500 million company who wanted 50 percent more than my client desired. We kept the process going forward despite this huge difference. By the end, both parties thought the fit was perfect and basically split the difference. This deal would never have come together if salary had been used as a yes/no filter instead of just an important discussion point. When it comes time to accept an offer, compensation is number five on the top five reasons why candidates accept offers. When you first call, it's number one. So don't talk about it first, and even if you have a problem, suggest it's still worth continuing exploratory conversations.

Under no circumstances should you wait until the end of the assessment process to begin negotiating the offer package. You've lost complete control of the process if you do, since by this time the candidate knows she's the only one left in consideration. To prevent this, discuss portions about the final offer at every step in the interviewing process and get agreement along the way. For example, "Our compensation structure is heavily based on bonus, with a low starting base salary. Is this something you would consider as we move on to the second round of interviews?" This type of approach minimizes the awkwardness of the typical negotiating session when everything is put on the table all at once and at the end. The key is to negotiate the offer and get some concessions along the way. You have more leverage this way. It's also more difficult for the candidate to backtrack if she's already agreed to move forward. You can negotiate every aspect of the offer this way and it's a great way to test sincere interest at each step. Using this parallel approach, you'll be assessing the candidate's competency at the same time you're recruiting and structuring the deal.

One of my associates used this approach a few years ago in negotiating an offer with a product manager for a health care products company. The candidate was very interested in the position after the first interview, and our client wanted to move quickly. We told the candidate that she was one of three people being invited back for a second round of interviews and the salary range was only slightly more than her current level. The job was an excellent career move for her and she agreed to return, understanding that if she were to get an offer it would be at a small increase. After a few more rounds of interviewing, it was clear she was the finalist and at that time upped her financial demands. We held firm though. We indicated to her that one of the reasons for proceeding was her prior agreement to continue the interview process knowing the tight financial situation. Although we didn't have any other candidates, we told her she would have to drop herself from consideration if she wanted to push the salary issue. She relented and accepted an offer consistent with our earlier discussions. This deal would have fallen apart or have become very uncomfortable if we hadn't discussed salary right after the first interview.

You must ask about salary history if you don't know it before you invite the candidate back for a second interview. If it's too high or if you have little room to maneuver, state your concern and ask whether this is a serious issue. Unless there's too much resistance, urge the candidate to come back in. Tell the candidate that while the salary could be an issue, the real evaluation will be about job stretch and job growth. Suggest that there might be other financial methods to compensate for a modest increase. On a recent director of marketing search, the candidate was given an early review and a significant sign-on bonus to compensate for a lateral move compensation-wise.

Use each subsequent interview session to gain more buy-in. If you sense sincere interest after the second interview, mention to the candidate what still needs to happen to get to an offer stage. This could consist of background and degree checks, reference checks, psychological testing, additional interviews, and a medical exam to ensure a drug-free workplace. Going forward is tacit acceptance to these conditions and the high likelihood the candidate is being honest about his interest and background.

The benefit package can either be used as a lure, or a way to relay nonpositive information if it's weak. Much of these discussions can be part of casual conversations as you're arranging other meetings. "Since we're growing, our benefit plan isn't as comprehensive as some of the larger companies." This way, by the time you're ready to make an offer, many of these potential deal-breaking contentious details have already been addressed.

A number of years ago, I had a strong candidate for the CFO position of a southern California-based retail-store chain. After his second interview with the CEO, I told the candidate the salary range (only a slightly higher percentage over his current package) and the next steps in the evaluation process. This consisted of a meeting with two board members on the East Coast, a half-day session with an industrial psychologist in the Midwest, and then a dinner with the chairman. This was before the medical and drug test, and a final meeting with the CEO. The candidate was very interested, but when he agreed to continue this arduous process, I knew the deal was almost done. Three weeks later, we finalized the package exactly as described. The candidate's decision to go forward under the conditions described was ample evidence of commitment and interest in the job. This is a great model on how all offers need to be tested.

■ STEP-BY-STEP THROUGH THE OFFER

Even though some of the components of an offer have been discussed, do not rush into presenting a formal offer until after completing the interview. You have fewer options then if the candidate responds, "I have to think about it." Once you make the formal offer, the applicant is now the buyer and the company the seller. This is a huge tipping point. At this point, open and honest communication stops. With an offer in hand, candidates stop thinking about why they want the job and now start thinking about why they don't want it.

Ample time to think about accepting an offer is fine, but you need to provide this time before the formal offer is extended if you want to get unbiased feedback. If you present the formal offer too soon, your attempt to find out the candidate's position is perceived as harassment, pushiness, or overselling. Negotiations then become awkward and stressful, with neither party wanting to lose face. Deals often fall apart at this point for petty reasons.

Never make a formal offer until every aspect of the offer has been tested and agreed on beforehand.

Never make a formal offer until every aspect of the offer has been tested and agreed on beforehand. Test offers every step of the way to gauge general interest. The following question allows you to differentiate between the job and the offer: "Assuming we can make an attractive offer, how does the job and challenge appeal to you?" This allows you to address any concerns about the job first. You'll eliminate many bad fits this way. You can also say, "Forget about compensation for a moment. Based on what you know now, is this a job you find worthy of serious consideration?" This is how you put compensation in the parking lot.

Compensation should not be the primary reason a person takes your job. You'll never be able to build a great team that way. By starting with job fit, you'll also be able to make the financial consideration a secondary component of the offer. Salary negotiations are usually easy if the candidate wants the position for personal growth reasons. Go back to this throughout the negotiating process if you get in trouble later on. Find out why the candidate really wants the job and be sure to remind him about these points often.

"We're thinking of putting an offer together for you, but we'd like to know your thoughts now about the job," is a good way to make a preliminary offer test. Use a trial close to get more specific. Something like, "What do you think if we could put a package together in the range of $_____ to $_____?" works well. You'll need to go back and forth with the candidate to test this range, but this gets both parties to start talking in an open manner. Add some competition, such as, "Although we're still seeing other candidates, I believe you'd make a great addition to our team. What do you think about something like . . . ?" Competition adds strength during the negotiating phase and makes the candidate more realistic. As mentioned earlier, you can also suggest that you like the person because of his potential, but to put an offer together you can't be as aggressive on the compensation side. Then explain how this will be balanced by more job stretch and job growth. On this basis, the candidate would then be able to command a bigger increase in a year or two.

Use a checklist like the following to test all aspects of the offer as you proceed through the interviewing process. Done properly, the candidate will have ample time to consider all aspects before the formal offer is presented and be ready to accept your offer within 24 hours. Cover each aspect shown in the following chart:

Target Offer	Summary Details	Test/ Agree	Objections/ Comments
Salary			
Bonus			
Car			
Other cash comp.			
Title—Position			
Benefits package			
Options			
Relocation package			
Next review			
Other			

Here's the basic question to use as you test components of the offer. "As part of a final offer, we're considering a relocation package that consists of [describe]. Is this consistent with your expectations?" Hesitation on any item means there are other issues to be considered, so continue probing. Objections at this stage often are due to lack of information. Don't move forward until these have been addressed. It's much easier to make tradeoffs at this time. Give something else if you can't meet a particular need, like a signing bonus instead of a higher salary. Find out whether this item is a deal breaker if you can't accommodate the candidate: "Does this mean you don't want to move forward if we can't resolve this issue?" Work these points until you obtain agreement. You'll discover this give-and-take process is easier when a formal offer is pending rather than in hand.

■ THE CLOSE: PUTTING IT ALL TOGETHER

Once all the aspects of an offer have been agreed on, you're ready for a preliminary close. You're still not ready to present a formal offer. This type of close gets the applicant to indirectly agree to the terms of the offer. Ask, "Since it seems like we're in agreement on all of the terms, when do you think you could start if we could formalize this package in the next few days?" In classic selling terms, this is called a *secondary close*, since giving a start date indicates total acceptance of all of the terms. If the person is reluctant to give a start date, there might be a big problem, so push for a date. Without a start date, the person is most likely considering other offers or a counteroffer.

These are things you would never learn about if you make the formal offer without testing it first. With a test offer, you can then start probing if the candidate is reluctant to provide a start date. Probing will uncover any potential deal breakers and give you the time you need to address them properly. If you obtain a start date, but still have some doubts, ask the candidate to walk you through the termination process. Find out how she'll tell her boss, the likely reaction, and ask about counteroffers. Leaving a company is a difficult process for many, so provide some guidance and a helping hand.

Now you're ready for the final close, but you're still testing so don't hand over the offer letter quite yet. As you review the final terms of the offer with the candidate, ask, "If we could put this offer in writing today or tomorrow, when would you be in a position to give us a formal acceptance?" Anything other than "immediately" or "by tomorrow morning" is a cause for concern. At this point, you've negotiated all the terms of the offer, the job scope, and provided streams of information on every point. And you have given the candidate time to think about it, in detail. Acceptance is assumed since you've been discussing the offer for the past few days; the person has seen the rough offer terms in writing; and has reviewed the terms with her friends, family, and advisors. Any backtracking now needs to be met with serious concern. Try this, "I'm concerned that you're now hesitant to move forward. I thought we had already agreed to all of the points in the offer. Has something happened to change your mind?" You'll need to find out the problem and then attempt to address it.

Done properly, this testing approach is a very natural way to share information in a nonpushy manner. You do want the candidate to think about your offer and all of its implications, but this process takes place before the formal offer is extended. If the offer is fair and mutually agreed on, there is no reason why the applicant still needs to think further about it, other than reading the fine print. More "thinking about it" at this point means you have a problem. In this case, don't push; instead, step back. Hesitation to accept your offer at this late stage typically involves a counteroffer or competitive offer. If you sense this is the case, tell the candidate that you are very concerned, and that you would like to understand what's happening.

This testing process is not a high-pressure approach. Making an offer and taking a job is a critical decision for both the candidate and the company. You want to give the candidate as much time as necessary to make a well-informed decision. That's why the informal offer and testing process is effective. It allows the candidate to do her research and consult with her spouse and other advisors throughout the interviewing process. By delaying the formal presentation of the offer until acceptance is guaranteed, the company keeps the lines of communications open and stays in a stronger negotiating position. You'll gain more unbiased information this way and have more flexibility.

There is no guarantee that all offers will be accepted or that everything will go easily. Our experience has been that more offers are accepted and that difficult problems often get resolved more easily when using this process. This is largely due to the open communications aspect of the process. Neither party loses face with the testing and give-and-take discussion of all issues.

■ OVERCOMING OBJECTIONS: WHAT TO DO WHEN THINGS GO WRONG

Occasionally, the closing process hits a snag or two. This is when some of the following advanced recruiting and closing techniques will come in handy.

➤ Close on an Objection

Use this technique to validate any objection or concern. If during the later phases of testing the candidate says she's concerned about the benefits package, just ask, "I assume if we can resolve this issue, you're in a position to accept all the other terms of the offer?" This narrows down the concern to this one issue. If the candidate hesitates to agree, this wasn't the real issue and you'll have to dig deeper to find the real problem.

We had a candidate who hesitated to accept an offer, stating he was concerned about the relocation package. We then asked whether he would accept the rest of the package if we could meet his needs on this, prompting him to reluctantly admit that the problem was that his wife had a good job and really didn't want to move. We couldn't resolve this issue and we were forced to drop an excellent candidate. Without this technique, we would have spent many more hours on a useless cause.

➤ Not Enough Money

There's never enough money in the budget; someone can always pay more, especially with competition for top talent increasing almost without limit. So if you don't present the job as a major career move, you're setting yourself up to lose the candidate over money. That's why you need to put money in the parking lot early and present the job as a growth opportunity. That's also why you must test all other aspects of the offer before finalizing the financial package. This is where the 30% PLUS Solution becomes extra important. If you've told the candidate early that you'll be using the interviewing process to demonstrate that the real increase is 30 percent comprised of job growth, job stretch, and compensation, you're in a good position when it comes to the final negotiations. By the time you make the formal offer, the person needs to clearly realize that the job is bigger (e.g., bigger team, bigger budget, bigger projects) and that there is more growth opportunity (e.g., part of a new company initiative). Under these conditions, a 7 percent to 10 percent increase is fully appropriate if the final package is competitive. However, there are still some things you can do if the candidate balks during the final testing phase.

Ask the person whether she would be open to accept the offer if you could provide an early review (less than a year) as a way to compensate for a lower-than-desired starting salary. Providing sign-on bonuses is also a great way to get around internal salary limitations. Make sure you review the benefits package in detail if it's better than the competition's.

Stop the process if the candidate doesn't appear to be flexible on salary. Since you haven't made a formal offer, it's easy to state that the compensation discussed is your limit. "I don't think we can go any higher." Get confirmation from the candidate. "Are you suggesting that if we can't meet your salary needs you're withdrawing yourself from consideration?" If the answer is "yes," you can either say you'll see what you can do, or terminate the process. Often the candidate will acquiesce.

Another way to negotiate salary is to introduce competition. Even if you don't have other strong candidates, you can still use the concept of indirect competition. A few years ago, I created a salary cap on a production manager's position in the food industry by telling the candidate that if we were to go any higher on salary we would be forced to look at candidates with more experience. The salary the candidate wanted was excessive. We had enough data to show him that the higher level was more consistent with directors than managers, and he had a few more years to go before he could get to this level. With this information and our strong stance, the candidate agreed to proceed within the salary range we targeted.

Presenting an experience gap is a great way to overcome salary problems and to create a compelling opportunity at the same time. Once, I worked with a strong candidate for a CFO position at a small company. She had some great Fortune 500 corporate experience, which drove her compensation up. A move to a smaller company with a broader focus would have been an essential career move for her, but she had to give up some salary to make the move. The company let her know that they were willing to risk her lack of experience in some important areas, since she had so much potential, but they could not meet her initial salary requirements. She recognized the opportunity and agreed it was a fair trade-off. From her perspective, she was getting something more important than salary if she were to get the job. She did get the job, and stayed there over seven years.

➤ Counteroffers

You need to confront the candidate early if you sense the possibility of a counteroffer. Be wary if the candidate hesitates to commit to a start date or is vague about getting back to you with a final acceptance. Ask the candidate about the chance that the current employer would present a counteroffer after resigning. Be concerned if the responses are vague or superficial. Ask the candidate how she feels about counteroffers in general. Explore the character issues. You defuse the threat of a counteroffer by exposing it as an inappropriate means to keep an employee. The long-term relationship is often weakened when an employee threatens to leave and is then lured back with a counteroffer. Cite examples as proof. Ask how she would feel if one of her employees had to be coerced into staying with a counteroffer. This is an indirect way of exposing the lack of integrity associated with accepting a counteroffer, especially if she has verbally agreed to your offer. This is the primary reason why you want to delay the formal offer until you obtain the candidate's agreement to accept it.

Counteroffers lack the negative stigma they had pre-2000. Company loyalty is no longer a big issue. If you haven't presented your job offer as a major career move, the potential for a counteroffer being accepted clearly exists. This is where the PLUS in the 30% PLUS Solution becomes important. If your candidate has strong ties to her current boss and team members, you'll need to counteract this by establishing a stronger bond with the new manager and new team. Present your offer over lunch or dinner, inviting the spouse if it helps. Make the person feel like part of the new team during the recruiting and testing phase. Have someone other than the recruiter help the new person understand the company culture, such as the new manager or a new colleague. These relationships are very important between the time the offer is presented and accepted and when the candidate starts. Talk with the candidate every few days after an offer has been accepted, discussing the future job. This minimizes the chance of buyer's remorse by making the future less risky and more exciting than accepting a counteroffer.

Handle counteroffers in a frank and direct manner. Most counteroffers occur during the period after a formal offer is presented, but not yet accepted. It's what happens during the "I have to think about it" time period. Testing offers minimizes this problem. Since the formal offer won't be presented until all objections are addressed, the candidate is less likely to be pressured into a difficult counteroffer position by the current employer. The candidate will either have to discuss the resignation beforehand without a formal offer, or state that a formal acceptance has already been given.

➤ Apparent Lack of Promotional Opportunities

This should never come up if you've presented the job as a career move, but to be safe, don't promise a promotion as part of your recruiting pitch. This can get you in trouble if the candidate isn't as strong as expected, or if business conditions worsen. Good recruiting comes into play here since you've been describing many of the long-range opportunities within the company as part of your push-and-pull interviewing process. To reinforce this, you can say that the candidate will be given as much responsibility as she demonstrates she can handle. Follow this up by stating that promotions are given to those who meet their performance objectives. If both the company and candidate meet their objectives, these promotional opportunities will certainly develop and the candidate will be in a great position to secure one.

Describe other people under your direction who have been promoted. This demonstrates that you're the type of manager who can develop people. Your personal mentoring is an important aspect of why a candidate might take your offer despite other problems.

Again, this is the PLUS in the 30% PLUS Solution. Good people want promotional opportunities. If the candidate believes you'll strongly support her and that there are realistic opportunities within your firm, you'll do well on this point. Presenting a realistic picture of how a candidate can grow, develop, and get promoted is the heart of effective recruiting. It is also the difference between building a good team and building a great one.

➤ Job Isn't Big Enough or Not Challenging Enough

If a candidate contends the job isn't big enough, make it bigger. This doesn't mean you need to give a bigger title or larger staff. Just add more work. Adding special projects works well. Assigning one-time projects of a critical nature are a great way to expand the scope of a job. These one-time efforts provide real meat to a position and can often help sway a candidate. Find out what really motivates a candidate to excel, and then assign projects that complement this. You can also tell the candidate that you'll assign special projects as soon as he gets up to speed. Be specific, since these projects are often the reason why candidates accept jobs. If they're challenging, important, and offer high exposure and learning, they become great means to expand a job's scope. You'll be able to pick up 5 to 10 percentage points in job stretch with these projects.

Discuss the strategic and tactical importance of the position if the candidate believes it to be beneath his or her competency level. This is a very important concern and must be dealt with directly. It affects the candidate's self-worth, so don't minimize it. Titles are important. If the job title is not comparable to the candidate's previous title, make sure to discuss the comparability of the job. Higher visibility, exposure, and impact on the organization can offset an apparently lesser job. Make sure you use this technique to clarify a job's scope if it's perceived to be too small. Of course, if the job is in fact a lesser position, you could have a real problem.

Don't create artificial job stretch or make false promises. If your job is beneath the candidate's competency, either make the job bigger or tell the candidate that he's too strong for what you now have available.

➤ Hesitating to Move to the Next Step

A candidate's hesitation to come back for another round of interviews is obviously a problem, but don't give up here. This is what recruiting is all about. If the candidate is a strong contender, it's worth the effort to get the person to reconsider. First, you must figure out the problem or concern. Often, it's a lack of information about a specific issue or some rumor the candidate has heard. Frequently, candidates remove themselves from consideration for the wrong reasons, so get in the habit of testing interest after every interview. You'll uncover issues that can be easily addressed before they become deal-breakers.

At the end of the interview ask, "Although we're still considering a few other strong candidates, I believe you're an excellent fit. From what you now know about the position, how would you rank your interest level on a scale of 0 to 10?" If it's in the 6 to 7 category, ask what it would take to get to an 8 or a 9. This will tell you what you need to work on. The key to good recruiting is an open, back-and-forth exchange of information. Losing a strong candidate for the right reasons is acceptable, but often, great candidates get away because nobody bothered to find out and address their concerns.

The same problems can occur when you're inviting a candidate in for the first interview. Significant objections can often be overcome with great opportunities. Always position the new opportunity in such a manner that the candidate will explore it objectively. I remember a great candidate who wasn't interested in a director of financial planning job with a big company because it was in downtown Los Angeles and would require relocating. However, I also knew if I could just get the candidate into the first interview it was a done deal because the job represented a great career move. I told the candidate he obviously wouldn't move unless this was a top 1 percent opportunity, so it was at least worth exploring. He agreed. After the interview, he called and loudly complained. It was a great job, and he knew he was going to be moving away from the suburban home he loved. Strategically, however, it was the right move. He's now the CFO at a Fortune 500 company, launched as a result of the connections he made at this company.

➤ Lack of Apparent Long-Term Opportunity

Lack of apparent long-term opportunity is another objection that should never come up if you included some strategic objectives in the performance profile. A performance objective like "Prepare a long-term facilities plan to support annual growth of 25 percent" instantly demonstrates the strategic importance of the job and the potential promotional opportunities. A good preplanned recruiting pitch can also help. Part of the performance profile preparation involves the creation of an employee value proposition. It starts by asking why a top candidate would want this job. Ignore the superficialities and "mom and apple pie" sentimentality. Use specifics, such as leading projects to increase market share by five points, introducing new technology, or a chance to rebuild your company after a fall. Include these in the performance profile and describe them throughout the interviewing process.

As you interview candidates, describe how the job relates to these strategic needs. Again, it's best to break down this recruiting pitch into short sound bites to use as prefaces to your actual questions. Here's a recruiting preface used at the beginning of a question for an accounting manager: "The company is planning to enter Europe in a big way later this year. We see enormous growth potential in this market. In fact, we expect it to represent 25 percent of our business in three years. This is why we need a strong person to set up our complete international accounting system. Can you please describe some of your international accounting projects?" This is a much better way of forming a question than the more common, "Tell me about your international accounting experience." The recruiting preface not only sends a great message about the importance of the job, but the candidate will be more expressive and open as she sells you on why she's qualified for the position.

➤ The Take-Away to Address Hesitation or Resistance

Just as your deal looks like it's about to fall apart, your last chance at recovery begins by retracting the offer. If the candidate has many significant objections or seems to be drifting away, it might be time for some drama. "I don't think we'll be able to overcome your objections on these issues, perhaps we should just agree to stop discussing a possible offer," might do the trick. If the candidate is seriously interested in the position and wants to really work something out, he'll pull it back. This could take the form of modifying his position or just agreeing to talk some more. Since you haven't made a formal offer, the take-away technique is a great way to test a salary cap or overcome some unreasonable objection. If the candidate still expresses interest, he's basically accepted your package with modest changes. Don't use this approach more than once with any candidate, and don't use it too soon. Use the take-away when it looks like the negotiations are about to fall apart. It can be the key to breaking a stalemate.

We used this approach once with a hot product marketing prospect from a top consumer packaged goods company. The candidate was exceptional, and he knew he was the final candidate. He kept on ratcheting-up his offer demands until the situation got tenuous. I called the candidate and told him he just broke the bank. My client had just retracted the offer and wouldn't go any higher. The candidate called back within four hours to see whether he could accept the previous offer. Retracting offers is one way to get back in the driver's seat.

➤ The Push-Away to Demonstrate Growth Opportunities

This is a good approach to convert a tactical weakness into a strategic strength. By raising doubt about competency in a certain area, you can often get the candidate to push back. This demonstrates an opportunity for growth and makes a job more appealing. If the financial package is a little tight, tell the candidate this is due to her lack of skills or experience in a certain area. Here's an example: "As mentioned during the course of the interview, we're a little concerned about your lack of international experience. This is a critical area for us and will represent a great area of personal growth for you. As you develop, we'll certainly compensate you accordingly, but right now we believe the offer is fair."

Candidates will view this as a great trade-off for giving up a little salary. By setting high standards, the candidate views the job as both a good growth opportunity and as a source of added compensation, once the skills are mastered. Balance both of these aspects as you put together a complete offer package. This is an area missed by many managers in the rush to the close. When you don't know enough about the candidate and ignore this vital area, you're left with compensation as the only negotiating lever.

■ DON'T STOP RECRUITING FROM BEGINNING TO END

Don't forget the candidate after an offer has been formally accepted. There's a natural tendency to let your guard down at this point. Nowadays, you must be extra vigilant. The best always have multiple opportunities, and the deal is not done until the candidate shows up for work. This is even truer as offers are played one against the other until the best rises to the top. Again, I can't stress strongly enough that you must differentiate your job as a career move, not a compensation increase.

A few years ago, an applicant called one night leaving an urgent voice mail, "I've got a problem. We need to talk." Since this candidate had already accepted an executive-level engineering spot but had not yet started, it was an unsettling call. It seemed that the candidate was getting a tremendous counteroffer that matched the salary and included a promotion. The candidate wanted my advice. The new position was a strategic move into a smaller company, but in a more impactful position. The counteroffer was a bigger individual contributor role in a large bureaucracy. The candidate knew this, but wanted reassurance. It was after 10:00 P.M., but I got my client, the CEO, who was also the hiring manager, to call the candidate and discuss all the issues again. We re-closed the deal without any changes to the offer, just constant attention. This demonstrates the importance of the need for continuous monitoring until the person arrives on the job. Here are some ideas on how to keep the person closed after the offer is accepted:

➤ *Jointly prepare the formal transition program before starting.* Meet a few times to review the performance profile and prioritize activities. This clarifies expectations before starting and it is something all great managers do.

➤ *Give the candidate an assignment before starting.* One of my Silicon Valley clients had a candidate review the strategic and annual plan to better understand department objectives.

➤ *Meet and call the candidate regularly and update her on what's happening.* This gives the new employee a strong understanding of what needs to be done before starting.

➤ *Let the candidate see his new office or workspace.* Let him even move in some things. This allows the candidate to visualize his role and strengthens the bond to the company.

➤ *Introduce the candidate to all the staff members, either in a formal or an informal way, before the start date.* This makes her a part of the team right away.

➤ *Send over reading material and new positive information.* Get your new employee up to speed as rapidly as possible. She'll stay excited and be ready to make an impact right away.

➤ *If convenient, send the candidate to a seminar or company event before starting.* We placed a sales manager who went to a company sales meeting before starting.

➤ *Have a social event, like a dinner with spouses.* This loosens tensions and is a good way to build understanding and a working relationship.

These things will help even if there's little likelihood the candidate would renege on an accepted offer. Staying in touch with your new employees sets the stage for a great working relationship once on the job.

➤ How to Shoot Yourself in the Foot and Other Recruiting Blunders

It doesn't take much to lose a great candidate. Recruiting is important, challenging, and difficult. Don't lose all of this effort with a dumb mistake. There are enough land mines around without you creating your own. Here are some of the biggest blunders I've seen in the past 20 years (It's a good checklist of what not to do):

Recruiting Mistakes to Avoid

➤ *Don't put a damper on the job.* Don't tell a candidate that there are few long-term opportunities or that they'll have to stay in the same job for at least two or three years. Maybe you think it's true, but jobs grow and change. The best employees always seem to see their jobs expand regardless of the situation.

➤ *If you're unprepared, appear unprofessional, and ask stupid questions, you'll drive away even average candidates.* The best candidates want to work for great managers. If you know the job, ask tough questions, and listen more than you talk, you've set yourself and the company up as a place where top people work.

➤ *Don't sell too soon.* You'll sound desperate if you start talking about the merits of the job within 10 minutes. This cheapens the job, you, and the company.

➤ *Don't talk about money too soon, or too late.* In the beginning, money is only used to filter in or out candidates. In the end, it's just a negotiating point. It's better to start with small steps at least by the second interview. By the time you make an official offer, it will be already done.

➤ *Stay away from personal, ethnic, or family matters.* They're against the law and in bad taste. If in doubt, ask your HR department for advice. Candidates frequently cite these faux pas as reason to withdraw themselves from consideration.

➤ *Don't demean the candidate or go overboard on the technical grilling.* Too many technical managers think they need to hire brilliant technologists. More frequently, they dig deep in the wrong area, which sends a terrible message of what's important and what's not to the candidate.

➤ *Don't wait until the end of the interviewing process to make an offer.* You've given up your bargaining position because the candidate knows he's the only one left.

➤ *Don't wait until the end to recruit.* Start the recruiting process with the first question in the first interview. Make the job compelling and the candidate important.

➤ *Don't stop recruiting after the offer is accepted.* These are tumultuous times. Great candidates get counteroffers and competing offers. Don't stop recruiting until the candidate starts the job.

■ RECRUITING BRINGS IT ALL TOGETHER

Recruiting is vitally important. First, it allows you to learn more about the candidate than you normally would by opening the flow of communications. Second, it allows you to control the terms of the offer. Finally, it allows you to better position your open job against all competing opportunities. This is why you must have a compelling job to offer and be better at marketing than selling. To recruit the best, you need to market yourself, the company, and the job as something valuable. The candidate needs to learn enough about the job to be in a position to trade off this opportunity against all others and against short-term financial needs.

Being a good recruiter is an essential component of good hiring. It's the key to building a strong team and the first step to becoming a top manager. Every college sports coach is rated primarily on being a good recruiter. If you can get the talent, being the coach is relatively easy. But even a great coach can't compensate for weak talent. The hiring manager must proactively take on the responsibility of recruiting. No one else is going to do it. A manager's personal success hinges on the ability to first build the team. As Jim Collins points out in his book *Good to Great,** no company became great without first building the team. It starts with good recruiting.

---

* Jim Collins, *Good to Great: Why Some Companies Make the Leap . . . and Others Don't* (New York: HarperCollins, 2001).

HOT TIPS FOR RECRUITING AND CLOSING

✔ Use the performance profile to create a compelling job. A compelling job is the foundation for the recruiting process.

✔ Create an employee value proposition by asking, "Why would a top person want this job?" and "Why is it better than competing jobs that offer more money?"

✔ Recruiting is not selling; it's career counseling and marketing. Use the "30% PLUS Solution" and create an opportunity gap.

✔ The best candidates make strategic decisions when considering an offer. Long-term opportunity is more important than short-term compensation.

✔ Use the interview to conduct a needs analysis to determine what motivates a candidate to excel. This allows the interviewer to create an opportunity gap showing a clear growth path.

✔ Unless leaving a bad situation, top candidates accept jobs for five reasons: (1) the strength of the job match, (2) the leadership skills of the hiring manager, (3) the quality of the team members, (4) the connection between the job and the company, and (5) the compensation. Make sure you recruit based on these same criteria.

✔ Remain the buyer throughout the interviewing process. You don't learn anything new when you're talking and selling.

✔ Assess, recruit, and negotiate at the same time. Don't wait until the end of the interview when the candidate knows he or she is the finalist.

✔ Use the "push and pull" questioning technique to create the opportunity gap. Ask challenging and recruiting questions to stay in control, create interest, and test motivation. The candidate needs to internalize the job by answering questions, not by hearing a sales pitch.

✔ Maintain competition. A job has more appeal and you'll have a stronger negotiating position throughout the negotiations if there are other candidates still in contention.

✔ Test all components of the offer before it's formalized. Candidates won't openly talk once the formal offer is in hand.

✔ The testing process is a great tool to identify and overcome objections. If you make the offer too soon, you'll never really know the candidate's other options.

✔ Don't shoot yourself in the foot. Move slowly. Keep an open mind. Don't sell too soon. Listen four times more than you talk.

✔ Recruit from beginning to end. Stay in touch with the candidate after the offer has been accepted and until the candidate starts. Great candidates will get pursued heavily once you stop the contact.

Chapter 8

Implementing Performance-based Hiring

It must be remembered that there is nothing more difficult to plan, more doubtful of success, nor more dangerous to manage, than the creation of a new system. For the initiator has the enmity of all who would profit by the preservation of the old institutions and merely lukewarm defenders in those who would gain by the new ones.

—Machiavelli

■ IS IT TOO LATE TO MAKE HIRING TOP TALENT A SYSTEMATIC BUSINESS PROCESS?

Since the second edition of this book came out in 2002, I've asked managers and recruiters at over two hundred different Fortune 1000 and midsized companies if they've finally won the war for talent. Only a handful said yes. In a March 20, 2006, USA Today/Gallup poll, 59 percent of managers said finding and training enough good people to fill current and future requirements was their most pressing problem. Worse, I can't find one company making the claim that things look like they are going to get better. This doesn't make any sense. Just consider the following major changes that have been implemented over the past 10 years:

➤ Technology is far better, when you consider the Internet, new advanced search techniques, candidate tracking systems, and automated employee referral programs.

➤ Companies now have in-house recruiting departments designed to compete with outside search firms staffed by experienced third-party recruiters (i.e., people who have agency experience).

➤ Companies have outsourced the entire recruiting function.

➤ New job boards have emerged for every niche market, and the major job boards have added a host of new features and functions.

➤ Managers have been trained in behavioral interviewing.

➤ New assessment tests have been introduced to prevent unqualified people from ever entering into your hiring process.

While all of these new programs have been tried, things haven't gotten any better on a sustainable level. The market for top talent is competitive and most companies haven't moved fast enough to get their fair share. Many companies have been misled, and they are trying to solve the wrong problem. While the old problems linger, new ones are cropping up. Whatever the cause, the complaints I hear today seem no different from the ones I heard 5, 10, or even 20 years ago. Based on current economic and workforce trends, I predict that hiring top talent will become far more difficult in the future than it is today. Unless something dramatic is done, the complaints will increase. Here's why:

➤ *Demographics and the aging workforce.* Baby-boomers are starting to retire from their primary jobs. The X and Y generations have different work experiences and different attitudes toward work than those they're replacing. On one level, the replacements are less than 1:1, both in quantity and in skills. The attitude change is more severe. Although I've seen no change in work ethic, the attitude part shows up as a decrease in company loyalty, more independence, a freelancer mentality, and an increased chance the person will leave a job when things get a little rough. Before the dot-com boom, most minor work-related problems either worked themselves out or people just suffered through. This is no longer the case. Few barriers to leaving a company now exist. All of these factors are having a profound effect on increasing workforce mobility. Few companies have built this huge demographic shift into their workforce planning models, nor have they addressed the accelerating increase in turnover this shift will cause. Worse still, very few companies have a comprehensive workforce planning model into which to plug these assumptions.

➤ *The impact of China and India has not been fully taken into account.* This is where most of the talent is being created, and they're not coming to the United States. By some reports, these two countries will be producing 10 to 20 times as many scientists and engineers as the United States.* While other reports indicate that these people are less qualified than their U.S. counterparts and many can't find jobs, there is a supply of talent that will impact where and how work is conducted in the future. The real point here is that there are huge global workforce changes taking place right now that need to be addressed to handle future hiring needs.

➤ *Technology has neither kept pace with hiring needs nor has HR/recruiting kept pace with technology.* Among all the major business functions (e.g., IT, finance, marketing, sales, operations), HR/recruiting is the least sophisticated user of technology—and the gap is widening. For example, candidate tracking systems have not evolved as rapidly as other business application software.† I attribute this to the users' (HR/recruiting) inability to push vendors in the right direction, not the vendors' lack of technical capabilities. In another example, company career web sites appear to be designed by amateur marketing people with little technical expertise. How else could you explain the difficulty candidates have in finding open jobs and in applying for them?

➤ *Anarchy rules.* At most companies, hiring is not an integrated system, but an out-of-control bunch of independent

---

* Vivek Wadhwa, "About the Engineering Gap," *BusinessWeek*, Dec.13, 2005.
† These are large database systems that keep track of job requisitions and candidates at every step in the hiring process.

processes and steps. Some of these processes in fact preclude the best people from ever applying. For one thing,
most job descriptions are boring. For another, they overvalue experience instead of potential. Making matters worse,
managers all interview differently, with few making complete
assessments and many letting emotions and intuition bias
the selection. They use a silly voting system to select one
candidate over another, recruiters are seen as administration, and candidates can game the system. This is anarchy.

➤ History is not on our side. The hunt for top talent has been going
on ever since candidate supply fell below demand. Lots of
money, resources, and effort have been thrown at the problem, yet there are no indications that things are getting better. If history is a guide, there is no reason we should be able
to do any better as the circumstances become more complex. Hiring is a business challenge that requires a business
approach and a business process to solve. Few companies
have viewed this problem in this way.

Collectively, this is why hiring will not get easier for anyone
other than hot companies, with hot products, in hot markets. The
purpose of this book is to provide every company the means to hire
top talent regardless of its business circumstances or the economic
cycle. This chapter ties all of the pieces together providing some
ideas on how any company, large or small, can implement Performance-based Hiring. To make hiring top talent a systematic business process, three big changes are required in addition to
implementing Performance-based Hiring.

First, executive management buy-in is required. Every executive states the importance of hiring top talent, but few match these
words with deeds. GE certainly does. I work with Wells Fargo and
know that they do. HealthEast Care System in Minneapolis does.
And so does the YMCA. The senior executives at AIG are getting on
board, and so are those at Cognos Software, Broadcom, and Quest.
Without executive commitment, you won't have the staying power
or resources to pull it off completely. If you don't have the buy-in
yet, you'll need to leave it to a few individual managers to take the
lead. In this chapter, we describe how to conduct a pilot program to
validate the effectiveness of Performance-based Hiring. In a few

months, you'll have the proof you need to demonstrate that hiring the best can be a systematic business process with an overwhelming return on investment (ROI). This is all it will take to get the executives to buy in.

Second, you must build a hiring culture that's talent-centric. Most companies today have an administration-driven hiring process (i.e., overly bureaucratic and very rule-bound), certainly not one that's market or talent-driven. Legal compliance and compensation and benefits drive how systems are designed and what can be done or not done. In this case, maintaining the status quo and avoiding problems dominate how decisions are made. A market- or talent-driven process means that every system and procedure is designed to address the needs of top talent. While you must be legally compliant, it doesn't mean you must be boring. In an administration-driven hiring culture, managers and recruiters have to put in extra work to overcome the inertia of a bureaucratic mentality to hire top talent. This is not possible on a long-term basis.

Third, workforce planning is a prerequisite. There is no way a company can hire top people on a consistent basis unless it can forecast its hiring needs at least one year out. This is not hard. Just have all department heads submit their hiring needs by quarter during the annual budgeting process. Changes (up or down) to this forecast need to be made on a quarterly basis, adding one additional quarter so you always have one-year visibility. A dynamic workforce planning process like this provides the time needed to tap into multiple sourcing channels, driving down cost and time per hire, while increasing candidate quality.

At its core, hiring top talent on a consistent basis requires a commitment from senior executives to providing resources, establishing a talent-driven mindset, and implementing workforce planning. Put this together with Performance-based Hiring and you'll be hiring top talent on a consistent basis before the year is out.

➤ Defining and Obtaining Management Commitment

It takes more than hype and hope to define and achieve management commitment; it takes focus and effort. When I was writing the second edition of this book, I had the chance to speak to a group of

35 CEOs through the Young Presidents' Organization (YPO).* At the beginning of the session, I asked about the importance of hiring top people to their company's success. Each believed it was essential. Yet, when I asked for examples of company initiatives underway to prove the claim, there was little in the way of substance either in place or underway. One was using a personality test to screen candidates, another was trying to get all managers to use a structured interviewing process that some managers used, and a third was starting to launch a company web site for posting jobs. This was about it. This surprisingly dismal state of affairs is representative of most of the 100 midsize and Fortune 500 companies we work with every year. While the Fortune 500s have more systems in place, most aren't too sophisticated. It's still difficult for them to find and hire top candidates quickly enough before they take other offers. Many of their internal systems and processes compete with each other (e.g., a great career event with an overbearing application process), and many line managers still do their own thing despite the constant threats from HR.

Wells Fargo, however, has a very impressive Right Fit program that's being implemented throughout their organization. The focus is on hiring and retaining top performers in every position. It seems to be working. As an example, I was invited to attend one of their three-hour group interview events where potential candidates had to demonstrate their stuff to their competition. The session was run by an exceptional young woman on their recruiting team who was a remarkable spokesperson for the company. I was impressed with most of the 15 candidates present, whose ages ranged from 25 to 50, but I found out later that only two were selected. During the opening round, the candidates had to describe why they had an interest in working for Wells Fargo and how they heard about the opportunities available. Most surprising, 12 of the candidates were referred by current employees who told them the opportunities for growth were exceptional. While the compensation is fair, the real reason these people were interested in Wells Fargo was the long-term opportunity to become better in a talent-centric organization.

---

* The Young President's Organization (YPO) is a group of presidents from midsize companies.

The YMCA already had a professional hiring process in place, but during 2002 to 2003, they asked us to implement Performance-based Hiring and train their 60-member volunteer board of directors. The YMCA knows it's only by striving to ensure that the best people run their branches will they achieve their aggressive community service goals. Go to any YMCA branch if you want to get a sense of how hiring top talent impacts business performance. Neil Nichols was named CEO of the YMCA of the United States in 2006. While Neil was the CEO of the YMCA of Greater Seattle, he implemented a very professional performance management and hiring process. This is a program that any business could implement and use to improve its performance. I suspect that Neil will accelerate these efforts at the more than 2,500 YMCA branches in the United States.

Hiring the best requires a dedicated executive management team who recognizes its importance as a core business process. They also must be willing to commit whatever resources it takes to create it, and then spend the time and effort to keep it going. Hiring the best must be a process, not an event. The pilot program described in this chapter provides you with the proof needed to validate Performance-based Hiring as the appropriate foundation for this type of business process. As you'll discover, the cost is lower than you're spending today. The real value of the proof is to obtain and sustain the commitment. Too many people in HR and recruiting somehow overlook this core business concept.

➤ Create a Talent-Centric Culture by Treating Candidates as Customers

Over the past 15 years, I've worked with hundreds of companies from small start-ups to those in the Fortune 100. Every one of these companies contends that they are focused on hiring the best, but when you peel the onion and see what goes on each day, it's very clear the processes don't match the rhetoric. Being talent-centric means that managers will willingly meet a candidate at inconvenient times, similar to how a sales representative would meet a customer. Being talent-centric means managers would be willing to invest their time conducting exploratory meetings with any candidate their recruiter suggested, and these same managers would allow their recruiters to set up interviews without any approval required. Being talent-centric means the company would invest as much money, time, resources, and talent in designing their career web site and writing compelling job descriptions as it does in advertising and marketing its products. On these measures, I suspect that hiring top talent doesn't even make the top-10 list of company priorities.

I had a chance to work briefly with Susan Burns when she was the director of recruiting for Federated Department Stores (the parent company for Macy's and Bloomingdales). Looking at the company web site gives you the sense you want to work there. Their career section is easy to find and compelling, and candidates can automatically schedule interviews with managers once the recruiting team has conducted a phone screen. This is the essence of a talent-centric culture—treating candidates as customers. According to Susan, they must, because their customers could be their candidates that afternoon. In companies where their employees work directly with the customer—like retail, restaurants, and hospitality—they tend to naturally treat their candidates with more respect. This idea of the "candidate is customer" is foreign to companies where few employees ever talk to customers. So if you want to start seeing and hiring stronger people, adopt some of the ideas you use to get more customers.

Understand How Top People Make Career Decisions

If you want to hire more top people, recognize that the time they invest in looking for a new opportunity is minimal. To address this constraint, publicize your jobs well and promote them quickly. Recognize that top people have multiple opportunities, so during the interviewing process you need to recruit and assess the candidate in tandem. Then, when you're negotiating the final offer, eliminate the competition and minimize the chance your hot prospect won't take a counteroffer. After the offer is accepted, you must make sure the candidate shows up, performs at peak levels while on the job, and doesn't leave prematurely for some better opportunity. This is not easy to pull off, but it's what it takes to hire and retain top people on a consistent basis.

The best people are more selective and more discriminating. When considering new opportunities, they balance short-term considerations with long-term opportunities. This is true whether they're active, passive, or in-between. If you want to make hiring top talent a systematic business process, redesign each step from beginning to end to address the needs of these best people. Unfortunately, most hiring processes today are designed to meet the needs of candidates actively looking for work and are based on criteria established by lawyers, compensation and benefits, bureaucratic rules, regulations, and administration-driven thinking. In Chapter 3, the point was made that there were five decision factors the best people use when evaluating career opportunities, including:

1. *The job match*: This included the short-term challenge and the long-term growth opportunities.
2. *The quality of the hiring manager*: The best people are looking for leaders and mentors to help accelerate their career growth.
3. *The quality of the team*: The best people want to work with other top people.
4. *The quality of the company*: The company doesn't have to be an industry leader, but it does need solid prospects and a plan to get better.
5. *The compensation plan*: As long as the compensation is in the upper third and the job provides real opportunity, compensation will not be the primary criteria.

When you put the job first, compensation won't be the determining factor in accepting or declining an offer. Shifting the decision criteria from compensation to opportunity is at the core of a talent-centric hiring model.

Offer Careers, Not Jobs
You don't need to compete on compensation if your job represents a strong career move for the candidate, and the manager and the hiring team are all professionals. Being talent-centric means that you don't post traditional job descriptions or conduct an interview if you're unprepared. This is equivalent to winging it during a product

presentation to a new customer. That's why every member of the hiring team, especially the recruiter and the hiring manager, must understand real job needs as described in the performance profile. With this, you can then use the interview to create an opportunity gap. As described in Chapters 4 and 7, this is the difference between the job stretch and job growth in your job and every other opportunity. Establishing this opportunity gap is how you negotiate on growth and challenge, not compensation.

The best candidates always have multiple opportunities. They want the best job available, or a significantly advanced role. Most jobs ads describe skills, duties, and responsibilities, but not exciting career challenges. This precludes the best from even applying. Writing performance profiles rather than job descriptions is the first step. Creating an employee value proposition (EVP) comes next. Combining the profile and EVP in creative and compelling advertising is how you turn boring jobs into exciting careers. It's what people do with their skills, not merely the skills they possess, that excites and motivates them to perform at peak levels. Clarifying expectations and providing people with work they like to do is also how you improve motivation, on-the-job performance, productivity, and reduce turnover in the bargain.

Performance Matters

Throughout this book, I've made it clear that understanding the performance needs of the job is essential to finding, assessing, recruiting, and hiring top performers on a consistent basis. I'll also make the claim that the quality of a company's ongoing performance management process is the core component of a talent-driven culture. Clarifying performance expectations has been shown to be the key to motivating people to perform at peak levels.* This is equivalent to the performance profile, not the job description. Clarifying expectations by defining the deliverables is how you should hire, onboard, manage, review, motivate, reward, and promote people. It starts by defining performance for every new job. This is a clear statement of what the person must do to be successful. It's not a list

---

*Marcus Buckingham and Curt Coffman, *First, Break All of the Rules* (New York: Simon and Schuster, 1999).

of skills, experiences, and academics. The basis for a complete performance management system is in place when these performance measures are tied to the company vision and broken down by functions and departments with a performance profile prepared for every job.

Implementing a talent-centric hiring process is not an event conducted by one manager, filling one position, working with one recruiter, and hiring one person. Although you might want to start here, the process is not sustainable unless your company has embraced the idea of creating a talent-centric culture. This requires an understanding that each job must offer the person filling it both a short- and long-term career opportunity. Implementing an end-to-end performance management system, with managers being evaluated on how well they hire and retain top performers, is part of this. The most important idea, however, is to treat all candidates as new customers, not vendors, and to treat the best candidates as potential major new customers. With this mindset, redesign every aspect of your hiring processes to attract the best people possible.

➤ Implement Workforce Planning

A key part of the transformation to a talent-centric hiring model is the need to be forward-looking and proactive at every step. You can't hire a top person when your only option is to run an ad. For many companies, hiring starts when someone quits or a requisition for a new employee is approved. The next step is to call a recruiter, or to post an ad, with the hope of finding a reasonably good person within 30 days. Unfortunately, unless you have a strong employee referral program, an effective networking process in place, and a database of great candidates ready to sign on, you're forced to settle for a compromise candidate. This is far too reactive. It doesn't give anyone enough time or options to find enough people. Although you might get lucky now and then, it's more luck than logic, and certainly not consistent or predictable. Yet, this is the default position most companies use.

To give yourself enough time to select the best available person, not the best person available, you need to be constantly forecasting at least 6 to 12 months. This gives you the time to set up the advertising, networking, referral, and nurturing programs needed to find top candidates. A rolling workforce plan should forecast all hiring needs by quarter and by position for the next 12 months. Update the plan quarterly, showing all quarter-by-quarter differences to the prior forecast. These differences are early warning indicators of big changes happening, and it gives the recruiting team ample time to modify their sourcing channels and tactics. This workforce plan needs to take into account company growth plans, internal movements and promotions, planned and unplanned turnover, retirements, outsourcing opportunities, and anything else that could affect hiring needs.

Once you have the annual workforce planning process in place, push it out two to three years, tying your workforce needs directly to your company's strategic plan. This gives you the chance to consider global shifts as part of your long-term hiring plans. Examples abound here. There was an article just recently about a push to place well-trained Russian software developers in the United States. What about using the thousands of underemployed Chinese engineers who just graduated in some off-shore design capacity? Or what about using the excess nurses from Bosnia to fill critical health care staffing shortages? The point here is that if you're reacting, you're not planning. If you want to hire someone for an important position six months from now, start the sourcing process today. Otherwise, you'll be left with just a few short-term options. That's why a workforce plan is so essential.

Your current employee base should represent a critical component of this workforce plan. It's obvious that in order to increase retention and maximize productivity, a company needs to train and develop its people to handle bigger and better jobs. For new hires, this was the promise made when you shifted the acceptance criteria from compensation to opportunity. Once they're on the job, you need to deliver on your promise. Create a formal program that gives you the ability to plug people into critical spots as they become available. A program like this is similar to a succession plan, but requires an internal talent database providing visibility to the skills and abilities of your best people. When a position opens up, you'll then have instant access to this pool of top employees. With a workforce plan in place, you can even begin grooming some of them for positions coming up 6 to 12 months from now.

Hiring processes need to be proactive and forward-looking. This gives you the time to find the best candidates available. If your hiring is reactive or short-term, you have fewer options to find good candidates, and you'll lower your standards as you succumb to business pressures. In addition to executive management commitment and a talent-centric culture, a strong workforce plan is essential if you want to make hiring top talent a more predictable business process.

■ THE BASICS STEPS: IMPLEMENTING PERFORMANCE-BASED HIRING

Start small. You might not be able to obtain executive-management commitment right away. If not, offer to conduct a pilot program to use as proof that Performance-based Hiring can be the foundation for a systematic process for hiring top talent. If you've never done it, implementing workforce planning for the whole company is a huge task. For the pilot or just as a mini-test case, start working with a few hiring managers and have them begin forecasting only their critical hiring needs. This allows you to establish the process and work the bugs out before you implement a companywide workforce planning process. Select the more "with it" hiring managers who clearly understand the importance of hiring top talent. Try to use a director-level person or a vice president who is willing to try a pilot program with the goal of creating a talent-centric hiring model and culture in their department. By starting small with a pilot, you can prove the process works.

➤ Start Using Performance Profiles

As soon as you prepare a performance profile, you'll begin to experience the benefits of Performance-based Hiring. If you're a manager, just follow the guidelines in Chapter 2 to prepare a performance profile for your next open position. You might even want to prepare one for your job to get started learning how to do this. If you're a manager, make one of the objectives "build and develop a strong team to meet all of this year's department objectives." Then figure out the two or three things you have to do in the next few months to pull this off. If you have an underperforming team member, you might want to create a performance profile that focuses on what the person would need to do to improve his overall performance. Work with this person both in the preparation of the profile as well as in monitoring performance over the next few months. At a minimum, you'll have the evidence needed to remove the person if performance has not improved. Once you are comfortable using performance profiles and clarifying expectations, you'll discover that not only will you hire better people, but you will become a better manager. Communication and clarifying expectations through the use of a performance profile is how real job needs are better understood. When interviewing, too many managers cannot specify the daily requirements of the job, confusing the candidates. A performance profile is written to address actual job needs, increasing both understanding and performance.

If you're a recruiter, use a performance profile when you take your next assignment. While the guidelines in Chapter 2 are useful, I would not approach a hiring manager and ask the questions without some up-front preparation. I suggest you prepare a preliminary performance profile for the open position before you ask your hiring manager client to review it. It's always easier to edit something than to create it. There are a few ways to prepare this type of preliminary performance profile. One simple way is to benchmark some of the best people you've already placed in similar jobs and find out what they're doing differently from average people. If you really know the job, you should be able to put together a performance profile without even talking to the manager. You'll certainly come across as an expert with great job insight when you present a performance profile that's pretty close to the mark.

➤ Try Out Everything for Just One Assignment

Performance-based Hiring is a complete system that can be used for just one assignment or for hundreds. You don't have to do much to test it out for just one assignment.

Prepare a Performance Profile Highlighting the Employee Value Proposition

Whether you're a recruiter or hiring manager, as long as you both agree to the basics of the performance profile, show it to the rest of the hiring team to get their buy-in. Everybody on the hiring team needs to understand real job needs. As they review the performance objectives, ask them what's missing from the profile and what shouldn't be there. If someone starts listing skills and personality traits as requirements, ask her to describe what the candidate needs to do with the skill, so it's more measurable. This is how you make the shift from *having* to *doing*. It's also how people who aren't familiar with performance profiles quickly learn how useful they are.

Once the performance objectives are agreed on, put them in priority order. Disagreement here is okay. Spend time on this so that all interviewers understand the real job on more than a superficial level. This will be critical when you start meeting some top people. Just like strong interviewers who can see through a weak candidate, strong candidates can quickly see through weak interviewers. Understanding real job needs make all interviewers stronger.

You'll need to convert the performance profile into a compelling employee value proposition and write a creative and interesting ad. If you're a recruiter, ask the manager and the hiring team why a top person would want this job. Don't accept superficialities, hyperbole, or general statements such as, "our company is a great place to work." Focus on the meat of the job. Something like, "the person will be a key member of the design team for our major new product line" is appropriate. When you can tie the job to some major company initiative, you enhance the long-term value of the position. Read Chapter 7 on recruiting for some other ideas on how to create this employee value proposition. Part of the reason to create a performance profile and the employee value proposition is to be able to write ads that are more interesting and that influence top performers to respond. Equally as important, you'll use this information during the interview and recruiting process to clearly demonstrate that you're offering a strong career move, not just another job.

Write a Compelling Ad That Can Be Found

Now you're ready to write your ad and post it where it can be found. The secret to your success is found in the title you choose and the first two lines you write. (Review Chapter 3 on sourcing for more details.) Because you're only testing the concept out right now, push the envelope and get creative. Here's the beginning of an ad we recently put up on craigslist.org for a telemarketing rep:

Telemarketing Representative, aka, Our Clients Will Soon Become Your Best Friends

If you want to work from home, in your slippers, and don't mind calling a bunch of preoccupied people all day, you might want to check this odd job out more closely. Here's the secret: the people you'll be calling really want to talk to you, they just won't know this until about five minutes into the call. Getting to that point is what we'll train you to do. So if you're interested in learning state-of-the art selling techniques and . . .

Within one day, we received a dozen great responses to this ad. The reason we chose craigslist.org is we searched Google for "telemarketing representatives jobs Chicago" and craigslist.org showed up a few times. This is an example of how to use reverse engineering and search-engine optimization techniques to make sure your ads are found. For your case study, include your email address to get the resume right away, rather than send the person through your normal application process. This alone will expedite the process and minimize opt-outs.

Screen and Interview the Candidate Using the Basic Performance-Based Interview

In Appendix C, there are three interview templates—the Phone Screen, the Basic Structured Performance-Based Interview, and the Second Performance-Based Interview. These all involve four core steps: (1) controlling biases, (2) conducting a work history review, (3) digging deep into a candidate's accomplishment to develop a trend line of performance over time, and (4) asking some type of problem-solving question. How to conduct these interviews is fully explained in Chapter 4. You can actually use the performance-based interviewing techniques without preparing a performance profile. You should do this as a test. You'll quickly discover that much of your fact-finding is based on understanding real job needs. Peeling the onion, digging deep into a person's accomplishments, and then comparing these to what's needed to succeed on the job is the fundamental concept behind the deep job-matching process involved in performance-based interviewing.

If a person seems to have the requisite background, my phone screens generally last 30 minutes. It takes about this long to

conduct a basic work history review and to discuss one or two accomplishments. This is enough for me to decide whether I should
conduct a full interview or not. I'll then either invite the person in
for a personal interview or schedule a more in-depth 60-minute
phone interview. I've discovered that a full performance-based interview conducted on the phone is actually more insightful than a
one-on-one interview. On the phone, it's all business. In person,
there is still some relationship posturing that occurs on both sides
of the desk that affects how the interview is conducted.

When you finally meet the candidate, make sure you don't make a
decision for at least 30 minutes. If you like the person, be skeptical.
Make the person prove his answers. If you don't like the person, give
the person the benefit of the doubt. Go out of your way to prove the
person is competent. This is a good technique to mentally put your
emotions and biases in the parking lot. Go out of your way not to
judge your candidate's answers. This is hard to do, but important if
you want an accurate assessment. If you treat the candidate as a customer, you'll actually listen more closely. Use the fact-finding tips on
the interview templates and in Chapter 4 as guides on how to dig
deep into each accomplishment. Develop your own probes as part of
your fact-finding. Your objective is to paint a complete word picture of
the candidate's most significant accomplishments. If you do this for a
few accomplishments, a pattern will soon emerge showing the trend
lines of the accomplishments over time. Remember to seek balance
among individual, team, and job-related accomplishments. If the candidate talks more about individual accomplishments, ask for examples of team accomplishments using the team fact-finding probes.

Toward the end of the first interview, ask at least one problem-
solving question. Pick something relevant to the job and ask the
candidate how he would solve the problem. This should be a give-
and-take discussion with the interviewer posing realistic "what if"
type questions. Good candidates have good questions of their own,
which need to be considered in your assessment. Remember that a
problem-solving question is designed to get at thinking, creative,
strategic, and planning skills. A good answer is not necessarily the
solution to the problem, it's how the person would go about getting
the information to solve the problem. That's why the problem chosen must be job-related. This is not a hypothetical question. It
needs to be a real problem the person is likely to face on the job.

For a technical person, ask how she would solve a design problem. For a manager, ask how he would determine whether the team is adequate. For an executive, ask how she would assess the strategic direction of the company.

Getting into a real work-related discussion makes this type of questioning insightful. I've discovered that the best candidates have the ability to visualize how they would handle a major task combined with a track record of delivering comparable results. Using the most significant accomplishment (MSA) question and the problem-solving question together will get at this critical capability.

Start to Complete the 10-Factor Candidate Assessment Template

In addition to the performance profile and the performance-based interview, the 10-Factor Candidate Assessment template is one of the three core tools in the Performance-Based Hiring system. Not only does it link all the tools together, it's also useful for just about every job from entry level to chairman. If you examine the 10-Factor Candidate Assessment form in Appendix C, you'll see that the rankings are based on a comparison to the real job needs as described in the performance profile. It also incorporates standard competencies and behaviors into this performance comparison. The guidance for each of the rankings also helps in increasing assessment accuracy. These notes provide specific guidelines on how you rank the candidate on the 1 to 5 scale for each of the 10 factors. Don't be easy on yourself or the candidate as you read these and rank the candidate. You need facts to justify your rankings, not feelings.

This 10-Factor Candidate Assessment form is designed so that a Level 3 ranking is a great candidate who can meet all job needs. Hire this person, unless you find a rare Level 4 or Level 5. A Level 4 ranking is a person who consistently does more work, does it better, or does it faster than described in the performance profile. If you hire this type of person, she'll need a bigger job or a promotion in the immediate future. A Level 5 is an all-star performer who will be promoted one or two times very quickly. If you can't deliver on this, the person will quickly leave your company. The Level 1 to Level 5 rankings are very important. Don't simplistically think that your hiring problems are over if you just hire a Level 4 or Level 5 person.

While these are great people, you'll need to provide Level 4 or 5 jobs to keep them excited and on your team.

Be extra diligent when you're trying to figure out the difference between a Level 2 and a Level 3 ranking. This represents the difference between a mistake and a great hire.

Here's the biggest hiring tip of them all. Successful hiring is not about hiring Level 3s or better. It's about not hiring Level 2s. These are people who are competent to do the work, but lack the energy or motivation to do it on a consistent basis. Be extra diligent when you're trying to figure out the difference between a Level 2 and a Level 3 ranking. This represents the difference between a mistake and a great hire. The 10-Factor Candidate Assessment template and the assessment techniques described in Chapter 5 will guide you through this critical area.

Remember to use the interview to collect information, not to make a final yes/no decision. At the end of the interview, complete the 10-Factor Candidate Assessment template based on your interview, but keep an open mind. Obtain the input of the other interviewers before you decide to move forward with the candidate.

Organize Other Interviewers and Conduct a Panel Interview

Chapter 5 described how to organize and assign roles to other members of the interviewing team. In essence, just assign a few of the 10 factors to each interviewer to make sure they're all covered. Overlap is okay. These other interviewers will still use the basic performance-based interview questions, but they'll be using different fact-finding probes and following different threads as they look for different capabilities and skills. As part of the organization, assign other interviewers different accomplishments from the performance profile to benchmark during their interviews. While the structure and questions of the interview used by other interviewers will be the same, the information gathered will be different.

As long as the other interviewers know the performance-based interviewing methodology, there will be some natural self-organization going on. For example, the second interviewer could ask the candidate what accomplishments were discussed in the earlier interview and what the focus was. Based on this, the second interviewer could then ask about different accomplishments and follow a different fact-finding thread.

As part of the interviewing process, you should also conduct a panel interview. This is described in detail in Chapter 6. The key here is to assign one person as the lead interviewer with everyone else in a support position. The support people need to be actively involved in the interview, but they can only ask follow-up and fact-finding questions to clarify the candidate's initial answer. The lead interviewer asks the basic questions and is the only person who can change topics. A panel interview conducted this way prevents interviewers from competing with each other or cutting the candidate off too soon. The real advantages of a panel interview are that it allows everyone to hear the same answers and weaker interviewers can participate. It also naturally prevents emotions and biases from affecting the final assessment.

Use the 10-Factor Candidate Assessment Template as the Basis for the Evidence-Based Assessment Process

After the first complete round of interviews, everyone on the interviewing team needs to get together and formally debrief. This is described in detail in Chapter 5 on implementing an evidence-based assessment process. Disallowing a yes/no voting procedure is the first step in increasing assessment accuracy. The point needs to be made that members of the hiring team are using the interview to collect information in their assigned areas and then sharing this in the debriefing session. Consensus will be reached on all of the 10 factors before deciding whether to move forward on the candidate or not. Removing the yes/no vote option helps interviewers focus on collecting unbiased information. Here are six guidelines to follow when you conduct the debriefing session:

1. *Make the point that the interview should have been used to collect information on each person's assigned area.* The team collectively will decide yes or no after they've heard everyone's input.

2. *Go around the room, starting with the lower-ranking people first and ask only for positive information.* This way, lower-ranking people

will be more candid with their assessments and not unduly influenced by a more senior manager. Starting with positives also establishes an open environment, without people thinking they made a mistake. If you allow the negatives to come up first, it'll poison the subsequent conversation.

3. *Don't accept any superficial or general statements, positive or negative.* Conclusions must be supported by facts, details, and examples. That's the whole purpose of the fact-finding process.

4. *Use the 10-Factor Candidate Assessment template as the basis of the debriefing, starting with the first factor of technical competency.* Have someone read the descriptions of the 1 to 5 ranking. These offer clues on the evidence needed to assess a candidate. Go around the room asking for information from those people who assessed this factor. Again, start with the lowest-ranking person. Make each person justify his or her ranking based on the notes. Ignore generalities. Done properly, the range in rankings will be pretty tight, like 2.5 to 3.5. If the range is wider than this after all information points are shared, it usually means someone is overly biased or emotional.

5. *Finish up all of the other factors the same way by sharing information and reaching consensus.* This normally takes about an hour the first time you do this, and about 45 minutes once people get the hang of it. You'll also discover that people become better interviewers as a result of the feedback given during these sessions. People learn what to ask and how to gain the right information after they've had to complete the 10-Factor Candidate Assessment form a few times.

6. *Lots of questions will be raised about the candidate after this session.* These can be used in later interviews if you decide to proceed with the candidate. You'll certainly have enough information to say no after this type of debriefing session.

Complete the Assessment

If you decide to move forward with the candidate, review Chapter 6 in detail. This describes everything you need to do to complete the assessment. At a minimum, you must conduct a comprehensive background check including degree verification, employment history, credit check, and criminal investigation. Add drug testing as a requirement for all new employees. Don't forget the performance-based reference checking. Have the hiring manager conduct at least two of these, and make sure you have the reference give examples of strengths and weaknesses using the fact-finding techniques from the performance-based interview. Use these reference checks to answer any of the questions raised during the assessment process. Add in a cognitive skills test of some type, like the one offered by Profiles International. This will increase overall assessment accuracy. You might want to use some type of personality or style test as well as a confirming indicator.

Recruit and Close Using the 30% PLUS Solution

While I've saved this section for the end of this summary, you've actually been recruiting throughout the process. It started when you created the performance profile and the compelling ad including the EVP. The hiring manager and those on the hiring team demonstrated professionalism by conducting an in-depth performance-based interview. Candidates experiencing this type of process know you and your company have high standards of performance. Candidates use this type of insight when deciding to accept one job over another.

During the actual interview, use the push-pull techniques described in Chapter 7 on recruiting to create an opportunity gap. The push-away is used to challenge or question the candidate's skills in a certain area. For example, if justified, you might say you're concerned about the breadth of the candidate's international experience since this is vital to the success of the project. Then ask the candidate to describe her biggest international project. Doing this a few times demonstrates the potential for growth the candidate will experience if the person were to get the job. You can do something similar using the pull-toward technique. In this case, describe an exciting project involved in the job and then ask the candidate to describe her most comparable accomplishment. This technique is better than trying to sell the candidate into the job, since the candidate has had to justify her capabilities to handle real job needs. As long as the job offers both short-term stretch and long-term growth opportunity, you're well on your way to closing this person on reasonable terms.

Remember to explicitly use the 30% PLUS Solution as part of your closing process. The best people need at least a 30 percent increase to move from one job to another. But this does not need to be all compensation. Some of this increase can be in job stretch (a bigger job) and some in job growth (better long-term growth and better prospects). If you can get these components into the 20 percent to 25 percent range, the compensation increase only needs to be 5 percent to 10 percent. If you're constantly offering too much to attract top performers, it's usually because you haven't demonstrated the growth and opportunity inherent in the job. Don't ignore the PLUS factor, either. This represents the hiring manager's total involvement in the hiring and recruiting process. A great job and a committed manager can go a long way in recruiting top performers without compensation being the deal-breaker.

Test every aspect of the offer before you put it in writing and sign it. When you're ready to put the final package together, just ask the candidate whether she would accept the offer on the terms outlined. If she says yes, ask her when she could start. Make sure you get a specific date or you're asking for trouble. Test the offer again just before you formalize it by asking the person how long she'll take before she signs the offer. If it's anything longer than "tomorrow," don't make the offer. In this case, the likelihood is that your candidate will take a competitive offer or a counteroffer is very high.

Sophisticated recruiting is not based on hardball closing techniques. It's a professional solution-selling process that must be used if you want to prevent your top candidates from going to the competition or taking counteroffers. Don't use these techniques if your job doesn't represent a strong career move. They won't work, anyway. While you want your candidate to have the time needed to make a complete evaluation of your job, you'll never learn what's happening once you finalize the offer. This limits your options. Stay the buyer as long as possible. You do this by holding the offer back. You'll close more offers if you're the last person making your candidate an offer. This way, the negotiation can be more about the opportunity and less about the compensation.

Try It a Few More Times until You've Mastered It

If you repeat the steps as described earlier for your next three to four hires, you'll pretty much have the process worked out. By this time, you'll have interviewed about 20 or so people, negotiated a number of offers, and have had a few turndowns. Not only will you have learned a lot, but you'll have some great anecdotal evidence to use to justify rolling Performance-based Hiring out to a larger group. For one thing, you'll be able to use the 10-Factor Candidate Assessment template as a means to measure candidate quality. You'll probably also observe an increased quantity and quality of the candidates sourced just because you have been starting to use better advertising techniques. The feedback you'll get from managers, recruiters, other interviewers, and the candidates themselves will help you hone the process. You might even notice that the accuracy of the assessment has increased because your new employees will already be working at higher levels. This should be enough to roll the process out to a bigger group in a more controlled pilot program test.

➤ Conduct a Pilot Program to Validate the Effectiveness of Performance-based Hiring

Every person who interviews a candidate for your company should be using the performance-based concepts described in this book. This process consists of three core tools—a performance profile, a structured performance-based interview, and a formal debriefing process using the 10-Factor Candidate Assessment template. If hiring top talent is the most important thing a manager can do to be successful, this does not seem like too much to ask. I contend that there is no simpler or more effective process around anywhere. Proving this is the reason you need to conduct a pilot program. Here are the primary objectives you'll be able to prove with this type of trial run:

1. Source stronger people and more diverse candidates for all positions.
2. Increase the accuracy of the interviewing and assessment process.
3. Minimize hiring mistakes.
4. Improve on-the-job satisfaction and performance while reducing turnover.
5. Obtain manager acceptance, from the first-line supervisor to the executive level.

6. Provide evidence that the process meets or exceeds all legal guidelines and minimizes liabilities.

7. Demonstrate suitability for all jobs from hourly and entry-level positions to senior management.

8. Make the business case that the cost of implementing the program is insignificant on an ROI basis.

This is quite a list, but conducted properly, you can validate the effectiveness of the pilot program in about six months.

Organize the Pilot Program and Validate the Creative Sourcing Program

Because you want to validate the process for different jobs, select managers from a number of different departments who have some significant hiring needs. Select managers for the pilot who are more forward thinking, open to change, and able to recognize the importance of good hiring decisions. You'll first need to prepare performance profiles for all of the open positions involved in the pilot study, plus write some creative ads. Break the pilot into two distinct parts, one focusing on sourcing and the other on interviewing and recruiting.

Start the pilot with 20 different managers and 20 different jobs. You'll probably be interviewing six or so candidates for each job, so this will be about 120 different candidates in total. Each candidate will probably be interviewing with two or three different people, so this in total will be about 250 to 400 different interviews. Keep a 10-Factor Candidate Assessment template for each of these individual interviews and also the combined group assessment. This will be enough information to develop accurate statistics and validate the process.

To validate the sourcing process, try out everything described in Chapter 3. If completed properly, the 10-Factor Candidate Assessment template provides a good measure of candidate quality. Using this, you can then track candidate quality to determine which sourcing channel provides the best candidates. To do this, put a table together with a column for the candidate's name and one for each sourcing channel you use to find candidates. In the first column, put the candidate's name and put the person's 10-Factor average score in the column representing the sourcing channel the candidate used to find the job. At the bottom of the column, show the average score and the spread. From this, you'll quickly see which channel produced the best candidates.

As part of the pilot, post some boring ads and compelling ads side-by-side to see the difference in pulling power between the two. Next, add a web analytics package to your career web site and start tracking opt-out rates at every step. This instant feedback will allow you to redesign each sourcing step to maximize the number of candidates who stay involved in the process. Use some of the search-engine optimization techniques described in Chapter 3 to push your advertising out to the right audiences and the right boards. These techniques, plus some compelling advertising, will increase your share of the strong semi-active candidates who use online techniques to find jobs.

As far as sourcing passive candidates, I'd restrict the pilot program to implementing a proactive employee referral program. To do this, ask the managers involved in the pilot program and their current team members to identify all of the best people they've ever worked with in the past. Then, begin contacting and recruiting these people for your open positions. Since you already know they're strong, you won't be wasting time targeting the wrong group. If the first group of referrals isn't interested in pursuing your open opportunities, get the names of other strong candidates from this initial group. These changes in your sourcing tactics will give you enough good candidates to begin validating the performance-based interviewing and selection techniques.

Validating the Interviewing and Assessment Methodology There are a few simple ways to validate the interviewing and assessment process. One way is to have the managers involved in the pilot program prepare a 10-Factor Candidate Assessment template for all of their recent hires using their actual performance to make the rankings. This will help you gain a sense of the quality of their past hiring decisions. Then, compare the prehire scores for all of the new people hired in the pilot program to the rankings of the past hires. Although rough, this does provide some insight in comparing the quality of past and current hiring decisions.

While this will get you started, the basic technique used to validate Performance-based Hiring is to compare the prehire 10-Factor Candidate Assessment results to the person's actual on-the-job performance using the same 10-Factor form. You can do this as early as 60 days after the person starts. You might want to do it again a few months later if 60 days is too short a period. With this data, you'll be able to calculate the actual correlation between the pre- and posthire 10-Factor scores. You can also compare how well individual managers did, as well as whether the group assessment was a better predictor.

Due to all of the variables involved in your company, your statistics might vary. That's the reason you need to conduct your own pilot and develop you own data. However, conducted properly, the performance-based interviewing and selection process should increase the overall predictability of the hiring decision into the 75 percent or better range. It will be in the 80 percent to 85 percent range if you conduct all of the background checking and testing as suggested in Chapter 6. This is very consistent with what the Hunter and Schmidt metastudy predicted. The data from your pilot program should be enough to validate the Performance-based Hiring on the eight core measures mentioned earlier.

You may choose to modify the processes used in your pilot program before making the business case to begin implementing Performance-based Hiring companywide. To do this, draw a table with the names of all of the people who were hired during the pilot program. Put their prehire score in one column and their posthire score in the next. Figure out what happened if there's a significant difference up or down. This is great feedback to use the next time you interview candidates to try to correct what's wrong. This is how you use process-control metrics for process improvement.

In the table, also highlight any hiring mistakes. These are the people you shouldn't have hired. You want to drive this down to zero. If there are only a few, you're okay. If there are more than four or five, you need to rethink everything you did during the pilot. It means something went wrong and the process is out of control. Your goal is make sure everyone who is hired has a prehire score of at least a Level 3 and this person's actual performance didn't decline after starting. Not hiring Level 2s is the other major goal of this pilot, so work hard to figure out what went wrong if you did hire some Level 2s. It is most likely that some of your managers weren't trained properly or took some ill-advised shortcuts.

Once you figure out how to hire Level 3s or better during a pilot, you're ready to implement Performance-based Hiring throughout your company. To calculate the ROI, just use the savings from reducing turnover and not hiring Levels 2s to the cost of training all of your managers. It's pretty easy to make the case that the cost of losing a good person due to turnover or not hiring an underperforming Level 2 is equivalent to the person's annual salary. Use your group of 20 managers as the "before and after" benchmark here. If in the past year this group lost six people due to turnover and this declined to three people, you've saved three times the average annual salary of the people leaving. Now add the impact of fewer mistakes to these total savings. If the group reduced the number of Level 2s hired from five to two during the pilot, you've saved the equivalent of three more annual salaries. Assuming an annual salary of $50,000, this is a total savings of $300,000 in the first year alone. If you keep the program up, you'll save this amount every year for just these 20 managers. This is a huge savings and easy to calculate. Even better, the training cost for these 20 managers is less than $15,000. That's a payback period of about three weeks and an ROI that's overwhelming.

Better yet, the managers involved in the pilot will tell their associates and they'll ask to participate. Once this happens, it will be easy to get the executive management buy-in you need to roll out Performance-based Hiring throughout your company.

■ GOLDEN RULES FOR HIRING GREAT PEOPLE EVERY TIME

Implementing Performance-based Hiring is as easy as described in this chapter. Start with one or two assignments. Work the bugs out. Hire a few great people. Then get more managers involved, covering more positions. In parallel, upgrade your sourcing capabilities. Work the bigger bugs out. Get buy-in from everyone, then implement these rules:

1. Prepare a performance profile before every new job requisition gets approved.
2. Everyone must use the performance-based interviewing techniques and ask the two core questions.

3. Do not hire a candidate unless a group 10-Factor Candidate Assessment template has been prepared during a formal debriefing session with all members of the hiring team.

4. Do not hire Level 2s.

That's it. Before you know it, you'll be hiring great people every time. The bottom line is that good hiring is no more than changing the selection criteria from assessing a candidate's ability to get the job toward the person's ability to do the job. Everything changes when this switch is made. We stop hiring people who are great at interviewing but weak on substance. We also reconsider those great candidates reduced to temporary nervousness by the glare of the spotlights. It's substance, not style that counts. As Red Scott said, "Hire smart, or manage tough," and you can never manage tough enough to overcome for a hiring mistake that you could have prevented. No Level 2s!

Appendixes

Appendix A

The Legality of Performance-based Hiring^{sm}

Robert J. Bekken, Esq.

For over 30 years, I have represented employers in hundreds of labor and employment discrimination complaints and/or lawsuits. I have also advised clients on how to terminate problem employees by placing them on the *George Washington Program* and making them part of history.

There is a common theme in virtually every situation: the employee *never* should have been hired in the first place. The employer disregarded *clear* warning signs that the applicant would *not* be successful, and it was not a question of "if" but "when" the termination would take place.

The litmus test of a successful hiring protocol is that it deselects the problem employee. The focus of a successful hiring program results in hiring top talent.

Robert J. Bekken is a partner in the Costa Mesa office of Musick Peeler & Garrett, LLP. He received his law degree from Emory University in 1976 and his undergraduate degree from Albion College in 1973. He has authored various publications on employment law and is a frequent lecturer to various business groups around the country on labor and employment law issues. He has conducted over 1,000 workshops and seminars and has spoken to numerous conventions and groups, both national and regional. Rob was selected by his peers as one of 30 Southern California *Superlawyers*, representing management in employment litigation. Only 5 percent of the California State Bar is awarded this honor.

What are the costs of hiring the problem employee? Managers spend more of their time parenting the bad employee, than focusing on developing and motivating new talent and existing top talent. It is axiomatic that it is easier to not hire an individual than hire him or her and face the legal risks of termination.

I have only represented five clients in allegations of discriminatory hiring. However, I have handled hundreds of cases involving allegations of discriminatory or unlawful terminations. The lesson learned is very simple: Rejecting the problem employee during the hiring process creates minimal exposure. The real exposure takes place when you hire the bad employee and subsequently fire him or her.

In virtually every case I have handled, the company failed to understand the profile for the successful candidate. Instead, the managers relied on their gut reaction and were motivated by the need to get a warm body in the door.

Performance-based Hiring represents a revolutionary breakthrough in terms of providing employers with a methodology to avoid litigation by not hiring the litigious applicant and providing a defense in the event that the employer's hiring decision is challenged. In essence, the Performance-based Hiring protocol is the "missing link" in the hiring process. It is both the practical and legal component of the hiring process that most employers overlook.

Employers must understand the legal landscape that they face in the employment arena today. By understanding this landscape, employers can better understand the importance of implementing an objective hiring protocol. Virtually all of the following laws provide that if the employee prevails, the employer must pay his or her attorney's fees.

■ WHAT LAWS ARE CAUSING EMPLOYMENT LITIGATION TODAY?

➤ Statutes

As discussed earlier, several statutes exist to protect employees from certain actions taken by employers. The following are just a *few* of the many major laws regulating the workplace:

Discrimination

Federal, state, and local laws prohibit employment discrimination based on enumerated categories, including race, color, ancestry, religion, sex, medical condition, physical or mental disability, national origin, age (40 and above), citizenship, sexual orientation, or marital status. Title VII of the Civil Rights Act of 1964 is the principal federal anti-discrimination statute, but there are many other federal and state sources of equal employment opportunity rights.

Individuals with a disability are protected by the Americans with Disabilities Act (ADA) and the Rehabilitation Act, both federal laws, as well as additional state laws. Generally speaking, the ADA and the Rehabilitation Act prohibit discrimination against a qualified individual with a disability with regard to job application procedures; the hiring, advancement, or discharge of employees; employee compensation; job training; and other terms, conditions, and privileges of employment.

Harassment

Under most federal and state anti-discrimination acts, employers, labor organizations, apprenticeship and employment training programs, other persons, agents, and supervisors can be civilly liable for harassment of an employee, applicant for employment, or a person providing services under a contract. Harassment, like discrimination, can be on the basis of race, religious creed, color, national origin, ancestry, physical disability, mental disability, medical condition, marital status, sex, age, or sexual orientation.

The Fair Credit Reporting Act and Other Laws Regulating Background Checks

The Fair Credit Reporting Act (FCRA) applies to employment-related decisions if the employer bases that decision on a consumer report or investigative consumer report obtained from a consumer reporting agency. Consumer reports generally include motor vehicle reports, criminal background checks, and credit history reports obtained from third parties. Investigative consumer reports generally include reference checks and other types of personal interviews. It is strongly recommended that all employers utilize background checks. In order to comply with the FCRA, however, the employer must have all applicants sign a separate form acknowledging that a report may be obtained. There is a sample disclosure included at the end of this report.

Federal and state laws also prohibit certain forms of background checks. For instance, the ADA prohibits employers from denying job opportunities to applicants who are: (1) rehabilitated drug users, (2) currently participating in a supervised drug rehabilitation program and are no longer using drugs, or (3) erroneously believed to be illegal drug users. Additionally, disqualification for employment based on past criminal behavior can violate federal law when the disqualifying criterion has a disproportionate impact on a protected class or has a tenuous or insubstantial relation to job qualifications. Also, employers may not ask disability related questions and may not conduct medical examinations until after they make a conditional job offer to an applicant.

➤ Common Law

Although most employers are aware of the exposure under common law claims of defamation, assault and battery, and infliction of emotional distress, most employers are unaware of the potential liability for negligent hiring. Negligent hiring claims are premised on the theory that an employer knew or should have known that an employee would engage in criminal, violent, or other harmful acts against a third party. The third party may be a co-employee, customer, or just a visitor to the employer.

The most astonishing aspect of a negligent hiring claim is that liability can even arise when an employee's acts are outside the scope of employment. Traditionally, the employer is only responsible for acts of its employees that occur during the course and scope of employment—meaning while in the employer's control. In negligent hiring cases, though, employers may be liable for acts where the employer did not exercise control over the employee. For example, if an employee follows a customer home and assaults that person, the employer will be liable if the customer can: (1) prove that the employee was unfit, incompetent, or dangerous, and (2) that the employer failed to protect the employee.

■ DESELECTING THE PROBLEM EMPLOYEE DURING THE HIRING PROCESS

If you look at successful companies, there is one underlying formula: they make it their mission to hire the best. Bill Pollard, the chairman of ServiceMaster, offers this very simple caveat in *The Soul of the Firm:*"I hope you believe that not everyone can work for your company."

This same principle is personified at Southwest Airlines, where only 4 percent of its 90,000 applicants are hired each year. The applicants are screened to ensure that they possess the right personality and character traits that permeate the existing employees of Southwest Airlines.

Frederick F. Reichheld, in *Loyalty Rules*, observes, "Loyalty leaders understand that they can and should treat everyone fairly . . . but they also understand that they can afford to be *loyal* only to those who can help build mutually beneficial relationships that reflect the principles of loyalty."

The implementation of Performance-based Hiring will result in the hiring of top talent and minimize the potential to have your company end up in the *lottery wheel of justice*.

➤ Using an Effective Application

In my years of practice, I have learned that the plaintiff virtually always provide false information during the interview process. As a result, I recommend that all of my clients use a comprehensive employment application that forces the applicant to reveal his or her true past.

In the event of litigation, the employment application will establish that the plaintiff misrepresented or falsified his or her past employment history to gain employment. During the discovery process, the true record of the plaintiff's past will expose a number of falsehoods. The exposure of these falsehoods allows the employer to utilize the *after-acquired evidence doctrine*. The United States Supreme Court has ruled that *after-acquired evidence* of misrepresentations during the hiring process can result in dismissal of the lawsuit or a reduction in damages that can be awarded to the plaintiff.

Most important, employment litigation lawsuits are normally won or lost based on the credibility or lack of credibility of the plaintiff. By establishing that the plaintiff is capable of mis- representation or falsification, the trier of fact will conclude that the employer's judgment in terminating the employee was justified.

➤ Background Checks

Background checks are critical to a successful hiring process. The background checks should include not only reference checks from past employers, but personal references as well.

Another component of checking the applicant's background is to determine whether the applicant has a criminal record. It is surprising the number of plaintiffs who have failed to disclose the past criminal record.

The application should contain a Notice that must be signed by the Applicant in order to obtain an "investigative consumer report" pursuant to the FCRA. This Notice must be signed by the applicant.

➤ Drug Tests

After 30 years of practice, I can establish that there is a common element among problem employees and plaintiffs—they all have drug or alcohol problems. Statistically, individuals with drug or alcohol problems use your benefits three times more than other employees. They file five times more worker's compensation claims and are absent from work five to eight times more than other employees. If they have an addiction to methoamphetmines or cocaine, there is a 38 percent chance that they will steal from their employer, and a 48 percent chance that they will sell drugs at work. If you are not drug testing, you are hiring all the rejects from your competitors who are drug testing.

➤ Removing your Company from the Lottery Wheel of Justice

After observing the inequity of the judicial system, I have determined that the most cost-effective and fair method of resolving disputes is binding arbitration. The reality is that our judicial system is broken. Plaintiff attorneys have learned that employers are eventually going to settle a case if they are forced to have a jury decide their fate. The unpredictability of the jury system creates settlement as the only logical business solution.

However, binding arbitration that is conducted by a former trial judge yields a much more predictable result. Plaintiffs are less likely to want to litigate before a judge who will not be swayed by emotion or bias.

➤ Establishing an At-Will Basis of Employment

The concept of at-will employment must be memorialized at the beginning of the employment relationship. Although employees can be terminated at will, the employer still must be able to demonstrate that the termination was not based on a discriminatory motive. However, the establishment of an at-will basis of employment will preclude an employee from contending there was an employment contract.

A sample Arbitration and At-Will Agreement is included at the end of this report.

■ COMPLIANCE WITH APPLICABLE LAW AND AGENCY GUIDELINES

The techniques espoused in *Hire with Your Head* and Performance-based Hiring not only represent an effective and practical means of hiring and recruiting personnel, but are also compliant with federal laws like the FCRA and guidelines issued by federal agencies such as the Equal Employment Opportunity Commission and the Office of Federal Contract Compliance. The table on page 272 highlights important legal guidelines and how the *Hire with Your Head* and Performance-based Hiring protocol complies with these guidelines.

■ CONCLUSION

The implementation of Performance-based Hiring will prevent companies from experiencing hiring and litigation nightmares. Instead, the company will hire top talent and not end up in the *lottery wheel of justice*.

Hire with Your Head

Performance-based Hiring Protocol	Law/Administrative Agency Guideline
Identifying the needs of the position to be filled: Identify the critical success factors of every job, and generate a performance-based job description that incorporates S.M.A.R.T. objectives (Specific, Measurable, Action-oriented, Result, and Time-based). Make these objectives the dominant selection criterion so decisions are based on a candidate's ability to meet the objectives rather than on other, subjective factors. Consider a performance objective of increasing workforce diversity. See *Hire with Your Head*, Ch. 2.	Selection criteria may be "objective" or "subjective." "*Objective*" criteria must be specific, clearly delineated, quantitative, objectively verified, and mechanically applied. See *Zahorik v. Cornell University*, 729 F.2d 85 (2d Cir. 1984). "*Subjective*" criteria are permissible but disfavored by the courts because they may mask the influence of impermissible bias in making hiring decisions. See *Atonio v. Wards Cove Packing Co., Inc.*, 827 F.2d 439 (9th Cir. 1987).
Evaluating the best recruiting options: When advertising, develop a marketing-driven performance-based advertisement that effectively describes a challenging position with a strong company that has growth opportunities. The advertisement should *only* focus on the performance needs of the job rather than experience or other requirements. See *Hire with Your Head*, Ch. 3.	Title VII and the Age Discrimination in Employment Act proscribe employment advertisements that indicate any preference, limitation, specification, or discrimination based on a protected classification (race, color, religion, sex, national origin, age), unless the classification is a bona fide occupational qualification. See 42 U.S.C. § 2000e et seq.; 29 U.S.C. § 623(e); 29 C.F.R. § 1604 et seq.
Using an effective application: Employers should make it clear to job candidates on the application that a background check will be conducted. Employers should also ask job candidates to reconfirm that everything on the application and all statements that are made during the interview are true and correct. See *Hire with Your Head*, Ch. 6.	State agency and federal EEOC regulations place strict express limitations on inquiries that attempt to identify protected characteristics such as race, religion, sex, sexual orientation, political affiliation, disability, national origin, and age. Inquiries relating to facially neutral criteria such as education, experience, height, weight, veteran status and military discharge, and financial status, are not impermissible per se. See 29 C.F.R. § 1625 et seq.
Conducting proper interviews: Questions should focus on fact-finding information about the candidate's past performance, team leadership ability, job competency, character and values, and professional accomplishments. See *Hire with Your Head*, Ch. 4. Use a telephone interview as a first stage to minimize personal bias. See *Hire with Your Head*, Ch 4.	
Checking all references and conducting background checks: Conduct a thorough background check on every finalist for any position in your organization. See *Hire with Your Head*, Ch 5.	The Fair Credit Reporting Act permits an employer to obtain a credit report on a prospective employee from a consumer reporting agency. See 15 U.S.C. § 1681b(a)(3)(B).

Sample Authorization for Background Verification

DISCLOSURE OF INTENT TO OBTAIN CONSUMER REPORTS OR INVESTIGATIVE CONSUMER REPORTS

For employment purposes, the Company may obtain consumer reports on you as an applicant or from time to time during employment. "Consumer reports" are reports from consumer reporting agencies and may include driving records, criminal records, and so on.

For such employment purposes, the Company may also obtain investigative consumer reports. An "investigative consumer report" is a consumer report in which information as to character, general reputation, personal characteristics, or mode of living is obtained through personal interviews with neighbors, friends, associates, acquaintances, or others. You have a right to request disclosure of the nature and scope of an investigation and to request a written summary of consumer rights.

AUTHORIZATION

I authorize the Company to obtain consumer reports and/or investigative consumer reports regarding me from time to time for employment purposes.

Signature: _____   Date: _____

Print Name: _____

Driver's License Number: _____   State: _____

Other Driver's Licenses Held in Past 5 Years: _____

Print Maiden or Other Names Under Which Records May be Listed:

_____

Date of Birth (to be used only for proper identification):

_____

Sample Comprehensive Agreement Employment
At-Will and Arbitration

1.   The undersigned Employee understands that the employment and compensation of Employee can be terminated by the Company or the Employee at any time, with or without cause and/or with or without notice, at the option of the Company or the Employee.

2.   The Employee further agrees and acknowledges that binding arbitration will be utilized to resolve all disputes that may arise out of the employment context. The Employee agrees that any claim, dispute, and/or controversy that either I may have against the Company (or its owners, directors, officers, managers, employees, agents, and parties affiliated with its employee benefit and health plans) or the Company may have against me, arising from, related to, or having any relationship or connection whatsoever with my seeking employment with, employment by, or other association with the Company shall be submitted to and determined exclusively by binding arbitration under the Federal Arbitration Act. Included within the scope of this Agreement are all disputes, whether based on tort, contract, statute (including, but not limited to, any claims of discrimination and harassment, whether they be based on state discrimination statutes, Title VII of the Civil Rights Act of 1964, as amended, or any other state or federal law or regulation), equitable law, or otherwise, with exception of claims arising under the National Labor Relations Act which are brought before the National Labor Relations Board, claims for medical and disability benefits under the Workers' Compensation Act, Employment Development Department claims, or as otherwise required by state or federal law. However, nothing herein shall prevent me from filing and pursuing proceedings before the state discrimination agency, or the United States Equal Employment Opportunity Commission (although if I choose to pursue a claim following the exhaustion of such administrative remedies, that claim would be subject to the provisions of this Agreement). In addition to any other requirements imposed by law, the arbitrator selected shall be a retired trial court judge, or otherwise qualified individual to whom the parties mutually agree, and shall be subject to disqualification on the same grounds as would apply to a judge of such court. The Federal Rules of Evidence shall apply to the arbitration. Resolution of the dispute shall be based solely upon the law governing the claims and defenses pleaded, and the arbitrator may not invoke any basis (including, but not limited to, notions of "just cause") other than such controlling law. The arbitrator shall have the immunity of a judicial officer from civil liability when acting in the capacity of an arbitrator, which immunity supplements any other existing immunity. Likewise, all communications during or in connection with the arbitration proceedings are privileged in accordance with the governing state laws. As reasonably required to allow full use and benefit of this agreement's modifications to the Act's procedures, the arbitrator shall extend the times set by the Act for the giving of notices and setting of hearings.

Sample Comprehensive Agreement Employment
At-Will and Arbitration (*Continued*)

Awards shall include the arbitrator's written reasoned opinion. **I understand and agree to this binding arbitration provision, and both I and the Company give up our right to trial by jury of any claim I or the Company may have against each other.**

3.   It is further agreed and understood that any agreement contrary to the foregoing must be entered into, in writing, by the President of the Company. No supervisor or representative of the Company, other than its President, has any authority to enter into any agreement for employment for any specified period of time or make any agreement contrary to the foregoing. *Oral representations made before or after you are hired do not alter this Agreement.*

4.   **This is the entire agreement between the Company and the Employee regarding dispute resolution, the length of my employment, and the reasons for termination of employment, and this agreement supersedes any and all prior agreements regarding these issues.**

5.   If any term or provision, or portion of this Agreement is declared void or unenforceable it shall be severed and the remainder of this Agreement shall be enforceable.

MY SIGNATURE BELOW ATTESTS TO THE FACT THAT I HAVE READ, UNDERSTAND, AND AGREE TO BE LEGALLY BOUND TO ALL OF THE ABOVE TERMS.

DATED: _____

                                           Employee's Signature

Appendix B

A Discussion of the Validity of the Structured Interviews Used in the Performance-based Hiring Process

Charles A. Handler, PhD

The purpose of this Appendix is to document the validity of the interviews used in the Performance-based Hiring system. This goal is accomplished via the presentation of three specific types of information:

1. Information about content validity (Section 1).
2. N2A summary of the research literature investigating the validity of structured interviews (Section 2).
3. Information summarizing best practices for structured interviews (Section 3).

The following sections provide an overview of each of these types of information as well as a description of the relevance of this information for demonstrating the validity of Performance-based Hiring interviews.

Charles A. Handler is the President and Founder of Rocket-Hire (www.Rocket-Hire.com).

■ SECTION 1: CONTENT VALIDITY

The information in this section provides evidence that the process used to construct the interviews used in the Performance-based Hiring system is consistent with established requirements for demonstrating content validity.

➤ Content Validity Defined

Content validity exists when it can be demonstrated that the content of a selection measure is related to the job for which it is being used.

➤ Requirements for Content Validity

The uniform guidelines on employee selection procedures present a set of standards for ensuring that selection procedures are content valid. The guidelines suggest that there are two critical aspects to constructing content valid selection measures:

1. The development of a clear definition of job performance.
2. The documentation of a clear link between job performance and the content of selection measures.

➤ Performance-based Hiring Content Validity

This Appendix provides evidence that the process used to develop the interviews used in the Performance-based Hiring is consistent with the specifications outlined in the uniform guidelines because it:

➤ Utilizes job experts to develop a clear definition of job performance by:

—Establishing job-related performance objectives for a given position.

—Ranking various aspects of job performance in terms of their relative importance.

—Linking all aspects of job performance to an underlying competency model.

➤ Links interview content directly to the definition of job performance by using job experts to develop interview questions that are based on concrete examples of job performance by:

—Using examples of job performance to develop detailed rating scales for each interview question.

—Using both examples of job performance and a competency model to create an overall form for rating each candidate's job performance.

➤ Further Evidence of Content Validity

This Appendix also suggests that consistency with the Uniform Guidelines requires that an empirical validation study be conducted to support each implementation of Performance-based Hiring structured interviews.

■ SECTION 2: OVERVIEW OF INTERVIEW LITERATURE

The information in this section summarizes literature providing evidence that interviews can be valid predictors of job performance. The implication of this information for the validity of Performance-based Hiring interviews is also discussed.

➤ Interview Validity Levels

Recent research has demonstrated that interviews used for the purpose of employee selection have shown validity coefficients that approach .60. This research also suggests that that there are two major determinants of interview validity:

1. The addition of structure to the interview process.
2. The use of job-related interview questions that examine an applicant's past job performance.

The interviews used in the Performance-based Hiring process incorporate both of these major determinants of interview validity.

Performance-based Hiring interviews contain a high degree of structure and make extensive use of questions requiring interviewees to discuss their past job performance.

➤ Additional Validity Information

Interview validation research also provides information that structured interviews such as those used in the Performance-based Hiring process:

- ➤ Provide incremental validity (i.e., predict a component of job performance not measured by cognitive ability and personality tests).
- ➤ Are unlikely to demonstrate differences in score based on race or sex.
- ➤ Will demonstrate validity in a wide variety of situations.

■ SECTION 3: THE BENEFITS OF STRUCTURE

This section provides a more detailed look at the impact of structure on interview validities by summarizing best practices in two critical areas: (1) structure related to the interview process, and (2) structure related to interview content. This section also provides information demonstrating that the interviews used in the Performance-based Hiring process are consistent with best practices in both of these areas.

➤ Content Issues

Content issues refer to anything related to the creation of questions used in the interview process. The interview literature outlines three major content issues that may contribute to increased levels of interview validity:

1. Using formal techniques such as job analysis to define job performance.
2. Asking the same questions to each interviewee.
3. Using questions that require interviewees to discuss their past performance in situations that are similar to those

they will face while performing the job for which they are interviewing.

➤ Process Issues

Process issues refer to all aspects of the process in which the interview itself is embedded. The interview literature outlines five major process areas that may contribute to increased levels of interview validity:

1. Rating each interview question individually and combining information from multiple questions when making final ratings.
2. Using rating scales that provide clear, job-related anchors.
3. Requiring interviewers to take detailed notes for each interview question.
4. Using multiple interviews to assess each candidate.
5. Providing extensive interviewer training.

The interviews used in the Performance-based Hiring process are consistent with best practices identified for both process and content, a fact that should contribute significantly to their validity.

■ CONCLUSION

The information summarized in this Appendix supports the fact that the interviews used in the Performance-based Hiring process are content valid, are representative of the most effective type of interviews available, and are consistent with best practices identified in the interview literature.

Finally, it is important to remember that interviews are just one source of data about the fit between an applicant and a specific job or position. A well-developed hiring process will provide multiple opportunities to collect additional data points from applicants. These may include tools such as screening questions, work history, and experience measures, assessments, and simulations. The goal being to provide decision makers with a wide range of job-related information that will help them systematically identify the best candidates and thus make sound hiring decisions.

■ REFERENCES

Campion, M. A., Campion, J. E., & Hudson, J. P. (1994). Structured interviewing: A note on incremental validity and alternate question types. *Journal of Applied Psychology*, 79 (6), 998–1002.

Campion, M. A., Palmer, D. K., & Campion, J. E. (1997). A review of structure in the selection interview. *Personnel Psychology*, 50 (2), 655–703.

Cortina, J. M., Goldstein, N. B., Payne, S. C., Davison, H. K., & Gilliland, S. W. (2001). The incremental validity of interview scores over and above cognitive ability and conscientiousness scores. *Personnel Psychology*, 53, 325–318.

Huffcutt, A. I., & Arthur, W. (1994). Hunter and Hunter. (1984). Revisited: Interview validity for entry level jobs. *Journal of Applied Psychology*, 79 (2), 184–190.

Hunter, J. E., & Hunter, R. F. (1984). Validity and utility of alternate predictors of job performance. *Psychological Bulletin*, 96, 72–98.

Janz, T. (1982). Initial comparisons of patterned behavior description interviews versus unstructured interviews. *Journal of Applied Psychology*, 67, 577–580.

McDaniel, M. A., Whetzel, D. L., Schmidt, F. L., & Maurer, S. D. (1994). The validity of employment interviews: A comprehensive review and meta-analysis. *Journal of Applied Psychology*, 79 (4), 599–616.

Motowidlo, S. J., Carter, G. C., Dunnette, M. D., Tippins, N., Werner, S., Burnett, J. R., et al. (1992). Studies of the structured behavioral interview. *Journal of Applied Psychology*, 77, 571–587.

Orphen, C. (1985). Patterned behavior description interviews versus unstructured interviews: A comparative validity study. *Journal of Applied Psychology*, 70, 774–776.

Weisner, W. H., & Cronshaw, S. F. (1988). A meta-analytic investigation of the impact of interview format and degree of structure on the validity of the employment interview. *Journal of Occupational Psychology*, 61, 275–290.

Appendix C

Forms and Templates

Structured Performance-Based Interview

February 2007.

the adler group

Note: This is a pre-scripted interview. It's important to follow the directions and ask the questions as written as closely as possible in order to insure an accurate assessment and legally defensible interview. **Do not end the interview too soon or assume competency too soon.** You must get specific examples of job-related accomplishments to determine competency. Then measure first impressions, AFTER YOU DETERMINE COMPETENCY. These two steps alone will increase accuracy.

Step 1	Welcome and Review Job/Motivation	Information & Hot Tips
Opening question to determine motivation	*Thank you for coming today. Based on your discussions please give me a quick overview of your thoughts about the job, and what you've discussed with others so far?* *What are you looking for in a new job? (pause) Why is having ___ and ___ important to you and why do you think this job meets that criteria?*	Find out what's already been covered. This way you'll be able to focus your questions and fact-finding. Asking the "Why?" follow-up question gets at the true source of motivation. Determine if person wants any job, or if person wants this job.

Step 2	Measure Impact of First Impression	*Information & Hot Tips*
Action, be aware of your biases	*Write down your immediate emotional reaction to the candidate – relaxed, uptight, or neutral. Write down cause. At the end of interview you'll measure the candidate's first impression again, when you're less affected by it.*	o Wait 30-minutes o Do opposite of normal reaction o Like: prove incompetency, be tough o Dislike: prove competency, be easy o Ask same questions to all o Be cynical, get proof, examples, facts

Step 3	Review Work History and Background	Fact-finding & Hot Tips
Use this to develop structure behind experience and accomplishments	*Please tell me about your most recent job. What was your position, the company, your duties, and any recognition you received? (do this for the past few jobs)* *Tell me about your schooling and advanced training.*	**For each job obtain** o Overview, title, type of work o Quick org chart o Dates, why left, explain gaps o Highlights, big projects, major focus o Recognition, raises, promotion **Education/Training** o Schools, degree, why, honors o What kind of training, why o How well did your do

Step 4	Assess 3-4 Major Accomplishments	Fact-finding & Hot Tips
Question for a few projects to determine impact and trend line	*Can you please tell me about a major one-time project or accomplishment? Or, consider a project or event that your quite proud of.* *One major project we're now working on is (describe). Please tell me about something comparable you've led.* Note: spend 10-12 minutes on 2-3 major accomplishments in order to develop a trend line of accomplishments over time. Make note of the accomplishments and type of work where the person excelled and/or was highly motivated to exceed expectations.	o Overview of job, company o Team and org structure o Environment – pace, resources o When? How long? Results? o What results were expected? o How did you plan project? o Obtain 2-3 examples of initiative o What did you change/improve o Big challenges or conflict faced o What did you learn about self o How did you grow as a result o What would you do differently o What (technical) skills needed o How were these enhanced o What (technical) skills learned o Describe likes, dislikes o Where did you exceed expectations o How did you improve yourself o What would you do differently o What recognition did you receive

Structured Performance-Based Interview
February 2007.

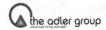
the adler group

Step 5	Assess 1-2 Major Team Accomplishments	Fact-finding & Hot Tips
Question for few teams & observe impact and trend line	*Can you please tell me about a major team accomplishment? Consider one where you led the team, and one where you were a key member of the team.* Note: spend 10-12 minutes on 1-2 team accomplishments. Observe trend line and changes in scope of team. Make note of the types of people on the team, variety of functions worked with, and how influential the person was in changing the direction of the team.	o Draw an org chart w/titles o What was your role, why you o What was plan & were results met o What were biggest team problems o How did you influence results o 3 examples of initiative helping others o Examples of being influenced o How could you have been better o Describe biggest conflict & resolution o Examples coaching others o Examples of being coached o How did you improve, learn o What did you like/dislike o Did you receive any recognition

Step 6	Discuss 1-2 Major Job-related Problems	Fact-finding & Hot Tips
Repeat question 1-2 times using real problems Anchor with real project	*One major problem we're now facing is _____. How would you go about addressing this? What would you need to know and how would you plan it out.* *What have you done that's most similar?* (Note: this is an anchor to insure that the candidate doesn't just talk a good game. This might have been covered above.)	o What would you need to know o What would you do first, why o Who else would you involve o How would you prepare o How would you prioritize tasks, why o How would you find out critical issues o What resources needed o How long would it take, why o What would you do if ..... o How would you make this trade-off o How would you make business-case

Step 7	Determine Interest and Recruit	Fact-finding & Hot Tips
Question & Discussion Create Job Stretch	*While I've seen a few other very strong candidates, I'm also impressed with some of the work you've done. What are your thoughts now about this job? Is this something you'd like to consider further? Why? Why not?* Note: only the hiring manager and recruiter need to ask this. Others can ask a softer variation, e.g., "what are your thoughts about the job?"	o State sincere interest o Make candidate earn job o Listen 4x more than talk, don't sell o Describe concerns to create gap o Mention other strong contenders o What other jobs are you considering o How interested on 1-10 scale, why o What's needed to know to get to 8-9 o Link job to big company projects o What else do you need to know o What do you like/dislike o How does job meets your needs o Compensation needs, availability o When can you come back, next steps o Provide collateral job profile, web site

Step 8	Measure First Impression Again	Information & Hot Tips
Compare candidate's true personality to 1st impression at opening of interview	*Measure first impression again at the end of the interview. Consider the actual impact on you, the actual impact on others (customers, peers, superiors, staff), and the actual impact of personality and style on performance.*	o Did candidate get better or worse o Become more/less nervous o Open-up more, talk more o Did you observe true personality in accomplishments o Were your biases controlled o Did this change your decision o Is true personality consistent with job needs

The 10-Factor Candidate Assessment

©2005. All Rights Reserved. The Adler Group, Inc. Rev Sept 05

the adler group
advanced hiring concepts

Candidate: _____ Position: _____ Interviewer: _____ Date: _____

	Factor	Competencies	Level 1 Unqualified	Level 2 Less Qualified	Level 3 Fully Qualified	Level 4 Highly Qualified	Level 5 Super Star	Rank
	General Evaluation Summary	Technical Motivation Cooperation Viewed by team Impact on team Planning Promotability	Incompetent Unmotivated Uncooperative Distraction Demotivating Reactive No potential to grow	Needs extra training Needs extra pushing Needs urging Avoided Neutral Passive Not promotable	Meets high standards Self motivated Fully cooperative A contributor An asset On top of issues Promotable	Does it better Does more, faster Initiates helping Trains, sought-out Influences others Anticipates issues Quickly promotable	Sets standards 120% committed Proactively coaches Asked to lead Motivates others Forward-looking Double promotable	
1	Technical Skills & Abilities	Basic knowledge Application Creativity, vision Learning ability Professionalism	Can't do the work. Doesn't meet minimum standards. Incompetent. A distraction. Avoided.	Can do the work, but needs added training, supervision. Struggles. Slow learner. Tolerated by others.	Can perform all required work very well. An asset. Requires minimal supv, can learn anything.	Does more than required, does it better, does it faster. Self-managed. Trains others. Learns fast.	Achieves another level. More creative, more insightful. Sets standards. Leader in field. Sought out.	
2	Motivated to Do the Work Required	Energy, Focus Commitment Initiative Work-ethic Self-development	Lazy, passive, doesn't want to do the work. No interest in position.	Will do the work if urged or pushed. Not a good fit for work. Avoids issues, reactive. Isn't improving.	Self-motivated to do this type work w/normal supervision. Proactively handles key issues.	Takes initiative to do more, faster, & better. Looks for problems to solve. Self-improves skills.	Totally committed to do whatever it takes to get it done. Wants to excel. Constant self-development.	
3	Team Skills (EQ) with Comparable Groups	Cooperate Motivate Assertiveness Sociability Influence, Lead Others	Uncooperative, bad attitude, negative. Hides problems. Or too individual. Cause of conflict. Antagonistic.	Will cooperate if asked. Needs urging to be involved with others. Avoids problems. Can't handle conflict. Passive.	Fully cooperates with others w/o urging. Openly addresses problems. Accepts conflict. Pushes viewpoint.	Takes initiative to help others. Anticipates problems. Persuasive. Motivates others. Handles conflict well. Takes lead.	Persuades, inspires, motivates, coaches. Minimizes conflict. Diplomatic. Proactively develops others. Asked to lead.	
4	Appropriate Problem Solving & Thinking	Intelligence Cause/Effect Analysis Logic Insight Process approach	Didn't understand any key issues or develop any solutions. Doesn't know how to start or collect information.	Understood most issues and developed okay solutions. Would need support. Random approach. Inconsistent.	Clearly understood all key issues and developed reasonable solutions. Logical approach. Will involve others.	Quickly understood all key issues. Works w/others. Developed multiple solutions. Sees secondary issues and impact.	Seeks out best solutions. Understood all issues, developed great solutions, & new insights. Sees cause & effect.	
5	Achieved Comparable Results	Decision-making Execution Achievement Commitment Experience	Experience and accomplishments are a complete mismatch.	Has some comparable accomplishments. Requires extra training & support to make it.	Accomplishments are comparable. Has handled similar projects with solid and comparable results.	Has achieved better results handling similar projects in similar environments.	Super fit. An MVP! Scope, span, size, scale, complexity, culture match with exceptional results.	
6	Planning & Executing Comparable Work	Organization Planning Workflow Decision-making Tough-minded Vision	Unorganized. Weak planner. Very reactive. Wastes lots of time. Misses most issues.	Okay organizer, knows how to plan, will do it, but needs help & pushing. Not as efficient as could be. Reactive.	Solid planner, organizer. Can handle all job needs. Anticipates issues. Gets it done. Efficient. Considers key issues.	Efficient planning, organizing, executing is strength. Anticipates, minimizes problems, overcomes challenges.	Coordinates, handles complex challenges smoothly. Makes it happen. Anticipates everything. Sees big picture & all issues.	
7	Environment & Cultural Fit	Decision-making Personality Pace Attitude Team Skills	Complete mismatch on culture and/or environment. Oil vs. water type. Has been cause of problems.	Reasonable match on culture and environment, but not perfect fit. Needs polishing. Limited track record.	Very close match on culture and environment. Smooth transfer. Has dealt well w/people, issues.	Track record indicates excellent match on culture and environment. Has made similar transfers.	Thrives in this type of environment, culture. Pattern shows extremely smooth transfer.	
8	Trend of Growth Over Time	Ambition Goal-orientation Commitment Responsibility Dedication Career Focus	No personal or business growth noted. Makes excuses. Not interested. Blames on others. Job trend is up and down.	Some professional and personal growth noted. Capable, but needs to be pushed to grow. Job trend is flat.	Job growth trend is slightly up or expanding role. Consistent positive pattern. Takes initiative to improve self.	Strong upward growth trend. Consistently does more. Takes pride in personal development. Pushes to excel.	Great upward trend. Great progress supported by results. Goes extra mile for personal development. Wants more.	
9	Character & Values	Honesty Integrity Professionalism Responsibility Commitment	Questionable character. This job does not compare with any values.	Reasonable character. Job somewhat fits values and needs. Will be a distraction.	Solid character. Job is a strong fit with values & motivating needs. Stabilizing presence.	Highly principled person. Job clearly meets values and motivating needs. Influences others.	Strongly committed person of great character. Role model. Impacts group. Sets standards.	
10	Potential and Overall Summary	Combo of ability, team skills, management, capacity to grow, vision.	This job is over person's head. Not a candidate. Multiple problems that are not correctable.	Can handle this job, but it will require extra training, supervision. Not likely to grow beyond job.	Can handle all critical aspects of the job and meet near-current needs. Has good upside potential.	Can handle all parts of job, will make quick impact, improve things, and has near-term upside.	Will make quick impact. Shows great potential to move up two levels. Potential super star.	

Total Score _____

The Adler Group, Inc. • Irvine, CA • www.adlerconcepts.com • 888.878.1388

Performance-Based Phone Screen

November, 2006.

Note: This is a 30-minute phone screen interview. **Do not end the interview too soon or assume competency too soon.** At the end of 30-minutes you'll be able to determine if the candidate is worth interviewing in more depth.

Step 1	Welcome and Review Job/Motivation	Information & Hot Tips
Opening question to determine motivation	*We're looking for a _____. The key aspects of this position include _____.* *Can you give me some quick highlights of what you've done in this area?* *Can you tell me why you're looking right now?* *What are you looking for in a new job?* (pause) *Why is having ____ and ____ important to you?*	Provide a two-minute short summary of the job and why it's important. Asking the "Why?" follow-up question gets at the source of motivation. Determine if the person is leaving something and wants to move quickly, or if the person is looking for a significant career move.

Step 2	Delay Impact of First Impression	*Information & Hot Tips*
Be aware of your biases	Since this is a phone screen the impact of the candidate's first impression will not be significant. Regardless, don't get swayed if the candidate sounds great on the phone, or the person is a reserved.	o Note your initial reaction o Be open-minded o Ask same questions to all o Make the candidate prove competency get details, proof, examples and facts

Step 3	Review Work History and Background	Fact-finding & Hot Tips
Spend 15 minutes on this. Get as much detail as possible.	*Let's review your resume in detail.* *Please tell me about your most recent job. What was your position, the company, your duties, and describe some of your big accomplishments? What did you start as? Any promotions or growth in the job? Why did you take the job? Why did you leave?* (do this for the past few jobs) *Tell me about your schooling and advanced training.*	**For each job obtain** o Overview, title, type of work o Quick org chart o Dates, why left, explain gaps o Highlights, big projects, major focus o Recognition, raises, promotion **Education/Training** o Schools, degrees, why, how well o What kind of training, why

Step 4	Assess Major Accomplishments	Fact-finding & Hot Tips
Use the work history review to select a task you want the candidate to describe in more detail.	Based on the work history review, you can either ask about an accomplishment that is most related to your open job needs, or ask the candidate to select one that's more comparable. *One of the big challenges involved in this position is _____. Can you please tell me about a major project or accomplishment where you've done something similar?* *Please tell me about a major project or task you were involved in where you really went the extra mile. This could be something that you're quite proud of. .* Note: spend about 8 minutes on this to gain a good sense of the scope and comparability of the task to your open position.	o Obtain overview of task o When did it take place o How long was the project o What impact did you make o Obtain 2-3 examples of initiative o What did you change/improve o Big challenges or conflict faced o What did you learn about self o What (technical) skills needed o What did you like most/least o Where did you exceed expectations o What would you do differently o Did you receive any recognition

Step 5	Next Steps	Hot Tips
Question & Discussion Create Job Stretch	*While I've talked to some other good people, I like your background. Is this something you'd like to pursue?* *From my standpoint it seems worthwhile at least taking the next step.* (Describe what this is.) *What are your thoughts based on what you now know about the job? How does this compare to other situations you're now considering?*	o State sincere interest o Mention other candidates o Determine interest o Ask about other situations o Ask about timing o Find out when the person would be available for an interview – this is good indicator or interest

Performance-Based Interview – 2nd Round

November, 2006.

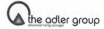

Note: The is a second round interview to be used by a person who has already interviewed the candidate. The primary purpose of this interview should be to validate strengths and concerns uncovered in the first round. Another important purpose of a second interview is to determine consistency of performance and breadth of capabilities. Part of this is requires focus on the problem-solving question. This could involve some type of take-home problem as described below.

Step 1	Welcome and Review Job/Motivation	Information & Hot Tips
Set stage. Validate interest and motivation	*It's good to see you again. Based on your discussions with others and the research you've done what are your thoughts now about the job?* *Where do you feel it's a good fit and what are some areas you're concerned about?* *We'll use this interview today to explore some of these issues and also for me to better understand how your personal objectives and capabilities fit with our job needs.*	Preparation is a better indicator of job interest in the 2nd round compared to the first round. Meaningful questions and any concerns reveal motivating needs. Consider if they are consistent with other things the candidate has said. Especially note comparisons to other jobs.

Step 3	Validate Work History - Especially Changes	Fact-finding & Hot Tips
Use this to develop structure behind experience and accomplishments	Make sure you review each major position the candidate has held. Build work charts to determine types of people the candidate has worked with and for. Ask about trends, promotions and recognition. *Why did you leave _____? Why did you take the position at _____? In retrospect was it a good move for you? Why/why not?* *Of all of the positions you've held, which one was most satisfying? Why?*	**Build a 360° Work Chart** o Who works for you – titles o Who do you work for – title o Who do you work with, inside and outside your department **Understand Why Changed Jobs** o Why did you leave o Why did you accept o Where was move good/not so good o What did you learn most in each job

Step 4	Assess 1-2 Comparable Accomplishments	Fact-finding & Hot Tips
Ask about job-related accomplishments to get at deep job matching.	Use this to revisit some accomplishments discussed earlier or to determine fit and interest on critical performance objectives. Brand the job by linking it directly to an important company initiative. *One major project we're now working on is (describe). This is an important project because (describe). Please tell me about something comparable you've led.* *What's the biggest task you ever volunteered for?* Make note of the accomplishments and type of work where the person excelled and/or was highly motivated to exceed expectations. Your looking at fit across a number of dimensions: scope, span of control, team fit, motivation to excel, complexity, breadth, technical, comparable results, culture fit and creative/strategic fit.	o How did you get the project o Describe the project o Get before and after snapshot o Peel the onion – dig deep o Describe environment – pace, how decisions are made, resources o Get examples of management style o Push away: I'm concerned you're a somewhat light in _____. o How did you grow o What did you like most/least o What would you do differently o What have you done differently

Performance-Based Interview – 2nd Round

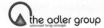

November, 2006.

Step 5	Job-related Situation Question or Take-home Problems	Fact-finding & Hot Tips
Repeat question 1-2 times using real problems Anchor with real project	If this is a take-home problem, ask the candidate to present a 10-minute summary of how he would go about resolving the problem. Then get into a give-and-take dialogue. Evaluate the process the person uses for getting at the solution. *One major problem we're now facing is _____. How would you go about addressing this? What would you need to know and how would you plan it out.* *What have you done that's most similar?* (Note: this is an anchor to insure that the candidate doesn't just talk a good game. This might have been covered above.)	o How would you find out real problem and develop a solution? Why? o What would you do first? Why? o Who else would you involve? Why? o How would you prioritize o How would you find out critical issues o What resources are needed o How long would it take, why o What would you do if ….. o How would you make this trade-off o How would you make business-case

Step 7	Q&A – Develop the Opportunity Gap	Fact-finding & Hot Tips
Question & Discussion Create Job Stretch	*What are some of the key questions you have?* *Do you see this job as a next step in your career?* *Some of my issues are:* *- Positive: (describe areas where you see a strong fit)* *- Opportunity for growth (describe areas where you see opportunities to grow, let the candidate respond)* *- Some big areas of concern are (describe some that are real stretches, not deal breakers)*	o What's your biggest positive o What's your biggest concern o What else would you need to know to get very serious about this opportunity o What do you think about others you've met o Do you have any questions about the company strategy or how this job fits into our department business plans

Step 7	Determine Interest and Recruit	Fact-finding & Hot Tips
Recruit and Advance to the Closing Process	*I'm impressed with what you've accomplished. Right now we're putting together a short list of candidates for a final round of interviews. Based on what you know now, is this something you're interested in pursuing?* *What is your timing?* *Are they're other situations your considering?* *What's going on at your current company that has gotten you to consider other opportunities? (Dig into this to validate reason for looking)* *Based on what you know how does this position compare to others you're considering?* *We'll get back to you in a few days, but don't hesitate to call or email me if you have any other questions.* Note: only the hiring manager and recruiter need to ask this. Others can ask a softer variation, e.g., "what are your thoughts about the job?"	o Try to pinpoint when the candidate is making a decision. o Find out how long the candidate has been looking o Determine whether the person is leaving something bad or looking for something better o Get specifics about job stretch in comparison to other jobs o Leave it on a positive, but explain that there are other candidates under consideration

Organizing the Performance-based Hiring Interview
©2006. All Rights Reserved.

the adler group

Position: _____ Candidate: _____ Date: _____

Interview Step	Hiring Manager	Interviewer 1	Interviewer 2	Interviewer 3	Interviewer 4
Introduction					
Emotional Control					
Motivation for Looking					
Work History					
10-Factor Assessment					
1. Overall Technical Competency					
2. Motivation for Required Work					
3. Overall Team Skills					
4. Problem Solving					
5. Achieve Comparable Results					
6. Planning & organization					
7. Environment/Culture					
8. Trend of Growth					
9. Character & Values					
10. Potential					
Team Projects, Tasks					
Tech Projects, Key Tasks					
Problem Questions: Thinking					
Recruit/Close					
Interest Level					

Summary and Evaluation:

The Adler Group, Inc. • Irvine, CA • 888.878.1388 • adlerconcepts.com • info@adlerconcepts.com

Index